Praise for *Richmond's Unhealed History*

"In these powerful and eloquent pages, Ben Campbell reveals a complicated history that has been hidden in plain sight. Campbell, long a brave and wise leader in Richmond, allows us to see an important and emblematic American city with new eyes. Though writing here as a historian, Campbell writes for the future, for the healing that is yet to come."

—Edward L. Ayers, President, University of Richmond

"Ben Campbell's book is an insightful and factual treatment of Richmond's history during the first four centuries of the city's existence. It is a must read that captures the spirit of conflict, rebellion and change from several perspectives. History aficionados will appreciate this timely book as Virginia commemorates the sesquicentennial of the Civil War."

—Senator Henry L. Marsh, III

"The history of Richmond, Virginia, encapsulates the history of the nation itself. For that reason, Richmond's story, or parts of it, has been the subject of hundreds of books, articles, and scholarly papers. Yet, no one has examined this history through the lens of Christian ethics---at least, not until Episcopalian priest, the Reverend Benjamin Campbell. Writing as a local pastor, theologian, and modern-day prophet, he exposes the ugly truth of Richmond's past and how the injustices of earlier periods haunt metropolitan Richmond today. Yet, he argues, what better place than Richmond for those unaware of the truth, those scarred by it, and those who deny it to listen to each other and engage in an honest conversation about the past and the inequities that divide the city today. Could not Richmond, Campbell asks, model for the rest of the country how truth-telling can lead to redemption and reconciliation? This is a unique book that should be required reading for every Richmonder, better yet, every American."

> —John V. Moeser, Senior Fellow, Bonner Center for Civic Engagement, University of Richmond, Professor Emeritus of Urban Studies and Planning, Virginia Commonwealth University

"*Richmond's Unhealed History* examines the struggles and wounds of the history of America as lived in Richmond for four centuries. It strikes and opens hearts, [and] illuminates both good and evil."

> —Philip J. Schwarz, Emeritus Professor of History, Virginia Commonwealth University, and Editor, *Gabriel's Conspiracy: A Documentary History*

"*Richmond's Unhealed History* persuasively shows how the divided, fragmented metropolis of today has its roots in . . . colonial times. Campbell takes readers on an informative, detail-rich tour through colonialization, slavery, war, segregation, urban renewal and suburban sprawl . . . Here at last is the honest re-telling of Richmond's past all our citizens need to comprehend our present—and to forge the moral vision that could change our future."

> —Thad Williamson, Associate Professor of Leadership Studies and Philosophy, Politics, Economics and Law, University of Richmond

Richmond's Unhealed History

Richmond's Unhealed History

By Benjamin Campbell

Brandylane Publishers, Inc.

ISBN 978-0-9838264-0-8
LCCN 2011939227

❀ *Brandylane*
Brandylane Publishers, Inc.
brandylanepublishers.com

Cover Art: "The Evacuation of Richmond."
Print by Currier & Ives, from the Library of Virginia, by permission.

For all of us.

When we got home, we laid the foundation of two large cities. One at Shacco's, to be called Richmond, and the other at the point of Appomattox river, to be named Petersburg. These major Mayo offered to lay out into lots without fee or reward. The truth of it is, these two places being the uppermost lading of James and Appomattox rivers, are naturally intended for marts, where the traffic of the outer inhabitants must center. Thus we did not build castles only, but also cities in the air.

William Byrd II

A city built on a hill cannot be hid.

Matthew 5:14

Contents

Acknowledgements

The story of this book begins early in my own life, with my father's and mother's distress about the relationship of the state and nation whose ideals they loved to the horrible, hypocritical realities of racism and segregation. Their names were Edmund Douglas Campbell and Elizabeth Pfohl Campbell. They were white Southerners—he a Virginian, she a North Carolinian—whose families had been in the South for six and four generations respectively. My own inner contradictions also intensified as, through our home and our church, I came to know the teaching and spirit of Jesus and the prophetic tradition of the Hebrew Scriptures. We said we loved Jesus. How did the rest of this happen? I became a priest. Finally, as you must do if you love and wish to understand Virginia, I came to Richmond.

My earliest connection with some of the details of Richmond's origins came from "Pope" Gregory, George Cleaveland, and Nancy Jo Taylor. Fr. Edward Meeks Gregory introduced me to his wonderful inter-racial network of Richmond people and stories, and brought me to Church Hill. Dr. Cleaveland was the official historiographer of the Episcopal Diocese of Virginia who, long before anyone seemed to care, had learned everything there was to know about the town of Henrico and shared with me his unpublished manuscript. I first encountered Ms. Taylor, a marvelous oral historian who taught generations of children in the Richmond Public Schools, when she was leading a tour of high school students on Grace Street outside Richmond Hill. I walked with her that day, and she described to me and her students the unmarked sites of African American history on Main Street and in Shockoe Valley. Her list of sites became the map of the first Richmond Unity Walk in 1993, the origin of the Richmond Slave Trail, and the initial outline of much of my own subsequent research.

As the stories began to unfold, I was privileged to talk with a number of folks who preserved pieces of them and shared them with me. I won't remember them all, but I do recall the gifts of Nessa Baskerville Johnson, Chief Anne Richardson, Deanna Beacham, Janine Bell, Pat

Hickin, Rev. Delmarshae Sledge, Elizabeth Kambourian, Jeff Ruggles, Ed Peeples, Henry Marsh, Chuck Richardson, Viola Baskerville, John Horner, E. Holcombe Palmer, Rutledge Dennis, Rev. Ed McCreary, John Franklin, Delores McQuinn, Ralph White, Will Sanford, Walter Kenney, Roland Ealey, Melvin Law, Maurie McInnes, Susan Sheppard, Lu Motley, Jeannie Welliver, Matthew Dolci, John Dolci, and Faithe Norrell Mickens. The Hope in the Cities team—Rob Corcoran, Rev. Sylvester Turner, Cricket White, and Rev. Paige Chargois—shared the journey from the beginning. John Moeser's work on annexation and on social and economic data has been indispensable. He, Philip Schwarz, and Ed Ayers have read all or part of the manuscript, although I do not charge them with any of its faults, analysis, or conclusions. All three are incredible scholars and teachers.

Four years of students have listened to this material in lecture form at Richmond Hill, and instructed me with their questions and comments. The Community of Richmond Hill has encouraged and supported me consistently and with kindness. Bill Walsh insisted that the lectures be videotaped. Robert Pruett has helped get the book into print. My son Philip spent a significant number of the days of his youth helping me explore many of the sites within walking distance of our home. My daughter Susanna has never relented in her encouragement, even though this publication will precede the completion of her own doctoral dissertation. And my wife Annie has shared every waking and sleeping minute of this journey with me.

Thanks to them, and to all who have cared.

Introduction

The Cross at the Falls
May 24, 1607

From May 21 to May 24, 1607, hundreds of citizens of Tsenacomoco watched along the riverbank as strangely clad oarsmen rowed a boat against the current, up the river's meandering course, to a small island at the falls. There the visitors disembarked, accompanied by Nauirans, the man who came with them as a guide. They fashioned a cross of wood, larger than a man, and planted it in the ground. One of the members of the expedition, Gabriel Archer, recalled the event:

> So upon one of the little islets at the mouth of the falls [Captain Christopher Newport] set up a cross with this inscription: "*Jacobus Rex* 1607," [Latin for "King James"] and his own name below. At the erecting hereof we prayed for our king and our own prosperous success in this his action, and proclaimed him king with a great shout. The King Powhatan was now gone and, as we noted, somewhat distasted with our importunity of proceeding up further, and all the savages likewise, save Nauirans, who seeing us set up a cross with such a shout began to [wonder]. But our captain told him that the two arms of the cross signified King Powhatan and [King James], the fastening of it in the middle was their united league, and the shout and the reverence he did to Powhatan, which cheered Nauirans not a little.[1]

Christopher Newport told Nauirans, Powhatan's representative, that the cross symbolized the partnership between King James and the Algonquian leader, and that the English troops were honoring Powhatan by their cheers. It was not true. He lied. The cross was planted to assert England's sovereignty and ownership of the land against the claims of her only real competitors in the law of nations: the other potential European claimants. The cheer represented their success in that achievement. No rights or title to the land on the part of its Powhatan inhabitants were recognized then or subsequently.

The planting of this cross was the planting of the seed that became Richmond and Virginia, and in stunningly pervasive ways, the United States of America. The growth of this seed into modern America has been told and retold by the chroniclers of Virginia history and American politics, religion, and education. They tell of the expansion of the nation to fill a continent; the vision of democracy in economics, property, politics, and religion; the extension of the vote across economic, racial, and gender lines; the establishment of a dynamic religious life under the banner of freedom of religion; and the growth of capital, immigration, and energy over four centuries to produce a wealthy and powerful nation.

The actual story bears some relationship to these tales, to be sure. But in the city where the seed of the nation was planted, the city now called Richmond, the underside of that great nation has shown a sickness and weakness that, from the beginning, has told another story—a darker tale not shared in public.

When you look back at the planting of the cross that day in May 1607, you can see the darkness around it, even as the company of English soldiers gave their cheer. They not only planted the seed of a great nation with unprecedented opportunity for all human beings; they also planted seeds of economic exploitation, racial discrimination, a hierarchical class system, and a heretical version of Christianity, seeds that have constantly threatened and retarded the development of the city with economic, racial, social, and religious diseases that could still destroy it.

The vision of a healthy and vital city at the falls of the James, like the vision of a healthy and vital nation growing from that original seed, captures our imagination. We can still feel the latency, the potential of this foundation, perhaps as those men standing on the island felt it. People still talk openly about the sleeping giant, the potential of Richmond, the city at the falls.

But there is an inexplicable resistance, a persistent negative force, which seems to hold the city back. Visitors and new citizens in metro Richmond say that the city is mired in its history—that it is, perhaps, still living the Civil War.

What is strange is that very few people know the real history of Richmond. This astounding reality began to emerge in the 1990s, as citizens began to discover that for a forty-year period in the nineteenth century Richmond had been the largest slave market in North America outside of New Orleans. In the peak period of Richmond's slave market, a population of enslaved Africans equivalent to the entire population of the city was "shipped downriver" each year. All traces of that trade had vanished from public and private school curricula and from popular histories, and all physical traces had been obliterated.

In 2011, barely five blocks away from where the slave trade flourished, the city jail overflowed with men and women, most of them African Americans. Adjacent to the jail was a portion of the city whose unemployment level ranged from twenty-two to fifty percent (a level regularly reported publicly as six to ten percent), and where household income was barely one-fifth of the region's norm.

But the city, now divided into as many as thirteen jurisdictions separated by race and income, seemed unaware—as unable to tackle the issues of these modern people as it was unable to remember its slave trading past.

If Richmond was mired in its history, it appeared, the bondage was greater than had been thought. This was not about the Civil War. This was about deeper and more fundamental flaws—issues which were present at the falls of the James on that day in May 1607, and which had not solved themselves.

The cultural assumption of the citizens of metropolitan Richmond of both major races has been that the future can hold hope only if the past is forgotten. Denial of history, not worship of it, is the anchor that has wrapped its seductive rope around the legs of metropolitan Richmond, pulling it down every time there is a positive initiative.

The fragmentation and competitiveness of jurisdictions, the repeated negativity of spirit, and the recriminations and insults of daily life among the citizenry indicate that there are things not known, stories not told. We are captive to forces we have not identified or remembered, forces that prevent us from being who we, in our best instincts, want to be. These forces are obvious to anyone who looks carefully at our history through five centuries. Our dysfunction should not surprise us. It is persistent and constant. If we address it, we will thrive. If we continue to deny it, we will fail.

From the beginning, from that day in May on the island in Powhatan's river, when Christopher Newport and John Smith laid claim to a land they did not even know was called Tsenacomoco, Richmond has been affected by major forces of destruction. These forces are economic exploitation, social class, racial discrimination, and heretical religion. No one unwilling to address these evils can build a healthy future for Henrico, Chesterfield, Hanover, Richmond, and the surrounding towns and counties.

Because these evils are buried so deeply, and have been so persistent in our history, the metropolitan city continually seeks to move forward while denying these problems and treating them as inconvenient nuisances on the road to progress. Seldom in any economic or political plan by any jurisdiction or major business association is an attempt made to address these issues either in whole or in part. But that strategy will never succeed. This is a spiritual and an absolutely practical issue. Denial destroys. Truth saves.

Metropolitan Richmond has within itself the capacity for its own redemption. It takes nothing more than the spirit of truth and hope, of repentance and forgiveness, of love and community. This metropolitan city has the power to claim its destiny in the world as a laboratory of racial and social justice—a city of once-great division and injustice where the races were reconciled by honesty, integrity, and truth. The spirit makes the difference. There is no substitute.

The Rev. Benjamin P. Campbell
Richmond Hill
June 1, 2011

1

The Reasons for Jamestown
1300-1607

Early European exploration of North America

In the mid-1500s, North Atlantic codfish accounted for sixty percent of the fish eaten in Europe. The fish came from the Grand Banks off Newfoundland and from the waters around Iceland. Basque fishermen may have been bringing the salted cod to European shores from North America as early as the fourteenth century.[2] Although it was not widely known, North America had been part of European commerce for several hundred years.

By the time the English came to Jamestown, four European nations—Spain, Portugal, France, and England—had been exploring the Atlantic coast of North and South America for more than a century. Columbus had come to the West Indies in 1492. John Cabot had visited in Nova Scotia and Newfoundland in 1497. By 1530 Henry VIII had sent an expedition to explore the American coast from Labrador to Florida,[3] as had France and Spain. Portugal's Brazil began in 1500. Spain had already established a colony in Havana in 1513 and in 1519 Cortez had begun his conquest of Mexico. Jacques Cartier and other Frenchmen explored the St. Lawrence River between 1534 and 1543 and attempted to establish colonies near Quebec. A French ship may have explored the Chesapeake in 1546.[4] From 1525 to 1550 the Spanish made several attempts to establish colonies in portions of Florida such as present-day Jacksonville and Mobile. Hernando De Soto spent four years between 1539 and 1543 with an army seeking to conquer indigenous tribes in what is now Florida, Alabama, and Mississippi. The French attempted in 1562 to establish a fort near Parris Island in present-day South Carolina.

As the sixteenth century progressed, New World settlements

became increasingly important to the European powers. By 1560 the Spaniards were taking twenty percent of their national revenue in the form of precious metals from Mexico and their newest conquest, Peru. Twice a year, in the spring and the fall, large armed convoys brought the treasure back across the Atlantic, and the Spaniards had to fight to protect the fleets against English and French attack. In 1555 the French attacked and burned Havana; the Spaniards attacked a French fort and massacred a colony at Jacksonville in 1565.

In the early 1560s, a Spanish ship came to the "Bay of Santa Maria" —the Chesapeake—and captured a young Paspahegh man who we now know was named Paquiquineo. The Spanish called him Don Luis de Velasco. Don Luis was taken to Mexico, where he was baptized and educated by Dominican friars, and then to Spain.

In 1570, by agreement with the Father-General of the Society of Jesus, Francis Borgia,[5] Spanish North American naval commander Pedro Menendez dispatched Father Joannes Baptista de Segura and seven other Jesuits, with Don Luis and a boy named Alonso de Olmos, to establish a settlement on the south bank of the York River near King's Creek. Five months later, Don Luis/Paquiquineo, who had left the settlement, returned with his tribesmen to kill them. Alonso was spared and lived two more years among the Indians. In 1572, Menendez came to seek the settlement. Finding the boy and hearing his story, Menendez' soldiers killed twenty native people in battle and hanged another eighteen.

Spain was anxious to control the Chesapeake, considering it not only a significant base for defense against English and French attacks on treasure shipments, but also a potential passage to the "Sea of the West."[6] In 1589, the King of Spain ordered two nephews of Menendez to establish a fort in the Chesapeake, garrisoned by 300 men, a plan that was never executed.[7]

The French and Spanish had tried different methods of dealing with Indian tribes in the first two-thirds of the century, ranging from massacre to negotiated settlement, but the relationship was always one of conquest, and enslavement of the population was sometimes attempted. The activities of the Spanish and French farther south were surely known to the native people of Tsenacomoco before the Spanish came to the Chesapeake, but not until 1570, so far as we know, did they threaten them directly.

The Spanish settlement and the deaths on the James River in 1570 directly involved the tribes coming together to form the Powhatan confederation, which included the Paspahegh. The Powhatan confederation was a group of thirty tribes extending from the Potomac to the northern reaches of the Outer Banks. There is some evidence that Paquiquineo may have been kin to the family of Powhatan, the supreme chief in Tsenacomoco when the English arrived. If Paquiquineo had still been alive, he would have been at least sixty years old in 1607.[8]

"Indian Man and Woman," an engraving by Theodor de Bry made in 1590 from a watercolor by John White, who accompanied the first Roanoke expedition in 1585.

The second recorded preliminary local skirmish with the Europeans occurred at Roanoke Island from 1584 to 1591, just twelve years after the Spanish massacre on the James. The English colony on the Outer Banks lived in peace with its neighbors the first year, but in the second year a new military commander, Ralph Lane, destroyed the host village and killed both the tribesmen and their chief. As had become the custom in their exploits up and down the coast, the Europeans took two natives back with them in 1584 to exhibit in England— Manteo and Wanchese—who returned with them in 1585. The war with the Spanish Armada in 1588 made it impossible to resupply the colony from England, and when English ships finally arrived in 1591, Fort Raleigh had been abandoned and the colonists had disappeared. Early English settlers at Jamestown sought the survivors of the "Lost Colony" but never found them.

Another Spaniard, Vicente Gonzales, sailed up the coast from St.

Augustine in 1588, looking for English. He did not see the settlement at Roanoke. He sailed the entire length of the Chesapeake Bay, took two Indians captive, and departed.

Sometime at the beginning of the seventeenth century another ship entered the bay and sailed up the Rappahannock River to what is now Tappahannock. It may have been the 1602 expedition of Samuel Mace sent out by Raleigh to find "Haterask." The European commander apparently killed a chief, thereby almost causing the death of John Smith six years later. When Smith came to Tappahannock in 1608, memories of violence were still fresh among the inhabitants. Smith wrote about the encounter soon after it happened.

> This kind king conducted me to a place called Topahanocke
> [i.e., Tappahannock], a kingdom on another river northward.
> The cause of this was that the year before a ship had been in the
> River of Pamaunke [i.e., the Pamunkey, an upper branch of the
> York River], who having been kindly entertained by Powhatan,
> their emperor, they returned thence and discovered the river of
> Topahanocke, where being received with like kindness, yet he
> slew the king and took off his people, and they supposed I were
> he. But the people reported him a great [i.e., large] man that
> was captain. And using me kindly, the next day we departed.[9]

England and Spain had been at war on the other side of the Atlantic. The English fleet defeated the Armada, but the ensuing conflicts delayed any English attempts to colonize America for the next decade. They also made colonization a more urgent goal of English policy. The formal treaty in 1604 did little to quell England's concern about Spain as a competitive power. Spain and France were claiming the New World, and under what Europeans regarded as the law of nations, any European nation could claim any territory not claimed and occupied by another European nation. During the 1500s the French had been planting stone pillars on the Atlantic coast of North America, and the Spaniards had been planting stone crosses, both claiming portions of the territory as their own. The Spaniards were coming toward the mid-Atlantic from the south, the French from the north.

The Doctrine of Discovery

European explorers in the New World were acting in accordance with what has been called the Doctrine of Discovery, a prevailing attitude in Europe that held that European "Christian" nations were entitled to claim as their own any property not held by other European "Christian" nations. Fifteenth century papal bulls defined the doctrine for the Europeans. In 1455 Pope Nicholas V, writing in *Romanus Pontifex*, specifically authorized Alfonso V of Portugal to "invade, search out, capture, vanquish, and subdue all Saracens and pagans whatsoever, and other enemies of Christ wheresoever placed, and the kingdoms, dukedoms, principalities, dominions, possessions, and all movable and immovable goods whatsoever held and possessed by them and to reduce their persons to perpetual slavery."[10]

In 1493, Pope Alexander VI, himself a Spaniard, granted Spain and Portugal rights to all lands west of a line drawn from north to south in the Atlantic ocean, splitting the entire New World between those two nations. The nations renegotiated the agreement in 1494 in the Treaty of Tordesillas. England, which was late getting into the establishment of settlements across the Atlantic, was placed at a severe disadvantage. Nearly a century later, in 1583, Queen Elizabeth was still careful to instruct Sir Humphrey Gilbert that in his expedition he should try to "discover, find, search out, and view such remote, heathen and barbarous lands, countries and territories" as were "not actually possessed of any Christian prince or people."[11]

Robert J. Miller, a Native American and a law professor who specializes in American Indian law, holds that the Europeans' Doctrine of Discovery had several distinct elements in practice, and he identified them for a conference in Williamsburg in 2008:

- First discovery. The first European country to discover lands unknown to other Europeans gained property and sovereign rights over the lands and peoples.
- Actual occupancy and current possession. To acquire complete title, a discovering country had to actually occupy and possess the newly found lands, usually by building forts and settlements.
- Preemption. The discovering country gained the power of preemption, that is, the sole right to buy the land from the native people.
- Indian title. Indian Nations were considered by Euro-American legal systems to have lost the full ownership of their lands. They only retained occupancy and use rights.
- Christianity. Religion was a significant aspect of the doctrine. Under Discovery, non-Christian peoples did not have the same rights to land, sovereignty, and self-

determination as Christians.

- Civilization. The Euro-American definition of civilization was an important part of Discovery and of ideas of Euro-American superiority. Euro-Americans thought that God had directed them to bring civilized ways, education, and religion to indigenous peoples and to exercise paternalistic and guardianship powers over them.
- Conquest. [M]ilitary victory in "just" and necessary wars [was] one way to acquire the Indian title. But conquest also described the property rights that Europeans gained automatically by first discovery; in essence, the first discovery was like a military conquest.[12]

Miller traces Discovery into American law, where, after years of implicit and explicit presence in Virginia practice, it found its way into the United States Code. In 1790, he notes, the first constitutionally elected Congress passed a law invalidating any ordinary land sale from an Indian or a tribe of Indians to anyone unless it was done specifically by federal treaty. In 1823, in the case of *Johnson v. M'Intosh*, the United States Supreme Court seems to have endorsed this doctrine. The court held that:

Discovery gave title to the government by whose subjects, or by whose authority, it was made against all other European governments, which title might be consummated by possession.... [Native property rights, however, were] in no instance, entirely disregarded; but were necessarily, to a considerable extent, impaired.... [Natives still held a legal right to occupy and use their lands but] their rights to complete sovereignty, as independent nations, were necessarily diminished, and their power to dispose of the soil at their own will, to whomever they pleased, was denied by the original fundamental principle, that Discovery gave exclusive title to those who made it.[13]

English leaders did not question the validity of the Doctrine of Discovery as a justification for ignoring the claims of the land's original owner/inhabitants. They sought only to ensure the validity of their own claims against those of other European nations. Using the euphemism "Discovery," the American court affirmed that the English conquest conferred full title to the conquerors.

Gathering momentum for colonization

Defeat of the Spanish Armada in 1588 energized the growing English ambitions toward the New World. The last quarter of the sixteenth century had witnessed repetitive, if inconclusive, expeditions and attempted expeditions by Englishmen to the western lands. Sir Francis Drake went around the globe from 1577 to 1580. Humphrey Gilbert claimed Newfoundland in 1583. Martin Frobisher sought gold and a northwest passage to the Orient on three successive voyages to what is now Baffin Island (1576-8). Following the failed enterprise at Roanoke Island, Christopher Newport (1592), Samuel Mace (1602), Bartholomew Gosnold (1602), Martin Pring (1603), Charles Leigh (1597, 1604), and George Waymouth (1605) all explored the western shores of the Atlantic for one purpose or another.

Richard Hakluyt (1552-1616) from a window at Bristol Cathedral.

The vision and excitement of the British nation was broadcast in 1599 in a monumental three-volume work entitled *The Principal Navigations, Voyages... and Discoveries of the English Nation made by Sea or over Land to the Remote and Farthest Distant Quarters of the Earth...within the Compass of these 1500 Years.* The author was Richard Hakluyt, a geographer and cleric, whom Queen Elizabeth appointed to the staff at Westminster Abbey. A student of economics and politics as well as geography and theology, Hakluyt befriended many of the explorers and mapmakers of the day, and became a leading advocate of western exploration.

His massive work reproduced documents from hundreds of explorations and many centuries of exploratory activity. One biographer calls it "the prose epic of the English nation."[14] Hakluyt was one of the chief promoters of the petition to King James to colonize Virginia, and when the London Company began to form under royal auspices in 1606, Hakluyt emerged as one of the four grantees for its charter to explore Virginia. He was nominally the clergyman in charge of Jamestown, appointing the Rev. Robert Hunt as his first representative on site.

In 1584 Hakluyt had written a report in support of the expedition to Virginia and Roanoke for Sir Walter Raleigh called *A Discourse on Western Planting*. The report was published in only four copies, one of which went to Queen Elizabeth. It did not gain her support for the Roanoke colony, but it did secure Hakluyt a favored place as an advisor to the monarchy.

Hakluyt's *Discourse* presented comprehensively the reasons for England to pursue its western explorations. The cause was urgent, he said, because other nations were active in the effort and moving to establish claims in the entire West Indies. The greatest concern was Spain. In 1584, Spain had just united with Portugal and its navy was unparalleled. The wealth of the Indies was filling the coffers of the Spanish king and bankrolling his imperialistic designs. Hakluyt urged exploration of the coast of North America in order to occupy the land before the Spanish and offset their power and wealth. The effort would, he said, cause England to build a stronger navy and to train both sailors and soldiers for the defense of the realm.

The search for a northwest passage, another route to the Orient, remained a significant concern for the English. It was one of the four instructions given in the "paper of advice" opened by Captain Christopher Newport upon arriving at Jamestown. The route had been an obsession of Europeans for more than a century. They sought to offset the unfavorable terms and disadvantages they experienced in commerce across the overland routes through Asia and Muslim lands.

Commerce, raw materials, and economic expansions of many sorts were major reasons for exploration and colonization, Hakluyt maintained. He detailed the prospects for trade, for markets for manufactured goods and woolens, and for sources both of raw materials and precious metals. He suggested that the English could charge duties to fishermen off the Grand Banks of Newfoundland. He pointed out that colonies in the temperate latitudes of North America were accessible by sea twelve months in the year and were a relatively short, four- to six-week journey from England.

He saw the colonizing efforts as a way of dealing with England's high number of unemployed persons: "This enterprise will be for the manifold employment of numbers of idle men," he claimed. "Spain and Portugal have taken care of their unemployed," he continued,

> but we, for all the statutes that hitherto can be devised, and
> the sharp execution of the same in punishing idle lazy persons,
> for want of sufficient occasion of honest employment cannot
> deliver our commonwealth from the multitudes of loiterers
> and idle vagabonds…. Thousands of idle persons are within
> this realm, which, having no way to be set on work, be either
> mutinous and seek alteration in the state, or at least very
> burdensome to the commonwealth, and often fall to pilfering
> and thieving and other lewdness, whereby all the prisons of
> the land are daily pestered and stuffed full of them.[15]

Hakluyt was not content to accept without challenge the right of Spain and Portugal to the New World by prior discovery under the provisions of the Law of Nations. Great Britain had gone there first, he claimed: "The West Indies were discovered and inhabited 322 years before Columbus made his first voyage."

A Welshman discovered America!

"We of England have…very ancient and authentic chronicles, written in the Welsh or British tongue, wherein we find that one Madock ap Owen Guyneth, a Prince of North Wales, being weary of the civil wars and domestic dissentions in his country, made two voyages out of Wales, and discovered and planted large countries which he found in the main ocean south westward of Ireland, in the year of our Lord 1170." The proof, he explained, is that the language of some people living on "the continent between the Bay of Mexico and the Grand Bay of Newfoundland"—that is, North America—"agrees with the Welsh language in some words and names of places."[16]

Hakluyt included the documentation for the expedition, from a history of Wales, as the first account of exploration of the Americas in his *Principal Navigations.*

Along with many of his contemporaries, Hakluyt dealt with the native population whose land would be taken and whose culture displaced in religious terms. He first accused the Spaniards of having killed more than fifteen million natives. "Upon these lambs…so meek, so qualified and endowed of their Maker and Creator…entered the Spanish…as wolves, as lions, and as tigers most cruel…. [They] tear them in pieces, kill them, martyr them, afflict them, torment them, and destroy them by strange sorts of cruelties, never either seen or read or heard of" before.[17]

Conquering the land would protect the native people not only against rapacious Spanish colonizers, English apologists said, but also against demonic spiritual forces. Historian Edward L. Bond describes "England's mission to the New World [as] part crusade." There was, he says, "a vast English literature on demonology [that] taught that Satan reigned in the world's remote and primitive territories."[18] King James himself was a student of demonology and had written a book on the topic in 1597.

William Crashaw, a cleric and a member of the council of the Virginia Company in London, wrote in his introduction to the promotional tract "Good News from Virginia" that "Satan visibly and palpably reigns [in Virginia] more than in any other known place of the world."[19] Alexander Whitaker, the Church of England minister at Henrico in 1612, had authored the ensuing tract. His words underlined the diagnosis of demonic relationship and the urgency of mission the English articulated:

> Let the miserable condition of the naked slaves of the devil move you to compassion toward them. They acknowledge that there is a great good god, but know him not, having the eyes of their understanding as yet blinded. Wherefore they serve the devil for fear, after a most base manner, sacrificing sometimes (as I have here heard) their own children to him....
>
> Their priests...are no other but such as our English witches are. They live naked in body as if their shame of their sin deserved no covering. Their names are as naked as their body. They esteem it a virtue to lie, deceive, and steal, as their master the devil teacheth them....
>
> But if any of us should misdoubt that this barbarous people is uncapable of such heavenly mysteries, let such men know that they are far mistaken in the nature of these men.... They are a very understanding generation, quick of apprehension, sudden in their dispatches, subtle in their dealings, exquisite in their inventions, and industrious in their labor.[20]

The Virginia cleric, soon to become Pocahontas' tutor, was confirming and continuing the view of the native population that Hakluyt had promulgated a quarter century before. As the first injunction in his *Discourse on Western Planting*, the geographer theologian of westward expansion had written "that this western discovery will be greatly for the enlargement of the gospel of Christ":

Seing that the people of that part of AMERICA from 30. degrees in Florida northward unto 63. degrees...are idolaters;... Then it is necessary for the salvation of those poor people which have sat so long in darkness and in the shadow of death, that preachers should be sent unto them. But by whom should these preachers be sent? By them no doubt which have taken upon them the protection and defense of the Christian faith. The Kings and Queens of England have the name of Defenders of the Faith.[21]

A special "collect," or formal prayer, was written for the Jamestown settlement effort. King James required that it be said at all services, and every soldier at Jamestown was required to use it at the beginning of the watch. The text reflects the theological judgments behind the mission:

Almighty God, ...seeing that thou hast honoured us to choose us out to bear thy name unto the Gentiles, we therefore beseech Thee to bless us and this plantation which we and our nation have begun in thy fear and for thy glory...and seeing Lord, the highest end of our plantation here is to set up the standard and display the banner of Jesus Christ, even here where Satan's throne is, Lord let our labour be blessed in labouring the conversion of the heathen, and because thou usest not to work such mighty works by unholy means, Lord sanctify our spirits and give us holy hearts that so we may be thy instruments in this most glorious work.[22]

Momentum for exploration and colonization in Virginia had been gathering in the British Isles for more than a century, from the time of Columbus and John Cabot through the reigns of Henry VIII, Mary, and Elizabeth I, until it finally burst forth at the beginning of the seventeenth century. It carried the dreams of a nation—ignorant and practical, imperialistic and self-serving, spiritual and material. To carry out these dreams, King James and his colleagues established a charter, and solicited private funds. The inevitable result, according to Susan Kingsbury, the scholar who compiled all the records of the Virginia Company, was to establish financial return to investors as a dominant goal for the settlement of Virginia: "To establish a settlement which should become a market for English goods, to advance the shipping, to spread the religion of the Kingdom were doubtless motives which aroused sympathy for the undertaking," she observed; but, she noted, "the arguments which brought investment were the opportunities for gain."[23]

The journey begins

> On Saturday, the twentieth of December, in the year 1606, the fleet fell from London, and the fifth of January we anchored in the Downs. But the winds continued contrary for so long that we were forced to stay there some time, where we suffered great storms; but by the skillfulness of the captain we suffered no great loss or danger.[24]

The narrator is George Percy, one of the voyagers. The colonists, all men, had left the Thames below London for Virginia in three ships. The largest, the *Susan Constant,* was 120 tons in capacity, 76 feet at the waterline, and carried 71 persons; the *Godspeed* was 48 feet long, 40 tons, and carried 52; and the *Discovery* was 38 feet, 20 tons, with 21 on board.

Three months later, on March 23, 1607, they arrived at the island of Martinique in the West Indies, a distance of 5,300 miles by way of the Canary Islands. On April 10, they left the island of Mona off Puerto Rico and headed north for the Chesapeake. On April 26, at about four in the morning, they saw land. Percy describes the first landing:

> The same day we entered into the Bay of Chesapioc directly without any let or hindrance; there we landed and discovered a little way, but we could find nothing worth the speaking of but fair meadows and goodly tall trees, with such fresh waters running through the woods as I was almost ravished at the first sight thereof.
>
> At night, when we were going aboard, there came the savages creeping upon all four from the hills like bears, with their bows in their mouths, [and] charged us very desperately in the faces, [and] hurt Captain Gabrill Archer in both his hands, and a sailor in two places of the body very dangerous. After they had spent their arrows and felt the sharpness of our shot, they retired into the woods with a great noise, and so left us....
>
> The ninth and twentieth day, we set up a cross at Chesupioc Bay and named that place "Cape Henry." ...The fourteenth day, we landed all our men, which were set to work

about the fortification, and others some to watch and ward as it was convenient.[25]

And so began the first permanent English colony in the New World.

Replica of the Godspeed *at Henricus Park on the James River south and east of Richmond.*

2

The Conquest of Tsenacomoco
1607–1644

Beginning the invasion

When Christopher Newport, John Smith, and their company returned to Jamestown on May 26, 1607 after their initial exploration to the falls of the James, they found that the fort had just barely survived an attack by about 200 Indians. Thus began what would be a bloody but intermittent struggle between a coalition of as many as thirty Indian tribes in Tidewater Virginia under the leadership of Powhatan, a Pamunkey chief, and colonists sent by the company chartered by King James I of England. The early years featured repeated violent encounters, marked by decisive battles in 1622 and 1644. European settlements, protected by military firepower, expanded steadily up the James River to the falls, and up the other tidal rivers, without treaty or permission from the incumbent occupants. By mid-century, most of the native people had been exterminated or expelled from Tsenacomoco by Virginia soldiers and settlers. English sponsors, both royal and corporate, drove the expansion of the settlement unilaterally, even as settlers and their governor went through rituals of conference and negotiation with the native inhabitants.

The language of the English adventurers in Virginia did not reflect a consciousness that they were invading the New World. The settlers believed that they, in the name of King James, were entitled to the land of Tsenacomoco, which they called Virginia. They considered the inhabitants of the land to be pagan savages. These inhabitants might be dangerous or helpful to them; they might be the beneficiaries of English Christianity and civilization; but they were not ever considered to have title to the land or to be persons of substance deserving respect.

Christopher Newport and John Smith did, in their initial dealings with the native people, act as if they respected Powhatan's preeminence in the land. At one point, they presented a crown to him on behalf of King James. A beautiful deerskin mantle in the Ashmolean Museum in Oxford, England is thought to have been a gift from Powhatan to Captain Christopher Newport. Although the parties may have had different intentions in these diplomacies, they were significant both to an Indian culture for whom protocol was important and to an English culture that respected formal rituals.

Even though the English did not consider themselves to be invaders, the initial Jamestown settlement was immediately fortified, and the leaders of the settlement assumed the likelihood of conflict. The English understood the conflict as the behavior one might expect from "savages"— the inconvenience of a wild and uncivilized land and people—rather than what naturally happens when an alien nation invades a people's homeland.

On January 2, 1608, about 120 new settlers arrived at Jamestown to join the forty or so who remained alive from the 144 that had arrived seven months earlier. In the first three years, a high percentage of the English immigrants and soldiers who reached the colony lost their lives—perhaps as many as ninety percent. Many were killed by native people. Many others were killed by disease, starvation, and various accidents. Some went voluntarily to live with the Indians or were captured. The propaganda in England did not disclose the dangers of the settlement.

A settlement at the falls

On August 11, 1609, two years after the founding of Jamestown, seven ships sailed up the James with 500 new settlers. The party was absent one of its ships, the *Sea Venture,* and 150 colonists who, with Captain Christopher Newport and the new governor of the colony, Sir Thomas Gates, had been shipwrecked on Bermuda during a hurricane.

The fleet brought instructions from the Virginia Company of London to move the headquarters of the colony upriver from Jamestown to a place more easily defended both from the Indians and, presumably, from the Spanish. Captain Francis West was sent with 120 men and six months' provisions to establish a new settlement near the falls.

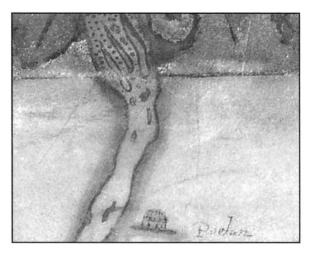

This detail is from the earliest map to show the James River up to the falls, prepared by Robarte (Robert) Tindall in 1608. Tindall drew so close to the edge of his sheet that the river runs into the decorative border of the map. The falls are clearly designated by the rocks and islands that fill the river. On the north bank of the river, a distance below the falls, is a hut symbolizing an Indian village, labeled "Poetan." Opposite the village is an island. The map is in the British Museum. Photo and caption by Jeffrey Ruggles, by permission.

West and his men built a fort, but it was a disaster. Men who left the fort were in danger; some never returned. The soldiers seemed to think their food supply should be acquired by looting the fields of the native people. The falls lay in territory governed by Parahunt, Powhatan's son. What had begun as a peaceful relationship between Parahunt's people and the English adventurers had clearly broken down. John Smith, who was president of the colony, came up to the falls to reestablish order. He found that the fort had been established on low-lying land, where it would be subject to flooding. He found several Indians kept as hostages in the fort.

West had been absent when Smith arrived, but when he returned, he and Smith argued heatedly. Smith then attempted to negotiate for the town the Indians had built on one of the hills near the falls. The town had two or three hundred acres of defensible, arable land around it. Smith offered to occupy the town and protect the Powhatans against their enemies the Monacans, who lived above the falls. He offered copper and an English boy named Henry Spelman, who had just arrived in Virginia from England several weeks earlier. In return he asked for an annual tribute to King James, a request that the chief summarily rejected. The town he purchased was called "Powhatan," and it was reputed to be the hometown of the paramount chief. Smith described it

16

in his later writings as a

> savage fort readily built and prettily fortified with poles and barks
> of trees, sufficient to have defended them from all the savages in
> Virginia – dry houses for lodgings, and near two hundred acres
> of ground ready to be planted; and no place we knew so strong,
> so pleasant and delightful in Virginia, for which we called it
> "Nonesuch."[26]

Smith embarked on a boat to return downriver to Jamestown, but
as he was sleeping in the boat he was badly injured by an explosion of
gunpowder. He jumped into the water to put out the fire and was fished
out of the river by the sailors. Tradition has held that it was an accident,
but at least one reliable scholar is convinced that West's men tried to kill
Smith. In any case, he was so badly injured that, on September 10, soon
after he had arrived back at Jamestown, he boarded a ship for England
to recuperate from his injuries. The colonists had forfeited their first
chance to establish a town near the falls of the James, but Smith had
nevertheless handed Henry Spelman over to Parahunt. Spelman, who
lived with Powhatan's people for two years, later recounted this initial
exchange.

> From Cape Henry we sailed up the River Powàhtan, and within
> 4 or 5 days arrived at James town, where we were joyfully
> welcomed by our countrymen, being at that time about 80
> persons under the government of Captain Smith, the president.
> Having here unladed our goods, and bestowed some ... fortnight
> in viewing of the country, I was carried by Captain Smith, our
> president, to the Falls, to the Little Powhatan [Parahunt] where,
> unknown to me, he sold me to him for a town called Powhatan.
> And leaving me with him, the Little Powhatan, he made known
> to Captain Weste how he had bought a town for them to dwell
> in, desiring that Captain Weste would come and settle himself
> there. But Captain Weste, having bestowed cost to begin a town
> in another place, misliked it.... [27]

Local Richmond tradition has placed Powhatan's village on present-
day Fulton Hill. There, at the beginning of the eighteenth century, stood a
large estate called "Powhatan Seat," with a stone before its entrance once
thought to have marked Powhatan's grave.[28] Another possible location is
the present site of St. John's Church on Church Hill, which William Byrd

referred to in 1741 as "Indiantown." But current archeological speculation centers on the site of "Tree Hill Farm," just to the east of Richmond in Henrico County, as the "Nonesuch Place" that Smith admired. His *Map of Virginia*, published in London in 1612, shows "Powhatan," the village at the falls, as its most prominent feature.

John Smith's 1612 Map of Virginia. The falls and "Powhatan" village near present-day Richmond are in the upper left quadrant.

Death and resurrection in Jamestown

Smith's departure from Virginia in the fall of 1609 was devastating for the remaining colonists, who soon faced their third, and most catastrophic, winter. Relationships with the native people, which ranged from desperate conflict to uneasy commerce, deteriorated. An expedition led by John Ratcliffe to Powhatan's retreat at Orapakes resulted in the death of as many as thirty-four of the fifty men who participated, including the death by torture of Ratcliffe himself. The expedition returned without acquiring any provisions.

There was little food. One man salted and ate his dead wife. Others appear to have dug up bodies and eaten them. By the time spring came, the Starving Time at Jamestown had claimed all but eighty of the settlers. The fort at Jamestown was wrecked. Doors fell off their hinges. Some of the houses were burned.

Then, on May 23, 1610, two ships arrived at the desperate colony. The *Deliverance* and the *Patience* bore the adventurers who had survived the wreck of the *Sea Venture* on Bermuda the previous August. They had constructed the replacement craft and now arrived, only to find the few remaining settlers near starvation. The new colonists were led by Sir Thomas Gates, the new governor of the colony. Among them was John Rolfe, whose wife had given birth to a first child, named Bermuda, during the time on that island. The child had died soon after birth, and Rolfe's wife died soon thereafter.

The Bermuda survivors shared their provisions with the desperate Jamestown inhabitants, but quickly determined that their supplies would not last more than two weeks. Gates decided that the colony must be abandoned. Tiny *Deliverance* and *Patience* took on board those who had survived the Starving Time, and on June 7, 1610 they set sail. They anchored overnight just downriver from the abandoned settlement. The next morning, as they prepared to set off, perhaps to seek support from English fishermen off Newfoundland, they saw ships in the distance. It was the fleet of Lord De La Warr, the latest governor of the colony, with provisions and about 400 new colonists and soldiers. All returned to Jamestown, and the colony began anew.

Tracts from Jamestown were a regular feature of the Virginia Company's program in London, seeking to raise money and settlers for the new colony. Stories of the Starving Time did not help—the tale of the man eating his wife was being told in every pub in London. The Virginia Company rushed out a new pamphlet which said that the man had killed and eaten his wife because of "mortal hatred," rather than near-starvation, and that he made up the starvation story as an excuse. Actually, the pamphlet explained, the man had a "good quantitie of meale, oatmeale, beanes and pease" on hand.[29]

To some, the rescue of the colony by the Bermuda survivors and De La Warr was seen as divine confirmation of the English mission in Virginia. In a tract published and widely read in London in 1613, William Crashaw, Anglican cleric and director of the Virginia Company, claimed the saving of the Jamestown colony was one of four acts of God that convinced him of divine purpose. They were, he said, "plain demonstrations that have convinced me to believe that assuredly God himself is the founder, and favourer of this Plantation."[30]

The first divine act, he said, was "the marvelous and indeed miraculous deliverance of our worthy Governors, Sir *Thomas Gates*, Lieutenant general, and Sir *George Somers*, Admiral, with all their company of some hundred and fifty persons, upon the feared and abhorred islands of the *Bermudas*, without loss of one person [sic], when at the same hour nothing was before their eyes but imminent and inevitable death."

The second was the discovery of Bermuda itself, by the potentially catastrophic wreck of the *Sea Venture* on its shores.

Third, and most convincing, was the arrival of the Bermuda survivors in Virginia just in time to save the colony. Crashaw spoke of

> the speciall and most fatherly providence of God over this action, in upholding it when man had forsaken it, and giving it life again when man had left it for dead: for had not Sir Thomas Gates and Sir George Somers come into Virginia from the Bermudas even when they did, the poor Colony...had been gone away, and our Plantation possessed by the Savages: and (which was much more miraculous) when they being come in, and...[all the settlers had] put themselves to the Sea to...quit the Country: and when...[there was] not an English soul left in James Towne, and, giving by their peal of shot, their last and woeful farewell to that pleasant land, were now with sorrowful hearts going down the River: Behold the hand of heaven from above, at the very instant, sent in the Right Honorable La-war to meet them even at the rivers mouth with provision and comforts of all kind; who if he had stayed but two tides longer had come into Virginia, and not found one Englishman: whereupon they all with as much joy returned, as with sorrow they had come away....
>
> And from that day by God's blessing..., they never wanted bread, for him that would take pains and do his duty. If ever the hand of God appeared in action of man, it was here most evident: for when man had forsaken this business, God took it in hand; and when men said, now hath all the earth cast off the care of this Plantation, the hand of heaven hath taken hold of it: God therefore be glorified in his own work.[31]

The fourth assurance of God's support, Crashaw maintained, was the number of voluntary financial contributions toward the endeavor: "the stirring up of so many honorable and worthy persons of all conditions to disburse so freely and so willingly such fair sums of money...."[32]

Crashaw's epistle, which was published immediately by the Virginia Company, was already known by the authorities to mask a desperate and more ominous reality lying behind the *Sea Venture* episode. While in Bermuda, the shipwrecked men organized at least three separate mutinies against the governor, seeing that life on the island and relative freedom from the social strictures to be anticipated in Virginia were to their advantage. Two of these persons were executed for rebellion—one by hanging and one by firing squad. [33]

The English-Powhatan War

English tradition consistently holds that the native people were hostile, murderous, and undependable, although the English did get much of their food from them during their first two years in Jamestown. But the native stories tell the same about the English. They suggest that John Smith and his armored soldiers, equipped with "firesticks," came to their villages and literally put a gun to the chief's head, taking the grain and leaving behind a few beads.

Both sides committed murder and atrocities against each other. But there is no indication that the English at any time honestly negotiated for land, agreed to pay for land, agreed to division of land, agreed to limit their own demands for land, or sought honestly to establish an equitable and mutually beneficial governing relationship. This is true even though Christopher Newport, John Smith, and their successors regularly represented themselves to native leaders as recognizing the Powhatan's position and the equitable relationship between the two peoples. The English did not consider the Powhatan people worthy of respectful relationship and mutual, legal covenant; and should it sometimes have been the case that colonial authorities were inclined that way, the English government and public-private Virginia Company of London would countenance no such outcome to the adventure.

On the other hand, it seems likely that the Powhatan people did intend, at least at some points in the story, to incorporate the English into their nation, and that Powhatan actually appointed John Smith a *werowance*, or leader, of the nation, and offered him a town on the Pamunkey River for settlement.

Powhatan could have killed both John Smith and Christopher Newport and did not do so. The threatened ceremonial killing and rescue of Smith when he was an unwilling guest at Werowocomoco, Powhatan's capital on what is now the York River, was most likely a demonstration of the tribe's intention to help him stay alive, a ritual of initiation. Far from being a disobedient savior of the alien white man, Pocahontas would have been in this drama a well-rehearsed bearer of her father's intentions for relationship and mercy. John Smith was returned safely to Jamestown in that second year of the colony after weeks of touring the various villages of the confederacy in the custody of the Powhatan's warriors.

The relationship between the Algonquian people and the English was extremely dangerous to the original inhabitants of the land, just as it was for the English invader/colonists. Colonists who strayed from the forts were constantly at risk of capture or attack. But so were native people. The English regularly threatened Indian villages, stole grain at gunpoint, and kidnapped Indian children to be their servants. With no English women in the colony for the first two years, and very few until 1619, Indian women were at constant risk of rape.

English leaders sought to compel the native people to allow them to take what land they wanted and simply trade with them for supplies, especially in the winter. Governor-general Lord De La Warr, after his arrival in 1610, sent a communication to Powhatan listing the crimes of the Indians. He knew, he said, that "these mischiefs were (not) contrived by him, or with his knowledge, but conceived them rather to be the acts of his worst and unruly people." He told Powhatan to return stolen swords, axes, and hoes, and any prisoners he might be holding. He reminded Powhatan that he had sworn allegiance to King James and had received symbols of "Civil State and Christian Sovereignty" from the English. Therefore, he should comply with De La Warr's demands. Powhatan replied in kind to the English message. According to William Strachey, secretary of the colony,

> [Powhatan] returned no other answer but that either we should depart his country or confine ourselves to Jamestown only, without searching further up into his land or rivers, or otherwise he would give in command to his people to kill us and do unto us all the mischief which they at their pleasure could and we feared; withal forewarning the said messengers not to return any more unto him, unless they brought him a coach and three horses, for he had understood by the Indians which were in England how such was the state of great werowances and lords in England.[34]

De La Warr responded aggressively to Powhatan's message. First his men attacked a village of Kecoughtan on the north shore of the James, killing five and capturing the grain fields of the village, ripe for harvest. A month later, on the night of August 9, 1610, English soldiers under George Percy attacked a town belonging to the Paspahegh tribe, at the mouth of the Chickahominy River. Percy described the attack:

> My lord general [De La Warr], not forgetting old Powhatan's subtle treachery, sent a messenger unto him to demand certain arms and divers men which we supposed might be living in his country. But he returned no other than proud and disdainful answers. Whereupon my lord, being much incensed, caused a commission to be drawn wherein he appointed me chief commander over seventy men, and sent me to take revenge upon the Paspaheans and Chiconamians. And so, shipping myself and my soldiers in two boats, I departed from James Town the 9th of August 1610, and the same night landed within three miles of Paspaha's town. Then drawing my soldiers into battalio, placing a captain or lieutenant at every file, we marched towards the town, having an Indian guide with me named Kempes, whom the provost marshal led in a handlock. This subtle savage was leading us out of the way; the which I misdoubting bastinaded him with my truncheon, and threat'ned to cut off his head. Whereupon the slave altered his course and brought us the right way near unto the town, so that then I commanded every leader to draw away his file before me to beset the savages' houses that none might escape, with a charge not to give the alarum until I were come up unto them with the colors. At my coming I appointed Captain William Weste to give the alarum, the which he performed by shooting of a pistol.
>
> And then we fell in upon them, put some fifteen or sixteen to the sword, and almost all the rest to flight. Whereupon I caused my drum to beat, and drew all my soldiers to the colors. My lieutenant, bringing with him the queen and her children and one Indian prisoner, for the which I taxed him because he had spared them, his answer was that, having them now in my custody, I might do with them what I pleased. Upon the same, I caused the Indian's head to be cut off; and then dispersed my files, appointing my soldiers to burn their houses and to cut down their corn growing about the town. And after, we marched with the queen and her children to our boats again where, being no sooner well shipped, my soldiers did begin to murmur because the queen and her children were spared. So upon the same a council being called, it was agreed upon to put the children to death, which was effected by throwing them overboard and shooting out their

brains in the water.

After burning the towns and crops in the surrounding area, they returned to Jamestown, with the queen still a prisoner. Percy concludes his narrative in this way:

> My lord general [De La Warr], not being well, did lie a-shipboard, to whom we rowed; he being joyful of our safe return, yet seemed to be discontent because the queen was spared, as Captain Davis told me, and that it was my lord's pleasure that we should see her dispatched (the way he thought best—to burn her). To the first I replied that having seen so much bloodshed that day, now in my cold blood I desired to see no more; and for to burn her I did not hold it fitting, but either by shot or sword to give her a quicker dispatch. So turning myself from Captain Davis, he did take the queen with two soldiers ashore, and in the woods put her to the sword.[35]

Percy's starkly unashamed account of the atrocity is itself noteworthy. No less striking is the attitude of Lord De La Warr, who was widely thought to have been brought to Virginia by God at just the right time to save the colony. De La Warr seems to have missed some of the glow of the divine blessing.[36]

The establishment of Henrico

Like his predecessors as governor of Virginia, Lord De La Warr sought to establish a headquarters at the falls of the James. After his massacre of the Paspaheghs, he went upriver with soldiers and established his residence at the fort built by his nephew, Captain Francis West, two years before. He spent the winter there, but on March 28, 1611, he left Virginia altogether. Seven weeks later, on May 19, he was replaced by Sir Thomas Dale.

Dale, a soldier, is known for his establishment of martial law in Virginia. Settlers were made subject to what he entitled the "Lawes Divine, Morall and Martiall, &c." They were, he said, " 'souldiers emprest in this sacred cause,' " answerable to " 'the King of kings, the commaunder of commaunders, and Lord of Hostes.' "[37]

Dale resolved to bring order to the Virginia Colony, turning his military discipline against settlers as well as native people. Severe laws were established against persons who would run away and join the original inhabitants—Dale is said to have tortured and killed persons he caught in that act at Henrico,[38] a town nine miles downriver from the falls of the James which he began to build in 1611, and to which he intended to move the headquarters of the colony. As governor, he was able to exercise in Henrico virtually absolute control over the town's inhabitants, which would not have been feasible in Jamestown. Dale's critics sent this account to England:

> Sir Thomas Dale removed himself with three hundred persons for the building of Henrico Towne, where being landed he oppressed his whole company with such extraordinary labors by day and watching by night, as may seem incredible to the ears of any who had not the experimental trial thereof. Want of houses at first landing in the cold of winter, and pinching hunger continually biting, made those imposed labours most insufferable, and the best fruits and effects thereof to be no better then the slaughter of his Majestys free subjects by starving, hanging, burning, breaking upon the wheel and shooting to death, some (more than half famished) running to the Indians to get relief being again returned were burnt to death. Some for stealing to satisfy their hunger were hanged, and one chained to a tree till he starved to death; others attempting to run away in a barge and a shallop...and therin to adventure their lives for their native country, being discovered and prevented, were shot to death, hanged and broken upon the wheel; besides continual whippings, extraordinary punishments, working as slaves in irons for term of years (and that for petty offences) were daily executed. Many famished in holes and other poor cabins in the ground, not respected because sickness had disabled them for labour, nor was there sufficient for them that were more able to work, our best allowance being but nine ounces of corrupt and putrified meal and half a pint of oatmeal or peas (of like ill condition) for each person a daye.[39]

Dale claimed divine warrant for what he was doing. Soon after Henrico was settled, on November 6, 1612, Henry, Prince of Wales, died. Henry had been Dale's patron, and Henrico was named for him. Dale wrote these words in tribute: "My glorious master is gone, that would have ennamelled with his favours the labours I undertake, for Gods cause, and his immortall honour. He was the great Captaine of our Israell, the hope to have builded up this heavenly new Jerusalem...."[40]

Dutch Gap, once the site of Henrico, is at foot of photo. Across the channel to the right is the point of Varina Farm. The point on which Henrico stood was later the site of a U.S. Light House Reservation, seen within a fence. On either side of that point are the abandoned channels of the James River which surrounded Henrico and Farrar's Island. The next large loop of the river above Dutch Gap encloses Hatcher's Island, and the final loop marks the end of Osborne Turnpike as the James turns north to the Falls and Richmond. The photo, from the files of Dr. George Cleaveland, appeared in the Virginia Magazine of History and Biography 30:164.

Our major source for information on the founding of Henrico is Ralph Hamor, who preceded Thomas Dale in Virginia, and published "A True Discourse of the Present Estate of Virginia" when he returned to England in 1615. Henrico was located on a narrow neck of land that was attached to the north shore of the James River at what is now Varina Farm. The neck, barely 200 yards wide, widened southward into a large bulb of arable land called Farrar's Island, covering seven acres and surrounded by a great seven-mile curve of the river.[41] Here is Hamor's account of the building of Henrico:

> At the beginning of September 1611, [Dale] set from James town, and in a day and a half landed at a place where he proposed to seat and build; where he had not been ten days before he had very strongly impaled seven English acres of ground for a town

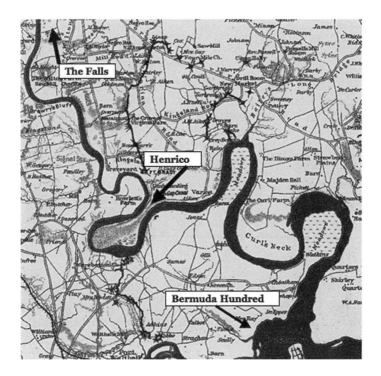

which, in honor of the noble Prince Henry (of ever happy and blessed memory, whose royal heart was ever strongly affected to that action), he called by the name of "Henrico."

No sooner was he thus fenced and in a manner secured from the Indians, but his next work without respect to his own health or particular welfare, was building at each corner of the town very strong and high commanders, or watchtowers, a fair and handsome church, and storehouses; which finished, he began to think upon convenient houses and lodgings for himself and men, which, with as much speed as was possible, were more strongly and more handsome than any formerly in Virginia contrived and finished; and even in four months' space he had made Henrico much better and of more worth than all the work ever since the colony began therein done.... [Henrico] stands upon a neck of a very high land, 3 parts thereof environed with the main river, and cut over between the two rivers with a strong pale, which maketh the neck of land an island. There is in this town 3 streets of well framed houses, a handsome church, and the foundation of a more stately one laid—of brick, in length an hundred foot, and fifty foot wide—beside store-houses, watch-houses, and suchlike. There are also, as ornaments belonging to this town, upon the verge of this river, five fair blockhouses, or commanders, wherein live the honester sort of people as in farms in England; and there keep continual sentinel for the town's security; and about two miles from the town into the main, a pale of two miles in length, cut over from river to river, guarded likewise with several commanders, with a great quantity of corn ground impaled, sufficient, if there were no more in the colony secured, to maintain with but easy manuring and husbandry more men than I suppose will be addressed thither (the more is the pity) these 3 years.

For the further enlargement yet of this town on the other side of the river, by impaling likewise—for we make no other fence—is secured to our use, especially for our hogs to feed in, about twelve English miles of ground, by name Coxen-Dale, secured by five forts called Hope in Faith, Charity Fort, Mount Malado (a retreat, or guest house, for sick people—a high seet and wholesome air), Elizabeth Fort, and Fort Patience.

And here hath Mr. Whitacres chosen his parsonage, or church land, some hundred acres impaled, and a fair framed parsonage house built thereupon called "Rocke Hall." Of this town and all the forts thereunto belonging hath Captain James Davis the principal command and government.[42]

An uneasy peace

An uneasy peace prevailed in the colony from the summer of 1613, due to the capture by the English of Powhatan's daughter Pocahontas. Pocahontas and John Rolfe, with their infant son Thomas, sailed for England on the *Treasurer* in April, 1616. Rolfe returned to the colony by himself at the end of May, 1617, his wife having died and his son having been left behind. Upon his return, Governor Samuel Argall, captain of the *Treasurer*, almost immediately led a raid killing a dozen Chickahominy Indians and taking another dozen prisoner, because they had not paid a tribute in corn they had promised to pay while he was gone.

In the winter, Powhatan retired from leadership. Opechancanough retained the military authority of the Powhatan tribes. He informed Argall that he would not agree to assign further lands to the English unless Thomas Rolfe were to come to Virginia to claim them.[43] Thomas was three years old at the time. In the response of the General Court of the Virginia Company to Argall concerning this information, we hear an incredulity that doomed any local negotiation between colonists and native people:

> Wee cannot imagine why you should give us warninge that Opachankano and the Natives have given their Country to Mr. Rolfe Child and that they will reserve it from all others till he comes of yeares except as some do here report it to be a Devise of your owne to some especiall purpose for yourselfe.[44]

In 1616 the Virginia Company had obtained a new royal charter, independent of any treaty with the Indians, which would unilaterally give "land patents" in Virginia to any person buying shares in the company. The policy was not put into effect for more than a year, but it encouraged expanding English seizure of land in Tsenacomoco and caused the establishment of as many as 40 new settlements there.[45]

By 1619, Argall had been recalled to England, and George Yeardley had become governor. Powhatan had died, replaced by his brother[46] Opitchipam. Relations between colonists and Indians were becoming increasingly tense, as we see in the trial of Henry Spelman in Jamestown on August 4.

Spelman, as a boy, had been given by John Smith to Parahunt at the falls of the James. Now, once more living with the English, he had visited Opechancanough's town when another English "interpreter" was present. According to the witness, Spelman "spake very unreverently and maliciously against this present Governor [Yeardley]" to Opechancanough, "whereby the honour and dignity of [Governor Yeardley's] place and person, and so of the whole Colonie, might be brought into contempte, by which meanes what mischiefs might ensue from the Indians by disturbance of the peace or otherwise, may easily be conjectured."[47]

The court opined that Spelman deserved to be executed "speedily," but instead sentenced him to seven years as a translator for the governor. The official record notes that Spelman "had in him more of the Savage then of the Christian," and that upon being sentenced he "muttered certain words to himselfe neither shewing any remorse for his offenses, nor yet any thankfulness to the Assembly" for not executing him.[48]

Soon thereafter, Spelman accompanied John Rolfe and another colonist named Thomas Hobson on a daring and unprecedented visit to see Opechancanough. They traveled up the Youghtanund River (now the York and Pamunkey) toward his headquarters, which lay some distance inland from the present town of West Point. Opechancanough met them and spoke with Rolfe. Rolfe reported back to Governor Yeardley that Opechancanough was adamant about not granting permission for further acquisition of land by the settlers. Similarly, he would not "upon any terms" allow children to be taken from their families to be brought up in an English-run school. But, he said, he would encourage entire families to settle near the school, if the English wished, so long as they were provided with houses, land and cattle. Their children could then go to the school and their board expenses would be borne by their own families, he suggested.[49]

The university at Henrico

The most idealistic venture of the English colony was the founding of a school and university at Henrico. The Virginia Company had determined, under the influence of Nicholas Ferrar and others, to build a university in the new colony that would serve both native people and the children of the English settlers. It was the hope of the English that they could ultimately pacify and incorporate the native people into their colonial society by taking Indian children from their homes and educating them in an English environment. The institution would also provide education for the children of settlers, who would otherwise have to be sent back to England. To support the university, they set aside 10,000 acres occupying the north bank of the James from Henrico town all the way to the falls. The present Richmond Hill was therefore the western terminus of the university lands.

Henrico did not flourish. When Dale left Virginia for good in 1616, just five years after building the town, much of it had already fallen into disrepair. Only thirty-eight men and boys were reported to be living there, half of whom were farmers. However, the dream of the university continued.

The idea gained significant strength when, probably in 1618, King James endorsed it and initiated a nationwide fundraising effort for the university through the Church of England. He asked the archbishops to hold a subscription in the parishes for that purpose in each of the next two years. They were to give the money to the Virginia Company to be "imployed for the godly purposes intended, and no other."[50]

The Virginia Company was expending energy and money on the project. Particular support was given by the Ferrar family of London.

The father, Nicholas, was a leading financier and had been an early member of the company. He gave 100 pounds to pay for the education of 100 Indian children. The brothers John and Nicholas were also members of the company. John provided his own ship, the *Bona Nova*, to bring settlers to the university lands in 1619. Nicholas, the son, was a theologian as well as secretary of the company, and was an eager supporter of the university.[51]

John Rolfe had written in 1617 that the native people were "loving and willing to part with their children."[52] In 1619, in the first meeting of the first European elected assembly in the Western Hemisphere, Virginia's House of Burgesses enacted a law that provided

> that for laying a sure foundation of the conversion of the Indians to Christian Religion, each town, citty, Borrough, and particular plantation do obtain unto themselves by just means a certain number of the natives' children to be educated by them in true religion and civil course of life—of which children the most towardly boys in wit and graces of nature to be brought up by them in the first elements of literature, so to be fitted for the college intended for them that from thence they may be sent to that work of conversion."[53]

Mismanagement of the college lands and preparations for the university led the Virginia Company in 1620 to send George Thorpe, who was a member of King James' privy chamber and of the Virginia Company, to run the project in the colony. Thorpe, living on the college lands, became known for his relationships with the native people, including Opechancanough. Thorpe planted 10,000 grapevines and also tried to produce silk. He was an advocate for the native people. In a letter to his patron, Sir Edwin Sandys, Thorpe wrote,

> There is scarce any man amongst us that doth so much as afford [the native people] a good thought in his heart, and most men with their mouths give them nothing but maledictions and bitter execrations, being thereunto falsely carried with a violent mispersuasion...that these poor people have done unto us all the wrong and injury that the malice of the Devil or man can afford, whereas in my poor understanding if there be wrong on any side it is on ours who are not so charitable to them as Christians ought to be, they being (especially the better sort of them) of a peaceable & virtuous disposition.[54]

Thorpe wanted the Virginia Company to make an official declaration to the settlers that its policy was the conversion of the natives. This would, he felt, help the native people trust the settlers. He was said to have threatened punishment to anyone who mistreated Indians, and even to have killed several dogs that were harassing native people. Thorpe thought that Opechancanough himself had admitted that his own religion was insufficient, and that he could be converted to Christianity. He related that he enjoyed his conversations with the native leader. He had built him an English-style house, revealing that he regarded his former habitation as a "denne or hog-stye."[55]

Good Friday morning, March 22, 1622, Opechancanough's men surprised and killed about 340 English. Seventeen settlers died on the university lands and the others fled. Thorpe was warned by a servant, but according to the official record, "out of the conscience of his own good meaning, and fair deserts ever towards [the Indians, he] was so void of all suspicion, and so full of confidence, that they had sooner killed him, than he could or would believe they meant any ill against him." The mutilation of Thorpe's corpse by the attackers was described as "unbefitting to be heard by any civil ear."[56]

Opechancanough's well-planned offensive probably was not intended to expel the English from Tsenacomoco. With a population at least ten times that of the English, the Powhatans could have attacked more broadly than they did. It is true that Jamestown had been warned by an Indian living with settlers across the river, but the Powhatans did not attempt to attack Jamestown in any case. The objective seems to have been more limited—punishment of the English for expanding unilaterally beyond the area that had been agreed to.[57]

Nonetheless, the colonists again saw in their survival the hand of God. In 1623 the governor set aside March 22 as a "day of prayer and thanksgiving to God for the merciful deliverance of many from the treachery of the Indians."[58] Far from being dissuaded from further settlement, they retaliated systematically, pursuing what scholar Edmund Morgan calls a policy of "extermination" of the native people. Killing a native person was not considered murder, nor had it ever been. Virginia Company records suggest that the colonists negotiated a series of sham treaties, deceiving the natives so that they might then attack them. They waited until the natives planted crops, settling in one place, and then attacked the towns.[59] In one particularly onerous case, a Dr. John Pott, who was both a distiller and a doctor, prepared a cask of poisoned sherry for a celebration with the Patawomeck tribe.

According to an account written in a letter by Robert Bennett,

> after a many feigned speeches, the peace was to be concluded in
> a health or toast in sack [sherry] which was sent of purpose in
> the butte [cask] with Captain Tucker to poison them. So Captain
> Tucker began and our interpreter tasted before the king would
> take it, but not of the same. So then the king with the king of
> Cheskake, [their] sons and all the great men were drunk—how
> many we cannot write of—but it is thought some two hundred
> were poisoned, and they coming back killed some 50 more and
> brought home part of their heads.[60]

Bennett concludes by saying "God send us victory, as we make no
question God assisting."[61]

Opechancanough's men had killed 340 settlers, scalping many.
The colonists retaliated in kind, also taking scalps (although apparently
this last fact scandalized the people back home in England). According
to Morgan, "within two or three years of the [1622] massacre, the
English had avenged the deaths of that day many times over."[62] Only a
relatively few Indians remained among the settlers—often as servants
or slaves.

King James dissolved the Virginia Company in 1624, changing
the whole governance of the colony and ending any effective efforts to
establish the university at Henrico.

Opechancanough succeeded Opitchipam as paramount chief of
the Powhatan tribes in 1629. On April 18, 1644, twenty years and a
month after the first attack, nearly ninety years old himself, half-blind
and "carried on a litter," Opechancanough ordered another attack on
the settlers. More than 500 English were killed, but by that time they
were less than five percent of the English population.

In 1645, English soldiers attacked Opechancanough's town and
fort on the upper Pamunkey River,[63] captured him, and imprisoned
him in Jamestown. Plans to ship him to England were cancelled when
a soldier shot him in the back.[64]

A new paramount chief, Necotowance, was chosen in 1646 and
signed a treaty with the English limiting English territory to what one
scholar has described as "an English reservation" on the Peninsula and
south of the James.[65] But at the same time the Virginia Assembly secretly
passed a law that abrogated those limits and opened up all the land
north of the York to settlers, effective in 1649. By 1665 the Indians had
been removed from most of Tidewater Virginia. A population estimated

at 15,000 to 20,000 in 1607 had been reduced to 2,000 to 3,000 in barely a half century. "In a very real sense," scholars Helen Rountree and Randolph Turner comment, "the Powhatans lost their land by being flooded out by settlers, not by being defeated in war."[66] In 1660, the European immigrant population reached 25,000.

What shadows remained on the land from the first forty years of English conquest and colonization! The colonists who survived were traumatized by years of combat, death, disease, and atrocity. Some had found life under the military rule of the colony so severe that they escaped to live in the swamps, or even with the constantly endangered native remnant. Hardly anyone of any race who lived in Tsenacomoco or Virginia was spared the trauma and the moral distortion of that period.

The English incursion had been founded on the assumption that land could be taken from its inhabitants without contract or remuneration. The relationship with these people was a perpetual state of war, in which no rights accrued to the people regarded as savages and no colonist was secure. There were no courts, no protective laws for the Powhatan people. Their religion was judged so defective as to assure them of damnation if they were not "saved" by baptism and conversion to the religion of the conquering people. Brutality and massacre were justified, and the natives were considered by the English settlers to be culturally and morally inferior savages. Relegated to permanent underclass status, they were safe only so long as they were invisible and not involved legally in property or the economy.

3

The Mystery of Pocahontas
1597–1617

The myth of the rescue

I n the Rotunda of the Capitol of the United States are three images of Pocahontas, who was the daughter of Powhatan,[67] the ruler of Tsenacomoco when the English arrived in 1607. One, entitled *Captain Smith and Pocahontas*, is in the great frieze that encircles the Rotunda.[68] A second, the *Preservation of Captain John Smith by Pocahontas*, is a sandstone relief over the west door.[69] The third, *The Baptism of Pocahontas*, is one of eight twelve-foot-by-eighteen-foot monumental oil paintings representing the early history of the nation that comprise the eight panels of the Rotunda itself.

Captain Smith and Pocahontas *as portrayed in the great frieze in the Rotunda of the Capitol in Washington, D.C.*

These official pieces of art represent the state-sanctioned story of the nation's origins as told by its leaders of European descent. The tale of the saving of John Smith's life by Pocahontas was taken from his *General Historie*, published in 1624. It has become one of the best known of all the stories of early Virginia. It is reproduced at length in the fourth-grade social studies textbook that was still required to be studied by all public school students in Virginia after 1965.[70]

The baptism of Pocahontas[71] is a less well-known incident than the rescue, but the commemorative painting of that event that hangs in the Capitol is intriguing if for no other reason than that it honors a major religious event in the central shrine of a nation that specifically separates church and state. The painting was installed in 1840, two years after President Andrew Jackson forced the Cherokee nation to walk the "Trail of Tears" to Oklahoma.

The Baptism of Pocahontas. *This monumental painting by John Gadsby Chapman, 12 x 18 feet in size, was placed in the Capitol Rotunda in Washington in 1840. It depicts Pocahontas being baptized "Rebecca" by Anglican minister Alexander Whitaker.*

An official pamphlet published at the time of the painting's unveiling called Pocahontas one of the "children of the forest" who had been "snatched from the fangs of barbarous idolatry." It congratulated the Jamestown settlers for inaugurating "the blessings of Christianity among the heathen savages."[72]

Pocahontas and John Smith stand as great mythic characters whose history lies at the foundation of European America's story of its beginnings. In particular, the Indian princess has intrigued and captured the fancy of the land's conquerors from the beginning. In her, perhaps, they saw the welcome they might have wished for and even thought they deserved—unaware as many were that they were invading and seeking to disrupt a culture as substantial and sophisticated as their own. In her they saw justification for their efforts on behalf of the savages, a vindication of the value of their civilization and their religion. The dominant American histories as told by the victors of European descent single out Pocahontas as the most admirable of her people.

Pocahontas' appeal in Virginia is striking. Careful genealogical studies list those persons who are entitled to claim descent from her through her son, Thomas Rolfe. Even at the most extreme point of early twentieth-century racial eugenics policy in Virginia, when "white" people were clearly distinguished from all others, the term "white" was legally defined to include "persons who have one-sixteenth or less of the blood of the American Indian and have no other non-Caucasic blood," a provision securing deliberate exception from the scandal of miscegenation for all who wished to claim publicly their descent from the Indian princess.[73]

The dominant American myth of Pocahontas, the dark-haired beauty from savage roots who provided welcome to strangers and sealed the legitimacy of the English settlement, is a piece of propaganda told to justify the effort and assuage the guilt of an unacknowledged war of conquest and extermination. Ninety percent of Pocahontas' people, those united under the paramount chief Powhatan, had been pushed out of Tidewater Virginia or killed in the first half-century of English conquest, under policies that in modern international law would be considered genocide.[74]

Preservation of Captain John Smith by Pocahontas. *Sandstone relief by Antonio Capellano, 1825. Located in the U.S. Capitol Rotunda, above west door.*

Nonetheless, for its own sake—and perhaps for her sake and the sake of humanity—the story of Pocahontas deserves to be told as best it can from the sources we have. She was clearly a remarkable woman. She lived the first two-thirds of her life in the language, religion, and culture of the Algonquians and the last third in the language, religion, and culture of the English. She was a charismatic figure in both environments. Her heroism is blasphemed if it is used to provide vindication for the violence and racism of her contemporaries and captors. Yet it is a tale with its own deep value, perhaps not yet fully appreciated at the beginning of the twenty-first century.

The daughter of Powhatan

Pocahontas was the daughter of Powhatan, a werowance of the Pamunkey tribe. Soon after her birth, her father became paramount chief of the tribes in Tsenacomoco—the land the English called Virginia. His new position required him to have many wives and many children, but Pocahontas remained a favorite.[75]

She was born around 1597, and called "Amonute." She spent her early childhood at her father's capital town, called Werowocomoco, on the northern bank of the Youghtanund (now the York) River. By the time the English arrived in 1607, she was known as Pocahontas, which meant "something like 'Mischief' or 'Little Playful One.' "[76] She probably first met John Smith and the English when Smith was captured and, after several weeks' guided tour of Indian towns, brought to Werowocomoco to meet Powhatan in January of 1608. It is this encounter that Smith later described as a near-execution in which he was rescued by Powhatan's daughter.

Few scholars believe Smith's story of a rescue. When Smith first told the story of his visit to Powhatan's town in his *True Relation,* published in 1608, he made no mention of a threatened death or of a rescue. The familiar story of his rescue appears in detail in his much more extensive *General Historie,* published in 1624.[77] There he described being seized before Powhatan by men bearing clubs who placed his head on two large stones, intending apparently to beat him to death. At that point the king's daughter took his "head in her armes and laid her owne upon his to save him from death."[78] By that point, Pocahontas had become a nearly mythic figure in England.

If this dramatic and life-altering event actually happened, scholars question why Smith neglected to include it in the first account of that particular visit to Powhatan. That account—his *True Relation*—is all the more credible because it appears to have been written without intention of being published. Moreover, persons knowledgeable of the Powhatan tribes and their traditions doubt that such an event could have been anything but an orchestrated initiation or rescue ceremony.

It would have symbolized the mercy and gentleness that the great chief had shown to the English visitor—a royal act of beneficence.

John Smith came back to Werowocomoco the next month, this time to bring his captain, Christopher Newport, to meet Powhatan. At this particular visit, Smith brought a white greyhound dog as a present, and Captain Newport exchanged some swords for corn. Following the visit, a dispute arose at Jamestown around the terms of trade between the colonists and the Indians. Smith took seven of Powhatan's men prisoner.

Now Powhatan sent his young daughter with some of his men to seek the return of the prisoners. Her visit would have been meant to assure the English of the peaceful intent of the visit, as well as to remind Captains Smith and Newport of the safe treatment which they had received when they were in Powhatan's own territory. She also probably served as an interpreter, having learned English from an English boy, Thomas Savage, who had been sent to live at Werowocomoco.

Smith described this visit in his earliest notes about Virginia, written several months later, in the spring of 1608:

> Powhatan understanding we detained certain savages, sent his daughter, a child of ten years old, which not only for feature, countenance, and proportion much exceedeth any of the rest of his people, but for wit and spirit the only nonpareil of his country. This he sent by his most trusty messenger, called Rawhunt, as much exceeding in deformity of person, but of a subtle wit and crafty understanding. He with a long circumstance told me how well Powhatan loved and respected me and, in that I should not doubt any way of his kindness, he had sent his child, which he most esteemed, to see me.....
>
> Now all of them...came amongst us to beg liberty for their men. In the afternoon,...after prayer [we] gave them to Pocahuntas, the king's daughter, in regard of her father's kindness in sending her. After having well fed them, as all the time of their imprisonment, we gave them their bows, arrows, or what else they had, and with much content sent them packing. Pocahuntas also we requited with such trifles as contented her....[79]

After that visit, apparently, Pocahontas visited Jamestown with some frequency, at least for the year and a half until Smith finally left the colony. After Smith's departure in the fall of 1609, relationships between colonists and settlers became increasingly hostile. In that winter, receiving little support from the Indians, the English almost died out.

But in the earliest colonial period the appearance of Powhatan's daughter in a visit signaled to the colonists that safety was present. Whether the English understood this as a deliberate signal from Powhatan is uncertain, but it is clear that they felt relief and enjoyment at the presence of this particular emissary.

William Strachey, who arrived aboard the rescue ships from Bermuda in May 1610, made famous the young girl's cartwheeling antics either from his own observation that summer, or from talking with some of the survivors of the previous year.

> Pochahuntas, a well featured but wanton young girl, Powhatan's daughter, sometimes resorting to our fort, of the age then of 11 or 12 years, [would] get the boys forth with her into the marketplace, and make them wheel falling on their hand, turning their heels upwards, whom she would follow and wheel so her self, naked as she was all the fort over.[80]

The only full sentences we have from the Powhatan languages may indicate that Pocahontas actually taught John Smith. Smith lists many words and phrases, as do other Englishmen reporting on the colony. But in his *Map of Virginia*, published in 1612, he gives these two examples of the language:

Mowchick woyawgh tawgh noerach kaquere mecher, which he translates as "I am verie hungrie, what shall I eate?"

Kekaten pokahontas patiaquagh ningh tanks manotyens neer mowchick rawrenock audowgh: "Bid Pokahontas bring hither two little Baskets, and I will give her white beads to make her a chaine." [81]

In his *General Historie* John Smith published a document written by Richard Pots, clerk of the Council, and three others that dramatized the role of the young woman even more, and spoke of charges that Smith wanted to make himself a king by marrying the king's daughter. Smith seems to have been interested in defending himself against these charges. Pots wrote,

> It is true she was the very nonpareil of [Powhatan's] kingdom, and at most not past 13 or 14 years of age. Very oft she came to our fort with what she could get for Captain Smith, that ever

loved and used all the country well, but her especially he ever much respected.... But her marriage could no way have entitled him by any right to the kingdom, nor was it ever suspected he had ever such a thought, or more regarded her, or any of them, than in honest reason and discretion he might. If he would he might have married her, or have done what him listed, for there was none that could have hind'red his determination.[82]

Indian tradition suggests that Powhatan was interested in showing his desire for a peaceful relationship with the English because he hoped they might become a part of his confederation and, with their weapons and ships, defend his nation against the Spaniards. Smith recorded such a suggestion in his writings. Powhatan's strategies in the first two years appear in retrospect to have indicated acceptance of the English presence, so long as they understood their subject status, while allowing them to fail if they could not support or defend themselves.

But the arrival of Lord De La Warr to rescue the departing, nearly dead colonists, on June 8, 1610, signified the end of any remaining Indian hope of a mutually beneficial arrangement between natives and settlers. De La Warr was aggressive, demanding tribute and subjugation from Powhatan, which the chief refused.

Pocahontas no longer came to Jamestown. In 1610 she married Kocoum,[83] a warrior who was probably a member of the Patawomeck tribe. There is some tradition that she had a son, also named Kocoum,[84] and there is speculation that they lived together for at least a time on the fringe of the Powhatan territory, in the town of Patawomeck.

Betrayal at Patawomeck

The Potomac River flows east in the first portion of its trip to the Chesapeake Bay from the mountains of Virginia, but when it reaches the fall line, the edge of Tidewater, just west of Washington, D.C., it runs south until it finally turns east again in Stafford County, north of Fredericksburg. This angular course brings the tidal Potomac within ten miles of the Rappahannock at Fredericksburg. The result was that in the seventeenth century, Indian people on the Potomac were close to the edge of the tribes concentrated around Powhatan's leadership, but also related to the tribes farther to the north.

At the corner where the great river turns east near Fredericksburg, Potomac Creek enters the Potomac River, creating a beautiful point opposite the great bend. On that point the Patawomeck Indians had a major town.[85] The fields of the Patawomecks were fertile and productive. Current tribal elders say that the tribe was a "semi-independent rival to the Powhatan Confederacy of Chief Powhatan to the south, but unlike many Native Americans who fought the white settlers..., a peaceful one."[86] This semi-independent tribe and its capital town provided the site for some of the most decisive events in the life of Pocahontas, Tsenacomoco, and the British colony of Virginia.

In the summer after he arrived in Jamestown, John Smith explored the Chesapeake Bay and visited Patawomeck. He arrived at what is now Potomac Creek on June 18, 1608. Hundreds[87] of wildly painted and shouting warriors hid in the woods near the anchorage, but the English musket shots quieted them. The Indians told Smith that they had been ordered by Powhatan to betray the English. After sailing all the way to the falls of the river near present-day Georgetown, Smith's expedition returned again to the Patawomeck, and were led by the chief on an expedition inland to a place where the tribe mined antimony.

A little more than a year later, an Englishman was living in or near the town. The young man was Henry Spelman, the servant-boy whom John Smith had given to Powhatan in return for the town at the falls of the James River. Spelman had gone to live with Powhatan at Orapakes for "24 or 25 weeks," when the "King of [Patawomeck] came to visit the Great Powetan." Orapakes, Powhatan's most secure retreat, lay in the north end of the Chickahominy swamp, only about ten miles east of the falls of the James, and was accessible only by trail and canoe.[88] The visiting Patawomeck king "showed such kindness" to Spelman and the other English boys that they "determined to go away with him," Spelman recalled in a written account. When the "king" left Powhatan's town, they sneaked out of camp to follow him. They were pursued. One was killed and one returned to Orapakes. But Henry escaped and eventually made his way to a Patawomeck town called Paspatanzie, where he stayed for more than a year.[89]

The next year, at the end of 1610, Samuel Argall, the ruthless and talented sea captain who had brought Governor De La Warr's ship to the colony that summer, sailed up the river to seek grain from the Patawomecks. The colonists were locked in a struggle with Powhatan over supplies, and nearly the whole colony had starved the previous winter. When Argall reached Patawomeck territory, he learned of Spelman's presence, and upon finding the boy, got him to negotiate with him for corn, peas, and beans from Iapassus, the werowance and brother of the chief of the Patawomecks. Argall then bought Spelman from the tribe, considering that the boy had more than earned his ransom by his skill at negotiating the price of the foodstuffs. Spelman traveled back to Jamestown with Argall, and soon was en route with him back to England.[90]

Two years later, on December 1, 1612, Argall, who now bore the title of Admiral of Virginia, headed up the bay to Patawomeck for more grain. This time he was in a warship, the 130-ton, 14-gun *Treasurer*. The giant war machine was probably the largest that had ever been seen in that part of the world, and must have had an impact on the native people who watched it sail up the river and approach their sanctuary. Despite relatively small numbers of warriors, English weapons and military power were daunting, and particularly intimidating to towns that were on the wide tidal rivers. Argall's soldiers were also now able to wear armor to protect against the arrows of Indian bowmen. Sir Thomas Dale, the new governor, had brought long unused armor from the Tower of London to protect his men and intimidate their opponents.

On January 1, 1613, the *Treasurer* reached the creek where the Potomac River turned to the north, and anchored outside the town. Iapassus seemed "to be very glad of my coming," Argall wrote his good friend Nicholas Hawes, "and told me that all the Indians there were my very great friends, and that they had good store of corn for me, which they provided the year before, which we found to be true."[91] Argall procured 1,100 bushels of corn on this trip. He left an ensign, James Swift, at the town and headed back to Jamestown.

Captain Argall made another trip up the Potomac in the *Treasurer* just three months later, on March 19, 1613. This time he explored the river northward to the falls, and when he returned he stopped upriver from Patawomeck, probably near present-day Aquia Creek. There, with Indian guides, he explored inland. It was on this trip that he heard the news that changed the life of Pocahontas, and perhaps of the entire colony, forever:

Whilst I was in this business, I was told by certain Indians my friends, that the Great Powhatans Daughter Pokahuntis was with the great King Patowomeck, whether I presently repaired, resolving to possess myself of her by any stratagem that I could use, for the ransoming of so many Englishmen as were prisoners with Powhatan; as also to get such arms and tools, as he, and other Indians had got by murther and stealing from others of our nation, with some quantity of corn, for the Colonies relief.[92]

Pocahontas must have arrived at Patawomeck soon after Argall's previous grain-purchasing trip. According to Ralph Hamor, she had come to the town in order to "be among her friends,...employed thither...to exchange some of her father's commodities for theirs; where residing some three months or longer."[93]

Argall was not going to let this opportunity go. He believed that if he could kidnap Pocahontas, he could put the Indians at a severe disadvantage and perhaps alter the negative course in which he and others felt the affairs of the colony were moving. He determined to force Iapassus to hand Pocahontas over to him, and developed an elaborate subterfuge to bring it off.

The Abduction of Pocahontas. *Engraving by Johann Theodore de Bry, 1619.*

Pocahontas, for her part, was "desirous to renew her familiarity with the English, and delighting to see them...would gladly visit as she did." She had not had any relationship with the English since Smith's departure and the increasing hostilities that followed. Since that time she had been married, and had lived with her own people. We do not know what had happened to her husband Kocoum, or whether or not she had borne a child. There is no indication in the written record of her family being present with her in Patawomeck, although it is suspected that her first husband may have been a member of that tribe. In any case, she seems to have been interested in having conversation with English people, perhaps in renewing as well her facility with the language.

Argall conspired with Iapassus and his wife to lure Pocahontas onto his boat, on the pretense that she would only go on it if they would accompany her. They ate supper and went to sleep. When they awoke, Argall informed Iapassus and his wife that Pocahontas was a prisoner but that they could go. He gave them what Hamor described as "a small copper kettle and some other less valuable toys so highly by him esteemed that doubtless he would have betrayed his own father for them." More likely, Iapassus and the Patawomeck Council had decided that they had little choice but to accede to the demands of the captain of the warship.

Argall told Pocahontas that she was being held hostage for eight English prisoners, and for swords, weapons, and tools that her father had taken. When he said this, the English account states, Pocahontas "began to be exceeding pensive and discontented."

Argall weighed anchor and sailed the *Treasurer* back to Jamestown with its precious cargo. Word was sent to Powhatan immediately of the capture and the demand for ransom. Powhatan did not reply for three months. At that point, according to Hamor, he returned seven men with seven broken muskets and a promise that when they returned his daughter he would give them 500 bushels of corn "and be forever friends with us."[94] Governor Dale replied that Powhatan's response was insufficient. He refused to release Pocahontas.

Imprisonment, baptism, and marriage

Pocahontas would have had ample reason to be afraid at the time of her capture. Rape of captured Indian women was common in the Virginia colony. The first British colonists were three shiploads of men and boys. The first two English women, Mrs. Forrest and her fourteen-year-old maid, Anne Burras, arrived in 1608, but it was not until 1619 and 1620 that significant numbers of female colonists arrived. Nonetheless, there is no indication that Pocahontas was mistreated.

On the contrary, Dale was so pleased by the capture of Powhatan's daughter that he gave special attention and protection to the prize his admiral had procured in Patawomeck.[95] After waiting three months to hear word from her father about ransom, he sent her upriver to the new town of Henrico, nine miles below the falls of the James River. On the south bank opposite Henrico was Rocke Hall, the parsonage of the Reverend Alexander Whitaker, the Anglican minister at Henrico. She lived in Whitaker's household while he taught her English and prepared her for baptism. Dale claimed he himself "caused [Pocahontas] to be carefully instructed in Christian religion ... [and] baptized."[96]

Meanwhile, John Rolfe had fallen in love with Pocahontas. Rolfe had been one of the survivors of the *Sea Venture* in its wreck on Bermuda, during which time a daughter was born and died. His first wife died soon after reaching Virginia. He now was in Henrico, and perhaps was working to raise tobacco at Varina Farm, on the north side of the James River just beyond Henrico's fortifications. Rolfe's proposed marriage to Pocahontas was radical and controversial. In any case, he could not marry her until she was baptized as a Christian. Rolfe wrote an impassioned, wordy letter to Dale expressing his reasons for wanting to marry the captive daughter of Powhatan. He said that he was striving to be

> in no way led [to this marriage]...with the unbridled desire of carnal affection, but for the good of this plantation, for the honor of our country, for the glory of God, for my own salvation, and for the converting to the true knowledge of God and Jesus Christ an unbelieving creature, namely Pokahuntas, to whom my heart and best thoughts have a long time been so entangled and enthralled in so intricate a labyrinth, that I was even a-wearied to unwind myself thereout.[97]

While Pocahontas was still under supervision near Henrico, in March of 1614 Thomas Dale and Captain Argall took the *Treasurer*, 150 armored men, and several other available ships deep into Pamunkey territory to challenge Powhatan directly with their military power, and to remind him that they held his daughter hostage. They took Pocahontas with them. Ralph Hamor also accompanied them. He wrote that the English "went up into [Powhatan's] own river where his chiefest habitations were, and carried with us his daughter, either to move them to fight for her, if such were their courage and boldness as hath been reported, or to restore the residue of our demands, which were our pieces, swords, tools."[98] Along the way they burned a town, killing "five or six" Indians.

The ship stopped at the town of Matchkot, on what is now the upper Pamunkey River beyond the present-day town of West Point. Powhatan was not available, and messages were sent to him. Finally, Hamor says, "Two of Powhatan's sons, being very desirous to see their sister, who was there present ashore with us, came unto us, at the sight of whom and her welfare, whom they suspected to be worse entreated (though they had often heard the contrary), they much rejoiced, and promised that they would undoubtedly persuade their father to redeem her, and to conclude a firm peace forever with us."[99] After that, Rolfe and one of the boy translators were led to see Powhatan.

They returned, having spoken not to Powhatan but to Opechancanough, who had said that he would represent the English demands to the paramount chief. Dale was incensed at the delay. He said that they would return downriver because it was planting season, but if Powhatan had not met their demands by harvest time, they would "return again and destroy and take away all their corn, burn all the houses upon that river, leave not a fishing weir standing, not a canoa in any creek thereabout, and destroy and kill as many of them as [they] could."[100]

At some point in the conversation, Ralph Hamor shared Rolfe's letter about Pocahontas with Governor Dale. "Master Rolfe had been in love with Pocahontas and she with him,"[101] Hamor said. Pocahontas gave her own version of the situation to her brothers there at Matchcot. Dale became "mild" as he realized the significance of the revelation, Hamor said, and agreed to return downriver with only the verbal pledges of the Indians that they would meet his demands.

Powhatan soon sent word of his approval of the marriage, and delegated "an old uncle of hers, named Opachisco, to give her as his deputy in the church, and two of his sons to see the marriage solemnized. Ever since," Hamor concluded in his account, "we have had friendly commerce and trade not only with Powhatan himself but also with his subjects round about us; so as now I see no reason why the colony should not thrive apace."[102]

One obstacle remained before Pocahontas could marry Rolfe. She had to be baptized. So far as the church was concerned, she was prepared. She had been catechized for nine months by Alexander Whitaker, the Anglican cleric. At her baptism, she was given the Christian name Rebecca. And at the same time, she revealed that her own adult name was Matoaka, a name that probably means "One who kindles." The English chronicler of the event, Samuel Purchas, said that the Indians had not revealed the name previously, "in a superstitious fear of hurt by the English."[103]

The English regarded the baptism of Pocahontas as the most important victory of all. The marriage of Pocahontas and John Rolfe might seal the peace, but the baptism vindicated the mission. Pocahontas' acceptance of English Christianity was proof that this had not been a mission of military and economic conquest, but rather a mission to save the savages. Sir Thomas Dale, in a letter, wrote that Pocahontas' baptism was his proudest achievement:

> Powhatan's daughter I caused to be carefully instructed in Christian religion, who after she had made some good progress therein renounced publicly her country idolatry, openly confessed her Christiann faith, was as she desired baptized, and is since married to an English gentleman of good understanding.... Her father and friends gave approbation to it, and her uncle gave her to him in the church. She lives civilly and lovingly with him, and I trust will increase in goodness as the knowledge of God increaseth in her. She will go into England with me, and were it but the gaining of this one soul, I will think my time, toil, and present stay well spent.[104]

We do not have any written documents from Pocahontas, and cannot therefore know the full motivation behind her formal acceptance of Christianity. The English saw it as a conversion and a renunciation of paganism. But this would not have been the normal meaning of such an act within her own culture. It was normal for captured women to join the religion of the tribe to which they now belonged. It was possible within Powhatan spirituality to add a god to the pantheon rather than replacing one god with another.[105] We do know that Pocahontas' agreement to be baptized and to marry John Rolfe caused Argall and Dale to withdraw the *Treasurer* and the armored men from Indian sanctuaries at the fall line, and to end their threats to destroy Indian towns. We do not know Matoaka's private understanding of her baptism.

Rolfe and Pocahontas were married in a church, most probably the church at Jamestown, on April 5, 1614, about a year after her capture at the Patawomeck village.[106] They settled on Rolfe's land, probably on Hog Island across the river from Jamestown. There Rolfe continued to develop not only the planting of tobacco but also its curing using methods developed by the Indians. He also became secretary of the colony.

Sir Thomas Dale was not finished with Powhatan's family, however. A month after the wedding Dale sent Hamor with Thomas Savage, a youth whom Christopher Newport had once given to Powhatan, to see the paramount chief. When they got to Matchcot, where Argall had brought his warships only several months before, Powhatan himself met their canoe. "His first salutation was to the boy," Hamor recalls, "whom he very well remembered, after this manner: 'My child, you are welcome; you have been a stranger to me these four years, at what time I gave you leave to go to Paspahae (for so was James town called before our seating there) to see your friends, and till now you never returned.'"[107] Hamor then read Dale's message to Powhatan, presumably with Savage translating:

> Sir Thomas Dale, your brother, the principal commander of the Englishmen, sends you greeting of love and peace on his part inviolable, and hath in testimony thereof by me sent you a worthy present, — two large pieces of copper, five strings of white and blue beads, five wooden combs, ten fishhooks, and a pair of knives.... He willed me also to certify you that when you pleased to send men he would give you a great grinding stone.

Hamor then came to the reason for the visit.

> The exquisite perfection of your youngest daughter, being famous through all your territories, hath come to the hearing of your brother Sir Thomas Dale, who for this purpose hath addressed me hither to entreat you by that brotherly friendship you make profession of to permit her with me to return unto him, partly for the desire which himself hath, and partly for the desire her sister hath to see her, of whom...your brother by your favor would gladly make his nearest companion, wife, and bedfellow.[108]

Sir Thomas Dale, the pious guardian of British rectitude in Virginia, who had a wife in England, wanted Powhatan to give him his twelve-year-old daughter as a wife. Powhatan angrily declined.

The voyage to England

Two years later, in April, 1616, a delegation from Virginia left Hampton Roads for the six-week journey to England. The ship was the *Treasurer,* the vessel aboard which Pocahontas had been kidnapped just three years before, captained by the man who deceived and imprisoned her, Samuel Argall. Aboard the ship were Sir Thomas Dale, who had completed his service as governor of Virginia; Pocahontas; her husband, John Rolfe; and their infant son, Thomas. They were accompanied by Tomocomo (Uttamattamakin), who was married to Powhatan's daughter Mattachanna, and seven other Algonquians, perhaps including Mattachanna.

The trip had been conceived by the Virginia Company as a form of publicity for the colony, and therefore Pocahontas' participation was not fully her own decision. She was a celebrity in the Virginia Company. They wished to use her to promote the colonial enterprise, as well as to raise money for the proposed school and university at Henrico. Tomocomo, and perhaps others of the Algonquians, had the specific duty, on behalf of the paramount chief, of reporting on the English culture. Tomocomo brought a stick to notch with the number of people he saw—which gives us a sense of what the Algonquian expectations might have been. They arrived at Plymouth around the first week of June, and continued by carriage the 173 miles to London.

The Virginia Company introduced them to many people during their visit. Initially, they stayed at La Belle Sauvage, an inn near Ludgate in London, but the trip and company became increasingly taxing. Pocahontas apparently suffered both from fatigue and from respiratory problems during those days, and was forced to go to bed.[109] To get respite from the London scene, they moved to Syon House, an estate in Brentford, nine miles from London, owned by the brother of George Percy, one of the original settlers and survivors of Jamestown, who had succeeded John Smith as president of the colony.

The Virginia Company wanted Pocahontas to have an audience with Queen Anne; some felt that she, as a member of the royal family of the New World, should properly have one. To secure this audience they enlisted Captain John Smith, her old acquaintance, who was in England preparing another expedition to North America. Smith's elegant letter to the queen describes the help that Pocahontas, although only twelve or thirteen years old, had given to him and the English. Her "compassionate pitiful heart of my desperate estate gave me much cause to respect her," Smith says.

Such was the weakness of this poor commonwealth as had the savages not fed us, we directly had starved. And this relief, most gracious Queen, was commonly brought us by this Lady Pocahontas. Notwithstanding all these passages when inconstant fortune turned our peace to war, this tender virgin would still not spare to dare to visit us, and by her our jars have been oft appeased, and our wants still supplied. Were it the policy of her father thus to employ her, or the ordinance of God thus to make her His instrument, or her extraordinary affection to our nation, I know not....[110]

Smith, about to leave on a voyage to New England, went to Brentford to see Pocahontas before he left. His description of the brief meeting is poignant, and leaves questions about how the two regarded each other at this point, some seven years after Smith's departure from Virginia.

Being about this time preparing to set sail for New-england, I could not stay to do [for Pocahontas] that service I desired, and she well deserved. But hearing she was at Brentford with divers of my friends, I went to see her.

After a modest salutation, without any word she turned about, obscured her face, as not seeming well contented. And in that humor, her husband with divers others we all left her two or three hours, repenting myself to have writ she could speak English.

But not long after, she began to talk and rememb'red me well what courtesies she had done, saying, "You did promise Powhatan what was yours should be his, and he the like to you. You called him father, being in his land a stranger, and by the same reason so must I do you"; which, though I would have excused, I durst not allow of that title because she was a king's daughter. With a well set countenance she said, "Were you not afraid to come into my father's country, and caused fear in him and all his people (but me)? And fear you here I should call you father? I tell you then I will, and you shall call me child, and so I will be forever and ever your countryman. They did tell us always you were dead, and I knew no other till I came to Plymouth. Yet Powhatan did command Uttamatomakkin to seek you, and know the truth, because your countrymen will lie much."

The small time I stay'd in London divers courtiers and others my acquaintances hath gone with me to see her, that generally concluded they did think God had a great hand in her conversion, and they have seen many English ladies worse favored, proportioned, and behaviored. And as since I have heard it pleased both the King and Queen's Majesty honorably to esteem her, accompanied with that honorable lady the Lady De la Ware and that honorable lord her husband, and divers other persons of good qualities, both publicly at the masques and otherwise, to her great satisfaction and content, which doubtless she would have deserved had she lived to arrive in Virginia.[111]

Portrait of Pocahontas from John Smith's General Historie, *1632.*

Whether Pocahontas had a private audience with the queen and king is in doubt. But we do know that she attended a special Twelfth Night revel, with a play written by Ben Jonson, at which the king and queen were present, on January 6, 1617. Historian Samuel Purchas, writing in 1625, said that Master Rolfe's wife

> did not only accustom herself to civility but still carried herself as the daughter of a king, and was accordingly respected not only by the [Virginia] company,...but of [other] persons of honor.... I was present when my honorable and reverend patron, the lord bishop of London, Doctor King, entertained her with festival state and pomp, beyond what I have seen in his great hospitality afforded to other ladies.[112]

Later Pocahontas and Rolfe, with young Thomas, visited the Rolfes' ancestral home at Heacham, about 100 miles east of the city, to meet Rolfe's family.

If Pocahontas demonstrated grace and presence to those she met, her brother-in-law Tomocomo showed another side of the New World to Londoners. Samuel Purchas said that he had "often conversed" with "this savage...at my good friend's, Master Doctor Goldstone, where he was a frequent guest, and where I have both seen him sing and dance his diabolical measures and heard him discourse of his country and religion...." He was, Purchas said, "a blasphemer of what he knew not, and preferring his god to ours because he taught them—by his own so appearing—to wear their devil-lock at the left ear."[113]

With half his head shaved and a lock hanging down from the left side, the Indian from Tsenacomoco also wore a breechcloth with an animal's head and tail on it, and a fur mantle, and painted his body and face.[114] He was upset at not having been allowed to see the king and queen of England, after the English visitors were allowed to visit Powhatan. When he told Smith of his disappointment, he reminded him of the greyhound the Englishman had given the Indian king.

> He told me [Smith recalled] Powhatan did bid him to find me out to show him our god, [and] the king, queen, and prince I so much had told them of. Concerning God I told him the best I could; the king I herd he had seen, and the rest he should see when he would. He denied ever to have seen the king till by circumstances he was satisfied he had. Then he replied very sadly, "You gave Powhatan a white dog, which Powhatan fed as himself. But your king gave me nothing, and I am better than your white dog."[115]

A number of artifacts remain from Pocahontas' trip to England. A pair of mussel shell earrings was said to have been reset for her by the Earl of Northumberland, who was at the time imprisoned in the Tower of London. A silver-mounted jug, said to have been given to the Rolfes by Queen Anne, is at Jamestown Festival Park, as is a blue onyx cameo brooch, also said to have been given by Queen Anne. A portrait was painted, and is probably the precursor of a black-and-white etching, which is extant.

Pocahontas, John Rolfe, and little Thomas, with Mattachanna, Tomocomo, and most of their fellow Indians, boarded the *George*, again captained by Samuel Argall, at anchor at Gravesend on the Thames east of London. On the day the ship was to weigh anchor, Pocahontas died. Her funeral was in the parish church of St. George at Gravesend on March 21, 1617. She was buried in the chancel, but the original church burned in 1727 and her grave is lost. The parish register still exists and carries this entry:

> Rebecca Wrothe[,] wyff of Thomas [sic] Wroth gent. a Virginia lady borne, here was buried in ye Chauncell.[116]

Tradition suggests that Pocahontas died of the respiratory illnesses with which London's foul air and damp, cold climate had afflicted her since her arrival. Some native people in Virginia may have thought that she was murdered.[117]

Argall's three-ship fleet, which still included the warship *Treasurer*, resumed its trip to Virginia. Little Thomas was sickly, and was let off at Plymouth, to be taken to the English Rolfe family to be raised. His father never saw him again.

In a letter written on June 8, 1617, to his patron, Sir Edwin Sandys, John Rolfe described the return passage to Virginia and asked Sandys to make sure that his son was taken care of. Rolfe explained his decision to leave Thomas behind, and spoke openly of his grief. He expressed hope that his child would be able to join him "when [he] is of better strength to endure so hard a passage."

"My wife's death is much lamented," he said. However, the young Thomas "greatly extinguisheth the sorrow of her loss, saying all must die, but 'tis enough that her child liveth." He went on to describe once more his grief at Pocahontas' passing. It is, he said, "much my sorrow to be deprived of so great a comfort and [the] hopes I had to effect my zealous endeavors and desires as well in others as in her whose soul, I doubt not, resteth in eternal happiness."[118]

John Rolfe returned to Virginia, became a member of the House of Burgesses, and continued his pioneering development of tobacco. In 1619 he was married a third time, to Jane Pierce. He died in 1622. Thirteen years later, in 1635, his son Thomas returned to the colony.

One who kindles

In August 2006, for the first time in the 390 years since Pocahontas' death, the chiefs of the Virginia Indian tribes visited Gravesend. There were two ceremonies—a large public one in a school hall with perhaps 500 people and a smaller one in the church. In the first ceremony, Chief Anne Richardson of the Rappahannock Tribe gave a ring to a representative of the queen, signifying the marriage that God had intended between the English and the native Americans to create a new nation. All in the hall were deeply touched by the spirit of the event, and many, including chiefs and the queen's representatives, wept.

Top: Chiefs of the Virginia Tribes gathered at the State Capitol in Richmond May 3, 2007, to welcome Queen Elizabeth. Below: Chiefs greet Queen, Governor Tim Kaine and first lady Ann Holton. Photos by Deanna Beacham.

Later in the church, in the midst of prayers and talks about the original intentions for the new nation, a similar event occurred. This time the chiefs themselves experienced a spirit of reconciliation of some of their own differences. Chief Anne said that what came to her in the visit was the sense, wherever she went, of what a loving person Pocahontas had been. The memory of her, and of her loving spirit, were still convincing over the distance of four centuries.

The following year, the Queen of England visited Virginia for the 400th anniversary of the founding of Jamestown. According to Chief Anne, Queen Elizabeth insisted that she first meet the chiefs at the Capitol in Richmond, before meeting the governor and his wife, and this occurred. They presented her with a copy of the original cameo brooch that Queen Anne had given to Pocahontas.

The undisputed facts of Pocahontas' life give a strong sense of her character and, perhaps, of her growing sense of her particular vocation. She was used by her father to symbolize the possibility of a common future of the Powhatans with the English. Her position as an emissary to feed starving colonists endeared her to them, but it is clear that her cartwheeling and her personality did as well. She also seemed ill at ease with the carnage of the early relations between her people and the settlers.

The tragedy of Pocahontas' life presented particular challenges. She was tricked and captured by persons she trusted. Her first husband was lost to her. In a two-year period after her captivity she learned English, was baptized, married an English husband, and gave birth. As a young woman, she was placed in the position of dealing almost singlehandedly, at times, with the catastrophic engagement between her family and culture and a strange and powerful invading nation.

What is remarkable about her is the way she seems to have gone ahead of events and attempted to find a courageous and creative way through almost certain tragedy. As an eleven-year-old, she was a translator and ambassador between the tribes and the Jamestown interlopers. As a captive, she delayed marriage and conversion until a treaty was concluded. As a wife and ostensible convert, she was a consistent representative for benevolence and understanding.

There is no way to know what Pocahontas' "conversion" to Christianity meant to her—and yet, she seems to have been a person whose spirit was deeply consonant with both the spiritual tradition of the Algonquians and the power of redeeming suffering that the Holy Spirit of Jesus engenders. Her experiences may have carried her to a profound truth of religion far beyond that of her mentors. She and her husband John seem to have had a deep and genuine relationship.

At the age of seventeen she became a royal representative of an entire nation in a totally different culture. Some accounts of her time in London are less than complimentary. The criticisms relate to a lack of British sophistication, the absence of the polish of London society. But many others express astonishment and appreciation at her grace and kindness.

Pocahontas was carried to London on a ship captained by the persons who had tricked, captured, and imprisoned her. Her visit was used to raise money for a school to educate Indian children, and to recruit more English colonists to Virginia, surely projects about which she must have had some ambivalence. Yet, in all her dealings, she appears neither to have betrayed her own people and heritage nor to have acted out of bitterness and hostility to the English.

The Christianity that the Europeans brought to Virginia presumed to claim God's warrant for seizing the land of another people without compensation or treaty and to treat those people as savages.[119] The religion of Pocahontas' birth regarded the land as being available to all, accepted the importance of community as fundamental, did not believe in the accumulation of land or of large amounts of money, and treated other cultures with respect. The spirit that was kindled in Matoaka appears to be the spirit to which both the Powhatans and the Christians were pointing, however feebly. In her, despite betrayals, deaths, and insults, the promise of the two cultures was represented.

Her life is justification neither for the imperialistic excess that began at Jamestown and may not yet have been fully renounced in America, nor for a romantic primitivism that longs for a pre-industrial village society. The Powhatan culture of Tsenacomoco would inevitably have had to yield to the more elaborate technologies and organizations of Europe. But ironically, the European colony will not ultimately survive without finally embracing values that were second nature to the people of Tsenacomoco. Four hundred years later, these values have still not fully penetrated the society at the falls of the James.

4

An Economy of Servants and Slaves
1607–1780

At its foundation, from 1607 to 1705, the British colony of Virginia constructed an elaborate class and slave system. The English class system, European prejudice toward non-European cultures, and the developing European slave trade in Africa were catalyzed into a toxic brew by the violence, greed, and trauma of the English settlement in the New World. The structure of the class system and the shadow of the slave system are still dramatically visible in metropolitan Richmond today. Their unremedied consequences still shape both the United States of America and American policy in the world.

At the end of his landmark book on the subject, *American Slavery, American Freedom,* Edmund S. Morgan asks the most important question about Virginia's original sin of race and class: "Is America still Colonial Virginia writ large? More than a century after Appomattox," he writes, "the questions still linger."[120]

Race is sometimes acknowledged, although underestimated, in its impact on America's stability. But class is, if anything, even more foundational, seldom acknowledged, and more insidious in its impact. To understand what developed in Virginia in the seventeenth century, we will look at the tobacco boom and bond servitude, at class warfare and Bacon's Rebellion, at the enslaving of Africans in Virginia, and finally, at the invention of the white race.

The tobacco boom and bond servitude

Mortality among English immigrants was incredibly high in the first twenty years of the Virginia colony. In 1624 there were still only 1,200 Englishmen, even though the Virginia Company had brought in

3,500 new settlers from 1619 through 1622. Of these, only about one-fifth were women.[121] Mortality was high among the native inhabitants of Virginia as well. Hundreds of native people were killed by the English colonists. There is some speculation, but no concrete evidence, that Europeans carried diseases that killed or debilitated many more.[122]

Meanwhile, developments in the economy of Virginia were setting the stage for the dramatic extension of Britain's hierarchical social class system into the new colony. In 1612, on Varina Farm adjacent to the town of Henrico, just nine miles downriver from the falls of the James, John Rolfe planted some West Indian tobacco in his fields. Rolfe's tobacco was far superior to the native variety. The local tobacco used by the natives had not appealed to the English, but the tobacco grown in Virginia from West Indian seed quickly proved desirable to importers in England. The first casks of the new tobacco were shipped to England in 1617, selling as a luxury item for three shillings for each pound.

Demand for tobacco exploded so rapidly that settlers who had not yet learned to plant enough food to feed themselves planted tobacco instead in every available corner. In his *General Historie,* John Smith described the scene that ship captain Samuel Argall came upon when he reached Jamestown in 1617:

> He found but five or six houses, the Church down, the Palisade broken, the Bridge in pieces, the Well of fresh water spoiled; the Store-house they used for the Church, the market-place, and streets, and all other spare places planted with Tobacco, the Savages as frequent in their houses as themselves, whereby they were become expert in our arms, and had a great many in their custody and possession, the Colony dispersed all about, planting Tobacco.[123]

Within less than a decade, tobacco had become the foundation of the economy of Virginia and its only major source of foreign exchange. Tobacco remained Virginia's major export, and a *de facto* currency, through the middle of the next century. The sudden and extraordinary success of Virginia tobacco had a decisive impact on the colony's social development.

The tobacco boom happened simultaneously with a change in England's development policy for Virginia. In 1616 the Virginia Company decided to distribute land to the surviving Virginians they called the "Old Planters" and to establish what they called a "headright" system.[124] The private economy was born. Hereafter, any person paying his own way to Virginia—called an adventurer—would be given fifty acres. More important for the future of the colony, anyone who paid for someone else to be brought to Virginia would get the fifty acres for himself.

The development of tobacco as a cash crop coincided with the decision of the Virginia Company to mount an aggressive campaign to send settlers to Virginia. Within three years the Virginia Company sent 3,500 new settlers. According to Edmund Morgan, secretary of the company Edwin Sandys "pressured every English parish to ship of its poor. He got the City of London to send a hundred destitute boys to serve as apprentices."[125]

Nearly all the people sent over by Sandys were men and boys, and nearly all were what the English called "servants." These servants had no property of their own. Since their passage was paid by someone else, they were bound to work for that person—or for whoever represented that party in Virginia—for seven years. The three categories of passage were tenants, bondservants, and apprentices.

- Tenants were, in theory, entitled to fifty percent of the proceeds of what they raised on the land they farmed.
- Bondservants belonged completely to their master during the time of their servitude.
- Apprentices were usually underage boys—called Duty Boys after the ship (the *Duty*) that some took to Virginia. To any planter who would pay ten pounds apiece for them, they would be bound as apprentices for seven years, and then for another seven years as tenants.

In early Virginia there was not as much difference between these three categories of bondservants as might appear on the surface. All three categories of servant were working someone else's land and subject to that person's rule. If the person for whom they were working should die, they belonged to someone else. They could be bought and sold. In addition, the rate of mortality was so high that relatively few survived their term of servitude. "Before 1624," Morgan says, "Virginia was a death trap for most of those who went there."[126] For the next thirty years, he says, the population was "dying rapidly" and was sustained only "by continuing heavy immigration."[127] If he survived, a servant's period of bondage was often extended for various reasons. The punishment specified for running away was an extension of the period of servitude.

The price of tobacco proved an irresistible incentive to Virginia's landowners to import labor from England. Owners calculated that a servant working in the fields could produce as much as 1,000 pounds of tobacco a year. At three shillings to the pound, the tobacco would be worth 150 pounds sterling. A landowner could import a servant from England on a seven-year labor contract at a cost of ten to twelve pounds sterling, and it would cost him about the same to maintain the servant for a year. Thus, in the first year, a new servant could earn for his master seven-and-one-half times his cost. In the second year, the value jumped to fifteen times his cost.

In the period from 1625 to 1640, 15,000 persons emigrated from England to Virginia, but the total immigrant population in Virginia increased by only 7,000. The high mortality rate in the first year after a new colonist's arrival increased the value of what was called a "seasoned hand," that is, a person who had survived the tobacco fields for one season. In the 1630s, '40s, and '50s, planters were willing to pay as much as three times more for a seasoned hand with three years left in his servitude than they would pay for a new servant with five years available.[128]

During the tobacco boom of Virginia's first fifty years, unlike later times, it was labor that was scarce, not land. The demand for servants imported from England continued unabated through at least 1654. The death rate meant that those few Virginians who owned land, had capital, and could import servants ended up with the headrights of their many deceased laborers. If a planter imported thirty servants a year and if half of them died, which was the case in the early years, he would acquire 750 acres of land simply by their deaths.

By 1660 Virginia's population was divided into six distinct social and economic classes: Indians, slaves, servants, freedmen, householders, and the Great Men.

1. *Indians.* Before 1646 Indians could be killed for no cause. In 1646, following the final defeat of Opechancanough in 1644, a treaty had been signed with the remnants of the Powhatan Confederacy. Under this law, Indians could no longer be killed for simply trespassing on the land that the English had taken from them; they could be put to death only for a felony. Many were made slaves. Others stayed to themselves in lands the settlers were not occupying.
2. *Slaves.* By 1660 the colony had from 500 to 1,000 African slaves, a small minority of the labor force. Not all Africans were slaves for life at this point; slavery for life was confined to Africans imported by the Dutch or from the West Indies, and to some Indians. Bond servitude was often indistinguishable

from slavery.

3. *Servants.* The large part of the labor in Virginia consisted of bondservants.

4. *Freedmen.* These were persons who had lived out their indenture but were in debt or unable to acquire land. Thus they were forced either to live off the land or to relate once more as tenants and debtors to those who did own land and property.

5. *Householders.* Freedmen who had succeeded in acquiring their own land and housing were classified as householders. A relatively small class, they were at great risk, because terms of trade and taxation negotiated by the powerful landowners frequently forced them back into debt, tenancy, and servitude.

6. *The Great Men.* This relatively small number of large and influential landowners, numbering no more than several hundred, controlled the economy and composed the House of Burgesses.[129]

The first fifty years of the Virginia colony were a violent, dangerous time, during which mostly unsuspecting and ill-equipped English settlers found themselves in desperate situations of conflict and struggles for survival. As many as fifty percent died during their first twelve months. Most had been members of the lower classes of England, living and dying like slaves after a brief sojourn in the New World. Virginia was an economic miracle for some and a death trap for many.[130] Ninety percent of the population was in bondage, while a tiny percentage of the population controlled almost all the land, production, and capital.

Some time in the middle of the 1640s and the beginning of the 1650s, the death rate began to subside. Virginia's English population jumped from 14,000 to 25,000 in just seven years, between 1653 and 1660. But by that time, the highly stratified, mostly enslaved society was about to explode.

Class warfare and Bacon's Rebellion

In 1660 what we now call Tidewater Virginia—the part of Virginia up to the fall lines of the rivers—was occupied mostly by English settlers. Toward the falls, freedmen might find some land for themselves and become householders, but the risk of attack from Indians was higher. There was no standing army to maintain security.

The majority of Virginians were bondservants, slaves, tenants, or freedmen without property. From 1658 to 1666 the assembly passed a series of acts that extended the term of bond servitude by three years for persons who arrived without specific indentures.[131] But even with these legislated extensions of bondage, an increasing number of Virginians of English descent were now surviving their apprenticeships or indentures and becoming free. Freedom seldom brought property or self-sufficiency, however. A number of freedmen left the land of their masters and lived off the land or in the forest. Many came to freedom early by trading their headright to their master. A massive land grab developed, in which the so-called Great Men accumulated vast acreage simply by purchasing headrights.

In 1661 the servants of York County started a rebellion, which was quelled. In 1663 nine servants were accused of planning an armed insurrection in Gloucester County, where the richest of the Great Men lived. Several of the instigators were hanged and the servant who betrayed them was rewarded with his freedom. The assembly established an official colonial holiday, "Birkenhead Day," named for the whistleblower.[132] In 1665 an uprising was threatened in Lancaster County, and in 1674 Sir William Berkeley, governor of the colony, put down two "mutinies" launched by impoverished freedmen.[133]

From 1661 until 1676 no elections were held in Virginia. But if they had been held, freedmen who did not own property would not have been allowed to vote—only the Great Men and the householders would have elected the burgesses.

In 1671 Governor Berkeley gave an interesting set of written answers to formal "Enquiries to the Governor of Virginia from the Lords Commissioners of Foreign Plantations." Some of the questions and Berkeley's answers follow:

15. *What number of planters, servants and slaves; and how many parishes are there in your plantation?*
    We suppose, and I am very sure we do not much miscount, that there is in Virginia above forty thousand persons, men, women, and children, and of which there are two thousand black slaves, six thousand Christian servants, for a short time, the rest are born in the country or have come in to settle and seat, in bettering their condition in a growing country.

16. *What number of English, Scots, or Irish have for these seven years last past come yearly to plant and inhabit within your government; as also what blacks or slaves*

have been brought in within the said time?

Yearly, we suppose there comes in, of servants, about fifteen hundred, of which, most are English, few Scotch, and fewer Irish, and not above two or three ships of Negroes in seven years.

17. *What number of people have yearly died, within your plantation and government for these seven years last past, both whites and blacks?*

All new plantations are, for an age or two, unhealthy, 'till they are thoroughly cleared of wood; but unless we have a particular register office, for the denoting of all that died, I cannot give a particular answer to this query, only this I can say, that there is not often unseasoned hands (as we term them) that die now, whereas heretofore not one of five escaped the first year.[134]

In 1675 conflict began between English settlers and the Susquehanna Indians, who had come south to Maryland, and other Indians on the Potomac. Five chiefs who had come out from their fort to negotiate peace were murdered by English forces. The conflicts continued and intensified. Virginians of English descent began to attack not only Indians from outside the colony but also Indians who remained peacefully within the colony. Nathaniel Bacon, a new settler and a friend of Governor Berkeley, came into the fray. Bacon lived on Curles' Neck on the James River, fifteen miles downstream from present-day

Nathanael Bacon   *William Berkeley*

Richmond. He also had property (Bacon's Quarter) on Shockoe Creek, near the present intersection of I-64 east and I-95 in Richmond.

Bacon had collected an army of freedmen, a situation Governor Berkeley feared. He arrested Bacon, but then pardoned him. Bacon's army was characterized by uncompromising hatred of Indian people. His men sought and received from the governor the right to enslave any Indian they captured. They made common cause with Occaneechee Indians against the Susquehannas in a battle that took place on an island in the Roanoke River near present-day Clarksville, and then turned and massacred the Occaneechees. Bacon promised freedom to any bonded persons, black or white, who would join his army. As the army came more and more to be composed of unemployed freedmen and bonded servants, they turned their enmity toward the tiny class of Great Men who had kept them in bondage and poverty.

Eventually Bacon returned to Jamestown with an army of 500, called "rabble" by the secretary of the colony. On September 19, 1676, Bacon's army burned Jamestown. The target of conflict had shifted decisively from the Indians to Governor Berkeley and his Great Men. What was referred to as his "Choice and standing Army" now included roughly equal proportions of black and white bonded men.[135] The worst fears of Virginia's tiny upper class had come to pass.

Fortunately for the owners of Virginia's servants and property, Bacon died on October 26. But behind him he left to defy the government an army of about 800 black and white, free, bonded, and enslaved men to whom he had proclaimed freedom. These rallied near present-day West Point, where the York River is formed by the Mattaponi and the Pamunkey rivers.

Captain Thomas Grantham sailed his thirty-gun *Concord*, a merchant ship enlisted by Governor Berkeley, up the York to confront this army on November 21. Grantham tricked 300 of them into surrendering. He later admitted that he had lied to the rebels to encourage their surrender, issuing "never to be performed promises" that he would pardon the freedmen for their rebellion, and give freedom to the English and Negro bondservants, many of whom had joined the army after the burning of Jamestown.[136] He then went farther upriver to the main garrison of the rebel forces, at the house of Colonel West:

I went to Colonel West's house about three miles farther, which was their Chief Garrison and Magazine; I there met about four hundred English and Negroes in Arms, who were much dissatisfied at the Surrender of the Point, saying I had betrayed them, and thereupon some were for shooting me, and others were for cutting me to pieces. I told them I would willingly surrender myself to them, till they were satisfied from his Majesty, and did engage to the Negroes and Servants, that they were all pardoned and freed from their Slavery; and with faire promises and Rundletts of Brandy, I pacified them, giving them several Notes under my hand, that what I did was by the Order of His Majestie and the Governor.... Most of them I persuaded to go to their Homes...except about Eighty Negroes and Twenty English which would not deliver their Arms.

Grantham deceived the remaining hundred men, placing them on a sloop that he said he would tow to a rebel fort, only to bring the sloop under the guns of another ship to compel surrender.[137]

Colonial Virginia progressed from the initial carnage of conquest, through the tobacco boom in which a few men prospered and thousands died, and into a twelve-month period in which hatred of Indians was transformed dramatically into a revolution of the disenfranchised mass of servants, slaves, and freedmen against the small, property-owning majority. What had begun as the last phase of a war against the "savages" very quickly changed into a class war of the landless poor against the privileged few.

Bacon's Rebellion, and the events leading up to and away from it, reveals a continued racism of all classes against the Indians, combined with a rapidly closing gap between disenfranchised whites and blacks, presided over by a small, white ruling class in which all political and economic power was concentrated.

It was a desperately unstable situation for those in control.

Enslaving Africans in Virginia

In August 1619 a Dutch warship had arrived in Jamestown with "not any thing but 20 and odd Negroes, which the Governor and Cape Merchant bought for victuals...at the best and easiest rate they could."[138]

Scholars now think that the Dutch ship, the *White Lion*, and an English ship, the *Treasurer*, had both pirated the Africans from a Portuguese slave ship, the *San Juan Bautista*, bound with 350 prisoners from the kingdoms of Ndongo and Kongo (modern-day Angola and Congo) to Veracruz, in present-day Mexico. The *White Lion* was first to deliver its human cargo to Virginia, and it is possible that the *Treasurer* followed several days later.[139] The *Treasurer*'s captain, Samuel Argall, was the same British gentleman who had been responsible seven years previous for the capture and imprisonment of Pocahontas.

These were the first Africans sold as slaves in Virginia. We do not know if any were ultimately freed, although it is clear that there were blacks of varying status in Virginia through much of the seventeenth century. For the first three-quarters of the century, although the Englishmen who were developing Virginia desired labor badly, they sought it primarily from England rather than from Africa.

England, suffering from major unemployment in the first half of the seventeenth century, provided plenty of labor to Virginia. England's enclosure movement had pushed subsistence farmers off the land and into the cities. The king looked to Virginia as a place to send these "masterless men"—whom he regarded as a problem—and Virginia's tobacco economy, with its ample land and high death rate, could use up as many immigrants as it could get. Often persons were brought involuntarily—felons, vagrants, debtors. English sellers wrote contracts with servant jobbers to deliver servants for a term. Many died before their terms ended; others were tricked into longer terms. The servant catchers and contractors often broke the contracts and many servants were duped. The death rate was so high and the price of labor so low that there was no need to seek the more expensive African slave labor being imported into the West Indies. For many or most of these "bonded servants," life in Virginia was slavery in everything but name, but no Virginia law officially established white European-American slavery. The African slave trade was in the hands of the Dutch; there was no English slave trade in Africa. By 1650, it is estimated that 500 Africans were enslaved in Virginia. That number would have represented two percent of the non-native population of the colony.[140]

In 1660 Parliament passed the Navigation Acts, prohibiting any Dutch ships from carrying trade to or from the colonies. This meant that Dutch slavers could not legally come to Virginia. In 1672 the English crown chartered its own company, the Royal African Company, and gave it a monopoly on transporting African slaves to the British colonies.[141]

Several other influences continued to retard the growth of the African slave trade in Virginia until the last decades of the seventeenth century. The British were less experienced in dealing with the African slave trade, and it took them some time to develop their own sources.

Moreover, major changes in the economy of the West Indies made those plantations the best market for English traders.

The islands had shifted in the 1640s to the production of sugarcane. At that point, any voluntary immigration to the islands by England's impoverished lower classes ceased. Compared with working in tobacco, cutting sugarcane was far harder work and the mortality rate was even higher. The West Indies became anathema to English labor. Only completely involuntary labor could fulfill the demands of English owners on the island sugar plantations. So the islands took all the enslaved African labor they could buy in those years, and relatively few Africans got through to Virginia. It was in the period from 1680 to 1700 that Virginia's switch to African slave labor occurred, and it occurred quickly and decisively.

In the first half of the seventeenth century the laws seem to have reflected only slight differences between Africans sold as slaves and other bonded servants, but by 1661 major legal distinctions were developing. A new law addressed the fact that indentured servants and African slaves often ran away together. The indentured servant, presumably English, was thenceforth to be subjected to the penalty of greater servitude if he participated in this, making it clear that the slave, presumably African or Indian, at least had a longer term, if not lifetime bondage.[142]

In 1662 one of the most definitive and insidious of the colony's statutes was enacted. It decreed that the child of an African woman who was a slave would be born as a slave, even if the father were a free Englishman. Here are the critical words:

> WHEREAS some doubts have arisen whether children got by any Englishman upon a negro woman should be slave or free, Be it therefore enacted and declared by this present grand assembly, that all children borne in this country shall be held bond or free only according to the condition of the mother, And that if any christian shall commit fornication with a negro man or woman, he or she so offending shall pay double the fines imposed by the former act.[143]

The use of the word "christian" to describe a person of English descent began to create some difficulty, since some colonists wanted to help their African slaves convert to Christianity. This prompted the legislature to enact in 1667 an "act declaring that baptism of slaves doth not exempt them from bondage." So far as Virginia was concerned, "christian" was a description of ethnic origin, rather than religious persuasion.

> WHEREAS some doubts have risen whether children that are slaves by birth, and by the charity and piety of their owners made partakers of the blessed sacrament of baptism, should by virtue of their baptism be made free; It is enacted and declared by this grand assembly, and the authority thereof, that the conferring of baptism doth not alter the condition of the person as to his bondage or freedom; that diverse masters, freed from this doubt, may more carefully endeavour the propagation of Christianity by permitting children, though slaves, or those of greater growth if capable to be admitted to that sacrament.[144]

Slavery in Virginia presented difficulties in the production of work that indentured servitude did not present. Indentured servitude had the possibility of freedom at the end, and therefore some incentive—if one survived—for behavior that would not invite the wrath of the owner. But the form of slavery that was developing had no such incentive. During the last decades of the seventeenth century the General Assembly passed laws reflecting the presumption that owners or masters might be inflicting violent punishment on their laborers. Thus, in 1669, we have this "act about the casual killing of slaves":

> WHEREAS the only law in force for the punishment of refractory servants resisting their master, mistress or overseer cannot be inflicted upon negroes, nor the obstinacy of many of them by other than violent means suppressed, Be it enacted and declared by this grand assembly, if any slave resist his master (or other by his masters order correcting him) and by the extremity of the correction should chance to die, that his death shall not be accounted [a] felony, but the master (or that other person appointed by the master to punish him) be acquitted from molestation, since it cannot be presumed that [premeditated] malice (which alone makes murder felony) should induce any man to destroy his own estate.[145]

The ability of owners to intimidate slaves and force them to work was further affirmed by legislation in 1680 and 1705 prescribing severe punishments for slaves who ran away. In 1680 the assembly said that a person trying to catch a runaway could kill him if he resisted, and in 1705 the language was made even more explicit. It became lawful

> for any person or persons whatsoever, to kill and destroy such slaves by such ways and means as he, she, or they shall think fit, without accusation or impeachment of any crime for the same.[146]

The 1705 act provided that the government would reimburse the owner for the loss of his slave, and if the slave were returned alive, the court could

> order such punishment to the said slave, either by dismembering, or any other way, not touching his life, as they in their discretion shall think fit, for the reclaiming any such incorrigible slave, and terrifying others from the like practices.[147]

In 1670 the legislature created a slightly less severe period of servitude for Indians who were captured and made slaves than for Africans arriving by ship.

> WHEREAS some dispute have arisen whither Indians taken in war by any other nation, and by that nation that takes them sold to the English, are servants for life or term of years, It is resolved and enacted that all servants not being Christians imported into this colony by shipping shall be slaves for their lives; but what shall come by land shall serve, if boys or girls, until thirty years of age, if men or women twelve years and no longer.[148]

In 1676, however, rage against the Indians spawned a series of laws decreeing that Indians captured in battle would be slaves for life. And in 1682, an ensuing statute redefined the status of Indians altogether.

> [B]e it further enacted by the authority aforesaid that all servants [who]...are not Christian at the time of their first purchase of such servant by some Christian...and all Indians which shall hereafter be sold by our neighbouring Indians, or any other traficking with us as for slaves are hereby adjudged,

deemed and taken to be slaves to all intents and purposes, any law, usage or custom to the contrary notwithstanding.[149]

In June, 1680, reacting specifically to the threats surfaced by the participation of African bonded servants in Bacon's Rebellion, the Assembly passed "An act for preventing Negroes Insurrections." The act restricted travel, judging the meetings of "considerable numbers of negroe slaves under pretence of feasts and burials" to be "of dangerous consequence." It prescribed that a "negroe or other slave" could not "presume to lift up his hand in opposition to any Christian [i.e., white person]," holding that the white person need only certify his charge against the slave by an oath and the penalty would be "thirty lashes on [the offender's] bear back well laid on." Furthermore, it was legal to kill "negro" slaves who had escaped, were hiding, and posed a threat to others.[150]

The invention of the white race

In 1705 the House of Burgesses enacted a comprehensive slave code. Entitled "An Act concerning Servants and Slaves,"[151] it carefully defined two distinct categories of bondage in Virginia, and carefully assigned the categories by racial origin. One category was "christian white servant." The other was "slave," a category reserved for a "negro, mulatto, or Indian, Jew, moor, Mahometan, or other infidel."

The code gives privileges to the "christian servant" that are expressly denied to the slave. A "christian" servant's indenture is limited by law. A dealer cannot sell a person into slavery who has been a free "christian" elsewhere. Masters and owners "shall find and provide for their servants wholesome and competent diet, clothing, and lodging." It is illegal to "whip a christian servant without an order from the justice of the peace." Servants have redress in court. If they are sick, they must be cared for by the churchwardens.

The act establishes several protections for "christian servants" that give them superior rights over persons of other races, regardless of the legal status of those persons. "For a further christian care and usage of all christian servants," the act declares, "no negros, mulattos, or Indians, although christians, or Jews, Moors, Mahometans, or any other infidels shall, at any time, purchase any christian servant." Moreover, no "negro, mulatto, or Indian, bond or free shall at any time, lift his or her hand, in opposition against any christian, not being negro, mulatto, or Indian." A "christian" need only swear an oath to a justice of the peace that such an offence has occurred, and the alleged offender will receive "thirty lashes...on his or her bare back." The 1705 code also confined free blacks accused of felonies to the same limited judicial process as enslaved blacks.[152]

The act consolidated the restrictions on slaves that had been developing over the previous fifty years. The category was specifically addressed to persons who were not "christians," and "christian" was defined not by baptism but by ethnic parentage. It prohibited intermarriage by "white men and women" with "negros or mulattos." It dealt at length with the problem of runaway slaves and their return. It addressed the evidently serious problem of "slaves [who] run away and lie out, hid[den] and lurking in swamps, woods, and other obscure places, killing hogs." It reaffirmed that the legal status of a child depended upon the status of the mother. And it provided that "for every slave killed, in pursuance of this act, or put to death by law, the master or owner of such slave shall be paid by the public."

The code introduced the word "white" into Virginia law. It prohibited any "negro," mulatto, or Indian, slave or free, from holding "any office, ecclesiastical, civil, or military." It also sought to clear "all manner of doubts [about] who shall be accounted a mulatto." A mulatto, the code said, is "the child of an Indian and the child, grand child, or great grand child, of a negro." That is, anyone of mixed race who is at least one-eighth African was considered "mulatto."[153]

Africans on the Upper James

Between 1680 and 1700, the population of African descent in Virginia doubled, to 6,000 persons. Forty years later it had ballooned to 60,000. In 1696 Chesapeake planters had successfully petitioned Parliament to take away the Royal African Company's monopoly on the slave trade to the colonies.[154] But at the same time the English began to trade in greater volume. English ships from Bristol and Liverpool plied the west coast of Africa and brought African prisoners into the tidal rivers of Virginia, stopping at plantations all along the way. By 1730, thirty-three percent of the colony's population were enslaved Africans.

Scholars currently estimate that approximately 114,000 Africans were imported and landed along the tidal rivers of Virginia from 1698 through 1774, the major years of forced African immigration.[155]

The British divided Tidewater Virginia into customs districts. The Upper James customs house was located at Bermuda Hundred. That plantation port became the primary western terminus of James River traffic from Africa because it lay at the end of the James River's broad sailing channel.

From Hampton Roads to Bermuda Hundred, the James is a wide arm of the sea, a tidal river as much as several miles in width, straight and broad, permitting easy access to large, ocean-going sailing vessels. At Bermuda Hundred, the river splits and narrows. The Appomattox River goes west from Hopewell and City Point to Petersburg and beyond. To the east, the James narrows in a series of five dramatic curls over a thirty-mile stretch until it straightens out and runs north ten miles to the falls at Richmond. Sandbars mar the channel,

Slave ships selling at Bermuda Hundred and Osborne's Landing July 1752-May 1772		
Ship	Shipped from	# of Africans
Ann Gally	Old Calibar	240
Hampton	Africa	273
Castleton	Africa	70
Thomas	Africa	60
Pompey	Africa	81
Apollo	Africa	197
Bassa	Guinea	108
Black Prince	Africa	120
Juba	Africa	300
Julia	Africa	100
Amelia	Africa	234
Industry	Africa	160
Speirs**	Gold Coast	15
Yanimarew	Africa	240
Aston	Africa	143
Martha*	Africa	148
Polly	Africa	430
Nancy**	Windward & Gold Coasts	250
Thomas**	Africa	200
Union**	Gold Coast	280
TOTAL	Ships: 20	Africans: 3649

**Osborne's Landing
*Sale moved to Osborne's Landing because many "will be deterred" by smallpox episode on *Yanimarew* from coming to Bermuda Hundred.
Sources: Philip J. Schwarz, "Richmond's Slave Trade," slide Show from Stratalum, Stratford Hall Seminar on Slavery (www.slideshare.net/stratalum/richmonds-slave-trade-strat-1009); Minchinton, ed., pp. 148-9; *Virginia Gazette* from July 7, 1752 to August 20, 1772.

which switches back and forth in 180-degree arcs. Tall trees block the winds for sailing, and the current moves downstream at a speed of several knots.

Henrico, the original English settlement near the falls, was located in 1611 on the fourth curl going upstream partly because that location made it defensible against the Spanish. Across the river, in what is now Chesterfield County, was Osborne's, a wharf begun in 1637 that became the secondary Upper James port of entry for enslaved Africans after Bermuda Hundred. It was here that two ships, probably the *Aston* and the *Martha*, were forced to bring their enslaved African emigrants for sale in September, 1770, after an outbreak of smallpox at Bermuda Hundred.[156]

Prior to 1735, only 400 Africans are recorded as having disembarked in the Upper James district, but following that year the number of Africans coming to the Upper James to be dispersed through sale at

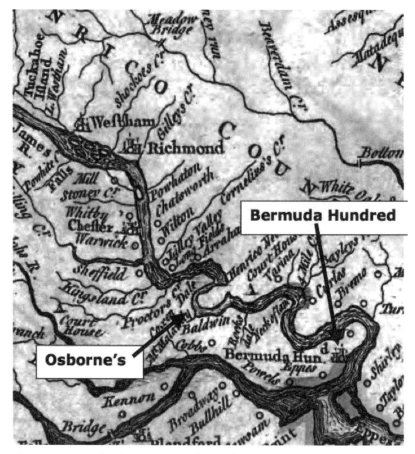

The upper James River between Bermuda Hundred and Richmond, from A Map of the most inhabited part of Virginia, by Joshua Fry and Peter Jefferson, 1754

Bermuda Hundred, Osborne's, Rocky Ridge (Manchester), and Henrico increased dramatically. By 1746 one-third of all Africans coming to Virginia came to Bermuda Hundred and Osborne's. Between 1735 and 1774 there are records of 127 oceangoing ships, almost all from Bristol and Liverpool, that brought nearly 16,000 imprisoned Africans up the James as far as they could sail.[157]

The African labor fed the region's growing economy. The central and southern piedmont areas of Virginia—the James River Basin west of the falls—were the best remaining "virgin tobacco lands" in Virginia and North Carolina. An annual export to England of six million pounds of tobacco per year from the Upper James in the 1730s increased to thirty million pounds annually in the 1770s. Exports of corn and wheat from the district increased dramatically at the same time. In the final

Enslaved Africans landed in the Upper James Naval District 1698-1774		
	Ships	Enslaved Africans
1698-1703	11	15
1704-1718	15	166
1719-1730	2	197
1731-1745	54	3405
1746-1760	28	5764
1761-1774	45	6732
	155	16279

Source: Lorena S. Walsh, "New Perspectives on the Transatlantic Slave Trade," *The William and Mary Quarterly*, 3rd Ser., Vol. 58, No. 1 (Jan., 2001), pp. 168-169.

fifteen years of the international trade, sixty-two percent of the Africans coming to enslaved life in Virginia set their first foot on the continent in what is now the Richmond metropolitan area.[158]

Even though Virginia prohibited any further involuntary importation of Africans after 1774, the enslaved population exceeded 300,000 by 1790. In that year, the total number of free and enslaved Virginians of African descent was nearly the same as the number of whites.[159] Fully two-fifths of the population, none of it white, was in legally defined and legally enforced slavery.

5

The Perfection Of Racialized Slavery
1720–1861

Poor whites and enslaved blacks

The number of captured Africans being delivered to the wharves of Tidewater Virginia plantations increased dramatically at the beginning of the eighteenth century. By 1720, 30,000 Africans were enslaved in the colony. The new labor from Africa seized the attention of Virginia planters for the first two decades, but soon the number of white servants purchased from England began to rise again. Between 1700 and 1775, more than three-quarters of the emigrants to Virginia were men and women, both black and white, in some form of servitude.[160]

In 1718 the British Parliament passed the Transportation Act. Under that legislation, over the next half century, English companies paid by the Crown brought approximately 40,000 convicts to Virginia and Maryland to serve out their terms in from seven to fourteen years of bondage.[161] Most worked in the fields of Virginia, often alongside other white bondservants or enslaved blacks. One-fourth of British emigration to America in the eighteenth century consisted of convicts. The trade did not end until war began in 1775.[162]

English merchants marketed indenture contracts to poor immigrants to provide passage from the British Isles to America. These indentures were longer than those in England, and condemned the signer to a state that, for a time, was not unlike slavery. Indentured servants were often mistreated on the passage across the Atlantic. Once in the colony they received no wages and could be sold, beaten, and punished for running away. But they also might look forward to receiving a payment called "freedom dues" when and if they completed the indenture.[163]

William Byrd, whose Westover plantation lay on the James River and who founded Richmond around his Shockoe Valley warehouse twenty miles upstream, made the multi-faceted labor situation sound idyllic in a letter to a friend: "Like one of the [Biblical] patriarchs," he wrote, "I have my flocks and my herds, my bond-men, and bond-women."[164]

But the reality appeared starkly different to others. A colonist who observed the sale of about 100 convicts in Williamsburg in 1770 was quoted in that city's newspaper with this description of the event:

I never see such pasels of pore Raches in my Life, some all most naked and what had Cloths was as Black [as] Chimney Swipers, and all most Starved by the Ill [usage] in their Pasedge By the Capn, for they are used no Bater than so many negro Slaves.[165]

Philadelphia was the primary port of entry for the indentured servants who began to pour into America from Ireland, Germany, and Switzerland, as well as Scotland and England. Pressure for immigration usually corresponded to various crises in the country of origin, such as famines and wars. Some of the German immigrants came under a new kind of contract as "redemptioners." Under these agreements, an immigrant had a certain amount of time after his arrival in America to collect from relatives or others the money he owed for transport. If he failed, he would spend years in bondage, working off the price of his passage.[166]

New immigrants also included free Scots-Irish and German settlers, who pushed the boundaries of Indian occupation westward, and opened the Valley of Virginia to a way of life that knew nothing of tobacco and little of slavery. Within the white European community in Virginia, these immigrants were a new class of people. Many were working people who had paid their own passage or engaged in a respectful and careful, legally enforced indenture relationship to gain their passage to the New World. Three great waves of emigration brought Scots-Irish from northern Ireland to the Shenandoah Valley. The first was provoked by the Irish potato famine of 1740–1741. A second influx occurred in 1754–1755, and the third between 1771 and 1775. The ships came into the port of Philadelphia, and the settlers then followed the so-called "Indian Path," also called by settlers the Great Wagon Road, the present-day route of U.S. Route 11 and Interstate 81 down the Valley.[167] These settlers were white, and they had three hundred years' harsh experience with the British class, race, and colonial systems behind them.

Virginia's slave codes had made a series of distinctions—some weighty and some subtle—between the status of African bonded persons and that of "white" bonded persons. The heaviest was that the black man's bondage was lifelong, unless he was freed at the discretion of the owner, and that any of his children would also be in bondage. More subtle were the provisions that allowed white bonded persons, no matter how low their status, to have automatic superiority in the court against a black person, and that established limits on violence by owners against white bondsmen but not black.

As the century progressed, an increasing number of white bondservants survived their indentures to become freedmen, expanding the population of free citizens who were not completely dependent on the Great Men. These small farmers and artisans joined with the new, free immigrants to form a growing buffer between the Great Men—who continued to control the colony, its economy, and its government—and the mass of servants who had neither rights nor wealth. With the other legal division—between black "slaves" and white "servants"—the growing success of the freedmen was crucial to the survival of the slave system. The alliance of white and black bondservants and propertyless freedmen, which had so dramatically threatened to overthrow Virginia's Great Men in 1676, could not resurface in eighteenth century Virginia.

The racialization of slavery reshaped the class system that had so dominated the colony in the previous century. The differential in wealth between the Great Men and ordinary persons continued to be massive. But racial privilege muted the class consciousness of whites. Along with expansion of voting rights and development of republican ideals, a feeling of solidarity grew among the majority "white" population. Freedmen, immigrants, and even indentured servants and redemptioners now had more in common with the Great Men than they had with the people still in slavery. By law they were given the gift of full personhood and citizenship—of being free and white.[168]

Slavery, which was a fundamental strategy if not a publicly stated goal of the initial conquest, had become an established part of the society. It was now reinforced by racial and cultural prejudice. The initial disregard for the culture and language of darker-skinned, communal land-sharing people, which English settlers had developed toward the Indians, was transposed to the African immigrants. Both African and Indian were now landless and without significant cash or capital. They could be controlled by a system of private ownership, enforced by the state.

By its slave system, Virginia codified, institutionalized, and regulated poverty. A state of minimal, landless subsistence for forty percent of the population was no longer to be an accident of the economy but a lifelong status required and justified by law.

Virginia's leaders racialized slavery, and reinforced the racial consciousness of the ordinary white persons who stood between the owners and the enslaved—a growing, seething class of hopeful settlers, landless immigrants, refugees from Europe, freedmen, voluntary indentured servants, and convicts working out their bondage. Virginia's slave laws of 1705 had declared them to be legally "white," privileged by ethnicity even when despised, imprisoned, or impoverished. White Virginians might be poor or in bondage, but they were not in permanent, mandatory poverty. They were not slaves.

Patrick Henry and other revolutionary patriots spoke of the need for liberty, and inveighed against enslavement by the king of England; yet they kept Americans of African descent in uncompromising bondage. In 1780, just before the final year of the American battle for freedom and independence, the Virginia assembly voted to "reward its soldiers in the fight for freedom with a bounty of 300 acres *and* a slave."[169]

The deepening conflict between freedom and slavery in Virginia created tensions in the population that were spiritual as well as political. Toward the end of the eighteenth century, Virginia came to the brink of a revolution that would establish freedom for all. But the high tide of religious and revolutionary thought crested short of universal freedom, receding by 1800 into a rigorous and hypocritical reaffirmation of a fully racialized slave system.

Religious revival and slavery

In the late 1730s and early 1740s Virginia experienced a spiritual change that historians now recognize was as important as any other factor in establishing the culture that separated the colony from England and built a new nation. Called the Great Awakening, it was a religious revival that brought about the development of American evangelical Christianity. Because it empowered persons separately from the hierarchy of the plantation culture, which had been blessed and maintained by the official Anglican Church, it became a source of democratic energy to the culture of Virginia.[170]

But the Great Awakening did not affect only the white culture. Beginning in the 1730s with George Whitefield, the Anglican clergyman who was one of the progenitors of the movement, evangelical preachers in Virginia addressed both black and white people, often together. One of their points of argument was the failure of the established Anglican Church to take seriously the spiritual needs of African Americans.

According to historian Charles F. Irons, "Virtually every well-known dissenter who preached or stationed himself in Virginia before 1770... attracted scores of black Virginians to his ministry."[171] Presbyterian Samuel Davies, one of the best-known evangelical preachers in Virginia in his time and the first non-Anglican to be licensed to preach in Virginia, came to Hanover County in 1747, preaching to both black and white Virginians. He claimed that 300 blacks were attending his service regularly by 1755 and that the number had grown to over 1,000 in 1756.[172]

Worship, prayer, and religious study outside the established church, led by someone other than officially established clergy, was strictly prohibited in Virginia. Hanover County authorities arrested and fined a bricklayer named Samuel Morris who began in 1743 to violate the prohibition against having ten or more persons in his house for a religious gathering,[173] although they subsequently licensed his meetings. The presence of increasing numbers of slaves in evangelical gatherings compounded the threat that these gatherings presented to authorities. In 1774, fifty Baptist ministers were imprisoned in Virginia for failing to obtain licenses to preach or for preaching in an unauthorized location.[174]

The time of the Revolution itself was marked by what is known as the "Great Revival," when the congregations of the Great Awakening experienced further growth. In the case of the Baptists and Methodists, this new energy gathered strength nearly equally among both African Americans and whites. In the decade of 1780–1790, the number of Baptists in Virginia tripled, from 7,208 to 21,317. Of these new converts, thirty percent were black.

Some white evangelical leaders advocated during the Revolutionary period for the abolition of slavery. John Wesley, whose presence was strongly felt in Virginia, had published his *Thoughts upon Slavery* in 1774, in which he strongly opposed the institution. Bishop Thomas Coke, appointed by Wesley as superintendent of Methodists in the New World and armed with an antislavery position adopted by Methodist leadership, traveled the state in 1785 promoting the position and recommended emancipation to the Virginia General Assembly. It was summarily rejected.

In 1790, the Baptist General Committee of Virginia resolved "that slavery is a violent deprivation of the rights of nature, and inconsistent with a republican government; and therefore recommend it to our Brethren to make use of every legal measure to extirpate the horrid evil from the land."[175] By 1793 the committee reversed itself, deciding "that the subject be dismissed from committee, as believing it belongs in the legislative body."[176] In 1797 the Dover Association of Baptists, the historic association of metropolitan Richmond, said, "We sincerely sympathize, both as Christians and Citizens, with those unhappy people.... We would therefore recommend to our Brethren, to unite with the Abolition Society, in proposing a petition to the General Assembly, for their gradual emancipation."[177]

Evangelical Christianity, which was a decidedly multiracial movement in Virginia, had by the last decade of the eighteenth century resolved to accept the status quo insofar as slavery was concerned. Initially, evangelical preachers had calmed anxious authorities by the contention that conversion would make their slaves more cooperative. In the period immediately following the Revolution, they determined that any discussion of the rights and wrongs of slavery belonged in civil, as opposed to religious, discourse.

Alone among Christian bodies, the Virginia members of the Society of Friends adopted and maintained a consistent witness against slavery. In 1782, they asked the General Assembly to emancipate slaves. The Assembly refused to do so, but it did pass a much more liberal manumission law that speeded up the path to freedom for a number of black Virginians. It was no longer necessary to send a petition to the governor seeking permission. Under that new law, the Virginia Yearly Meeting of Quakers decided in 1784 to require its members to free their slaves within ten years and to refuse to hire the slaves of others. Quakers abided by this practice, and some worked to support the persons they freed. In 1790, Quakers were instrumental in founding the Richmond branch of the nation's new antislavery society, originating in Philadelphia, called The Society for the Relief of Free Negroes Unlawfully Held in Bondage.[178]

Slavery and revolution

In American civil society at the end of the eighteenth century, revolution was in the air, and slavery was a part of the discussion. From the point of view of Virginia's enslaved Africans, the best opportunities for freedom were provided by disputes among the white citizens. The departing British governor of Virginia, Lord Dunmore, as he was being chased out of Williamsburg, embarked on his sloop of war *Fowey* and cruised the lower James and Hampton Roads proclaiming freedom to African Americans. Slaves joined his flotilla, and an army of black men wearing sashes proclaiming "Liberty to Negroes" fought an engagement on his behalf. Five years later, in 1780, Benedict Arnold brought a British army of 1,600 men up the peninsula to Richmond, and on the way was joined by hundreds of slaves seeking freedom.

Other white leaders of the state questioned the institution. George Mason, who was a slaveowner, nonetheless spoke frequently of his opposition to slavery. His comments in 1773 were trenchant:

> [Slavery is] that slow Poison, which is daily contaminating the Minds & Morals of our People. Every Gentlemen [sic] here is born a petty Tyrant. Practiced in Acts of Despotism & Cruelty, we become callous to the Dictates of Humanity, & all the finer feelings of the Soul. Taught to regard a part of our own Species in the most abject & contemptible Degree below us, we lose that Idea of the Dignity of Man, which the Hand of Nature had implanted in us, for great & useful purposes. Habituated from our Infancy to trample upon the Rights of Human Nature, every generous, every liberal Sentiment, if not extinguished, is enfeebled in our Minds. And in such an infernal School are to be educated our future Legislators & Rulers.[179]

Three years later, in 1776, Mason presented to the Virginia convention a Declaration of Rights which began by saying that "all men are by nature free and independent," a statement that aroused controversy among his colleagues.[180]

In 1793, Judge George Wythe of the Virginia Court of Chancery in Richmond cited Mason's language in holding that because of that free nature, the burden of proof must fall upon someone who claimed the right to enslave another. Wythe's opinion was overturned by a higher court.

Gradual emancipation was the overt prescription of some. In 1783 Thomas Jefferson drafted such a proposal. In 1796 St. George Tucker, a professor at the College of William and Mary, published *A Dissertation on Slavery, With a Proposal for the Gradual Abolition of it*. He submitted it to the General Assembly, which promptly tabled it.

Revolution and rebellion

Meanwhile, the new urban centers of a formerly rural Virginia were producing a different situation for African Americans. Under the 1782 law, private emancipations increased significantly. By 1800, nearly twenty percent of the black population of Richmond was free.

In addition, working conditions for urban slaves became more flexible. Many, especially artisans, were hired out by their owners. Living with little supervision, they were often essentially on their own. Black family structures, even though not sanctioned by law, had become more definite during the eighteenth century, and the areas in which black people lived were essentially private communities. Although as few as five percent could read and write, these served as eyes and ears for the remainder of the enslaved community.

The situation in the last decade of the eighteenth century was made more volatile by continuing disputes within the white leadership of the state and the nation. Some politicians discussed secession from the Union, and the party in power attempted to make it a crime to criticize the government. The Republicans, who counted Virginia as a stronghold, courted relationship with the French. James Monroe, former ambassador to France, became governor of Virginia in 1799.

From 1791 to 1793 the French island of Saint Dominique, with 600,000 black and mulatto slaves, burst into revolt. Toussaint L'Ouverture became the leader of the colony. Whites in the new capital city of Richmond soon became aware of the implications for their own slave republic. Official state records from August 1792 to December 1793 document warnings to the governor and state officials about plans for slave rebellions. Officials of Richmond, Norfolk, and Petersburg were worried about an "insurrection of negroes." In a deposition given July 22, 1793, John Randolph of Richmond attested that he had been awakened between ten and eleven at night by the sound of people in the street:

> I rose & went softly to my window, where I discovered two negroes close to the wall of my house nearly under me; the one spoke to the other telling him that the blacks were to kill the white people soon in this place. The other asked how soon; the other replied, there must be a day set. He said when; & the other answered, between this and the 15th day of October. The other said, what do you give them so long a time for; he replied, it would take some time for us to get ready. The other

said, you won't kill them; his reply was, I'll be damned if we don't on the 15th of October. In this time another had joined them—it still remained a doubt with two of them whether the plot would be put in execution or not. The one who had been chief speaker said he would bet them what they pleased—the other asking him what he had to bet; he answered, pointing his finger down street, saying that is to be my house, & this my house—meaning, as I expected, the house I live in. & now you know my houses; yes, replies one of the others. The one who seemed to be chief speaker, said, you see how the blacks has killed the whites in the French Island and took it a little while ago.[181]

In 1794 the French Convention voted to abolish slavery in its Caribbean territories, and white French refugees came to Tidewater Virginia, bringing their household slaves with them. By 1795 as many as 12,000 Dominican slaves had been brought to the United States from a nation where black slaves had successfully overthrown their white masters. Some of these mingled with the general population in Virginia's urban centers of Richmond, Petersburg, and Norfolk. Governor James Monroe articulated the growing anxiety of the white population:

The scenes which are acted in San Domingo must produce an effect on all the people of colour in this and the States south of us, more especially on slaves, and it is our duty to be on our guard to prevent any mischief resulting from it.[182]

On August 30, 1800, after months of planning and communication with colleagues in Richmond and its surrounding counties, and in the cities of Charlottesville, Petersburg, and Norfolk, enslaved Africans in Richmond sought to initiate a revolution, led by a powerful blacksmith named Gabriel, who lived on Brook Hill north of the city. They intended to capture the city of Richmond, to kill some of the persons they felt had oppressed them, and to establish a free society of working people of all races.

It rained. It rained so badly that the would-be soldiers could not gather properly. Many did not come out. Those who did could not all meet where they intended. Signals became confused. And the loss of time made the betrayal of the conspiracy almost inevitable.

Since 1692 Virginia law had provided for courts of *oyer* and *terminer*, special courts in which slaves were tried by five justices of the peace. The law prescribed hanging as the punishment for rebellion. The courts were required to reach their decision within ten days after arrest, and the penalty, if death, was to be carried out immediately.

Convictions and executions began soon after the plot was discovered. Gabriel had escaped by ship to Norfolk but was captured there. On October 10, 1800, he was the twenty-fifth conspirator to hang. His lieutenants had carried a banner with the message "Death or liberty." Their hanging was intended, along with other punishments, to intimidate the enslaved population. Bodies of the conspirators were distributed among several hanging grounds in and around Richmond to make certain that the consequences of the challenge were fully understood.[183]

Gabriel was placed on a cart and driven to the foot of a steep hill near the corner of 15th and Broad streets in Shockoe Valley to Richmond's "Burial Ground for Negroes." There, in the center of the sacred ground of the Africans of Richmond, he was hanged on the city gallows.

The burial ground itself was in disrepair from floods and extensive use. According to Christopher McPherson, a free black clerk in Richmond,[184] the cemetery lay

directly east of the Baptist meeting house, unenclosed, very much confined as to space, under a steep hill, on the margin of Shockoe Creek, where every heavy rain commits ravages upon one grave or another, and some coffins have already been washed away into the current of Shockoe stream, and in a very few years the major part of them will no doubt be washed down into the current of James river; added to this, many graves are on private property adjoining, liable to be taken up and thrown away, whenever the ground is wanted by its owners..., and furthermore, we may add the humiliating circumstance, that this is the very express *gallows ground where malefactors are interred*. I ruminated on this ghastly scene, and now, thought I, were I in a barbarous land, and such a sight like this was to present itself to my view, I should exclaim to myself, these are a poor, ignorant people.[185]

The white population of Richmond, which had only been the capital of Virginia for twenty years, was shaken by the near success of Gabriel's plan. Richmond was a city of 5,537 persons, of whom 2,900—just over half—were black, and 2,293—forty percent—were slaves.[186] In a pattern that would be repeated periodically over the next six decades, authorities reacted by establishing restrictions on the enslaved black population. A city guard force was posted; the local abolition society was repressed; teaching blacks to read was discouraged; and, in 1806, the 1782 manumission law, which made it easier to free slaves, was tightened. From that point forward, a slave could only be freed if he would leave the state within twelve months.[187]

The colonization movement

Four years after Gabriel's death, in 1804, a young enslaved man named Lott Cary came from Charles City, east of Richmond, to Richmond's Shockoe Valley, to work for hire in the tobacco warehouse. Cary was about twenty-four years old. In 1807, he was converted in a sermon in First Baptist Church and baptized. His life began to change. He learned to read and write, and he read voraciously. In the warehouse, Cary began to do work that involved reading, writing, and keeping ledgers. His employer gave him extra money for the work, and by 1813 he was able to purchase his freedom and that of his two children for $850. He was ordained and began to preach at the First Baptist Church, an interracial congregation that counted 1,200 black members.

With two other black men, Collin Teague and John Lewis, and with the active support of William Crane, the white member of First Baptist who was teaching a class in mission to black members of the church, Cary formed on April 26, 1815, the African Baptist Missionary Society. The society was formed for overseas mission to Africa, not explicitly for colonization of Africa by freed American slaves. Crane was the official head of the society, so far as authorities were concerned. "This was necessary," one historian notes; "Since the various uprisings of Negroes were making Virginia a hotbed of discontent, the city of Richmond was wary of having Negro meetings unless they were sponsored by white persons."[188]

On December 12, 1816, the Virginia House of Delegates, after a one-day secret session, passed a unanimous resolution asking the Governor to ask the President of the United States to obtain "a territory on the coast of Africa, or at some other place not within any of the states or territorial governments of the United States" for "free or emancipated Virginia Negroes." The Senate concurred, with only one vote in opposition. [189]

The vote was used to support a movement, begun by Virginia politician Charles Fenton Mercer, to form the American Society for Colonizing the Free People of Color of the United States, known as the American Colonization Society (ACS). This was accomplished in

Washington on December 21, 1816. George Washington's nephew, Supreme Court Justice Bushrod Washington, agreed to be president. He was joined in the foundation by Rev. William Meade, later to be Episcopal bishop of Virginia, who became one of the society's major advocates.

From the beginning, the society's supporters argued over whether the society would help to end slavery or whether, by deportation of free blacks, it would actually strengthen it. Following the advice of Henry Clay that they "sidestep the 'delicate question' of slavery altogether," the delegates to the Washington meeting founded the society without resolving the contradiction inherent in the policy.[190]

Lott Cary saw himself not as a colonization person, but as a missionary to the people of Africa. "I am an African," he said, "and in this country, however meritorious my conduct, and respectable my character, I cannot receive the credit due to either. I wish to go to a country where I shall be estimated by my merits, not by my complexion, and I feel bound to labor for my suffering race."[191]

In 1821, Cary, Teague, and their wives left for West Africa aboard the *Nautilus* in a delegation of twenty-eight adults, with their children. The delegation was cooperating with the colonization movement, but was not sponsored by it. The American Colonization Society did not yet have any land, so the missionaries disembarked in the British colony of Sierra Leone, and were given a farm to work. Mrs. Cary died soon after the arrival. President Monroe sent U.S. Navy captain Robert Stockton to West Africa on the armed schooner *Alligator* to obtain territory. In a negotiation conducted by holding a gun to the head of a chief whom the English called King Peter, he obtained for the Colonization Society an area for settlement called Cape Mesurado. The land included ninety miles of coast, and went seventy miles inland. Cary was pleased to note that there were 125,000 natives of the Bassa, Vey, Dey, and Kroo tribes among whom to do missionary work. On February 7, 1822, the colonists arrived at the Cape.[192]

Lott Cary's Richmond missionaries may not have come to West Africa primarily to establish Liberia for the American Colonization Society, but it is doubtful if the colony would have been established without their strong leadership. The ACS sent an agent, Jehudi Ashmun, to be in charge of the colony, but his leadership was not always effective. When surrounding tribes sent a force of 1,500 men to attack the colony in 1822, Ashmun seems to have disappeared. Cary rallied thirty-seven men and boys, armed with guns, and turned back the attack. In 1823, Cary represented the needs of the settlers against repressive policies of the Colonization Society. Although this initially alienated him from the society, by 1826 they had appointed him vice agent of the colony, and when Ashmun left because of health problems in 1827, Cary took charge of the 1,200 settlers.

Two other Virginians had leading roles in the colony. Hilary Teague of Richmond edited the newspaper in Liberia and eventually wrote the Liberian Declaration of Independence. Joseph Jenkins Roberts of Petersburg became the first president of Liberia. Between 1820 and 1830, 1,670 Americans emigrated to Liberia, and more than a quarter of them died of disease. At least 720 were free persons, representing a highly educated group, who emigrated voluntarily.[193] More than 6,000 persons ultimately emigrated to Liberia before the end of American slavery, a third of them from Virginia.

Opposition to the colonization movement began to build among blacks during the 1820s, particularly as information coming back to the community told of the many deaths and hardships of the settlers. In 1826, Richard Allen, the founder of the African Methodist Episcopal Church, spoke out in Philadelphia against the movement, but some momentum continued. Cary himself wrote a letter to a friend in Richmond in September, 1827, seeking to counter some of Allen's views. Gilbert Hunt, a well-known free black member of First Baptist who had been rewarded with his freedom for saving white Richmonders in the Theater Fire of 1811, visited the colony in 1829, but returned in 1830 with a less than enthusiastic report. In November, 1828, the colonists faced another threat from the native tribes in the area they had settled. Working to prepare ammunition, Lott Cary was injured, and on November 10, 1828, he died.

The anxiety of the slave-owning community and the white leaders of the state remained in a cyclic state of turmoil for the entire period from 1800, the year of Gabriel's Insurrection, until war finally broke out in 1861. National struggles over slavery had regular effect on the mood in Richmond. But there were local issues, too, which showed the volatility of the population.

Writing from Monticello, Thomas Jefferson expressed the anxiety of the period explicitly in a letter to a friend in 1820 regarding the national debate over slavery in Missouri:

> This momentous question, like a fire bell in the night, awakened and filled me with terror. I considered it at once as the knell of the Union. It is hushed indeed for the moment. But this is a reprieve only.... I can say with conscious truth that there is

not a man on earth who would sacrifice more than I would, to relieve us from this heavy reproach, in any *practicable* way. The cession of that kind of property, for so it is misnamed, is a bagatelle which would not cost me in a second thought, if, in that way, a general emancipation and *expatriation* could be effected: and, gradually, and with due sacrifices, I think it might be. But, as it is, we have the wolf by the ear, and we can neither hold him, nor safely let him go. Justice is in one scale, and self-preservation in the other.[194]

In 1829 David Walker, a free black man living in Boston, who had come from North Carolina, published a pamphlet entitled *Appeal in Four Articles Together with a Preamble to the Colored Citizens of the World, But in Particular and Very Expressly to Those of the United States of America*, which white Southern governments regarded as incendiary. The pamphlet turned up in Wilmington, North Carolina, and in Savannah, Georgia. The magistrate in Wilmington told the governor that the document spoke "in most inflammatory terms of the condition of the slaves in the Southern States exaggerating their sufferings, magnifying their physical strength and underrating the power of the whites, containing also an open appeal to their natural love of liberty; and throughout expressing sentiments totally subversive of all subordination in our slaves."[195]

The mayor of Savannah asked the mayor of Boston to arrest Walker. The governor of Georgia sent the document to the state legislature. Then, in early 1830, the Virginia General Assembly was again called into secret meeting. Governor Willliam B. Giles told the assembled legislators that an agent of the mayor of Richmond had "found a copy of the dreaded publication in the home of a free Negro."[196] The House of Delegates responded, passing a law "making it criminal to write, print, or circulate among slaves seditious writings. The teaching of slaves to read and write, whether in Sunday schools or by private instruction," was "also strictly forbidden." The delegates' resolution, passed by a single vote, was rejected by the Senate.[197]

Legislative debate over slavery

In the fall of 1831, the event that Virginia's slaveowning population most feared came to pass. In Southampton County, seventy-five miles southeast of Richmond, on August 22, enslaved Africans under the leadership of Nat Turner killed fifty-five white persons. Turner was finally captured on October 30, tried, hanged on November 11, and then skinned. By the time the events were over, the state had executed at least twenty-three men, and mobs had killed as many as 200 more. Many free black persons remaining in Southampton County wanted to emigrate to Liberia to find safety.

The General Assembly met in December, and was presented with a petition from Hanover delegate William Henry Roane, grandson of Patrick Henry, on behalf of the Virginia Orthodox Quakers, seeking the gradual emancipation of slaves. Free blacks and newly emancipated blacks would be sent out of state. Other similar petitions came to the Assembly. The Richmond *Enquirer,* one of the two major newspapers in the city, advocated the removal of free blacks and attention to "the greatest evil which can scourge our land."[198] Two hundred fifteen women from Augusta County even submitted a petition to the Assembly saying they were willing to give up their slaves in order to prevent insurrection.[199]

The petitions to alter or abolish laws on slavery were referred to a select committee, which was instructed to examine the causes of the insurrection in Southampton County and to propose strategies for the deportation of free blacks.[200]

On January 16, 1832, the select committee made its report. It asked the Assembly to agree that it was "inexpedient for the present legislature to make any enactment for the abolition of slavery." A preamble, inserted as a concession to opponents, declared that the House was "profoundly aware of the great evils arising from the condition of the colored population of this commonwealth," and agreed that it was a good idea to export both free Negroes and 'such as may hereafter become free.'[201] The House resolution observed, however, that the removal of free Negroes might "absorb all our present means; and that a further action for the removal of the slaves should await a more definite development of public opinion."[202] Debate was lengthy and heated.

Finally, the Assembly voted 65-58 to support the select committee resolution and to continue state authorization for the enslavement of Virginians of African descent. The primary opposition came from legislators representing communities west of the Blue Ridge, where there were few slaves. They emphasized the need to build in the Valley and western parts of the state a strong, non-slave, white working man's society with a diversified economy. After the defeat of the antislavery resolution, the House of Delegates passed by a significant majority a resolution to assist free blacks who wished to emigrate to Liberia. But the Senate killed the measure when conservatives said the funds could not go to anyone who was not free at the time of the bill's passage.

The Assembly then tightened the so-called "black codes" of the state—this time with a sixty percent vote in favor. The laws held that

- Neither enslaved nor free black persons could preach or attend religious services conducted by a black person.
- A slave who wished to attend a religious service conducted by a white man had to have the consent of his owner.
- Free blacks charged with a felony or larceny would be tried in the same system as slaves.
- It was illegal for either whites or blacks to write, print, or circulate advice to slaves to rebel.[203]

The Assembly also reiterated and strengthened a provision of the Virginia code of 1819 that made it illegal for either blacks or whites to teach slaves to read or write. The 1831 statute specified that the blessings of literacy should be denied not only to slaves, but also to "free negroes or mulattoes, at any school-house, church, meeting-house or other place..., either in the day or night, under whatsoever pretext."[204]

None of the public or politically supported proposals to end slavery in Virginia contemplated the mandatory freeing of enslaved Africans or their continuation as residents of Virginia. The Virginia proposals always called for gradual elimination of slavery and the deportation of newly freed slaves and even blacks who were already free. Scholar Patricia Hickin, who studied the antislavery movement in Virginia extensively, explains that "fear of future ... insurrections gave antislavery Virginians the courage to speak out against the 'peculiar institution,' and for two weeks in January of 1832 the legislature seriously discussed the possibility of eventually abolishing slavery. But no one in the legislature suggested that the freedmen be allowed to remain in Virginia; what anti-slavery men in the legislature were chiefly interested in was the banishment of all blacks, slave and free. The strategy of "Virginia emancipators," Hickin says, was to deport both free and surplus enslaved Africans from the state, reducing their proportion in the population, until most were removed, or until it was "safe" to emancipate the remaining black population.[205]

During 1832, after the Assembly had left Richmond, legislative support of the colonization movement gained momentum. Virginians learned that hated Northern abolitionist William Lloyd Garrison had condemned the movement. Nothing could have been more helpful to the Virginia sponsors. Retired president James Madison, living at Montpelier west of Richmond, signed on as president of the American Colonization Society. In 1833, the legislature appropriated money to support the colonization of black persons who were free at the time of the bill's passage.

Virginians reacted angrily to increasing pressure from Northern Abolitionists over the next few years. In the summer of 1835, the American Anti-Slavery Society sent large amounts of abolitionist literature into the state. In 1836 the General Assembly made it illegal for a member of an abolitionist society to cross the state line to advocate abolition, or to distribute literature promoting it. They asked state governments in the North to make it a criminal offense to form an abolition society, suppress "all associations within their respective limits, purporting to be, or having the character of, abolition societies; and [to] make it highly penal to print, publish, or distribute, newspapers, pamphlets, or other publications, calculated or having a tendency to excite the slaves of the southern states to insurrection and revolt."[206]

Meanwhile, Richmond's white church leaders defended themselves against increasingly aggressive attacks on slavery by Northern Christians, justifying the institution by calling attention to the charity and paternalism of southern Christians. An August 1835 meeting of Baptists, Methodists, Presbyterians, and Episcopalians in the Richmond offices of the *Southern Churchman*, the Episcopal publication, criticized Northern evangelicals for their opposition to slavery. The abolitionist was "the enemy of the black man," the Virginia white Christians said, because he denies him opportunity for religious development. Citing the "example of our Lord Jesus Christ and his Apostles, in not interfering with the question of slavery, but uniformly recognizing the relations of master and servant," they resolved unanimously "that we earnestly deprecate the unwarrantable and highly improper interference of the people of any other State, with the domestic relations of master and slave."[207]

The Virginia apologists attracted national attention, but there is no indication that their opponents were allowed to present their positions in any safe forum in Richmond or Virginia. William Meade, an early supporter of the colonization movement, became assistant bishop of the Episcopal Diocese of Virginia in 1829 and succeeded as the Bishop of Virginia Episcopalians in 1841. Meade became an outspoken proponent of a paternalistic religious justification for slavery. He preached, and then printed, several sermons on the topic in a volume entitled *Sermons,*

Dialogues, and Narratives for Servants To Be Read to Them in Families (1836) and in a compendium called *Sermons Addressed to Masters and Servants.*²⁰⁸ Meade's sermons circulated widely and came to the attention of the famed abolitionist Frederick Douglass. Douglass seized on them as an object for instruction and ridicule in his speech on American slavery entitled "Love of God, Love of Man, Love of Country," which he delivered in Syracuse on September 24, 1847. Douglass began by quoting Bishop Meade:

We have men in this land now advising evangelical flogging. I hold in my hand a sermon recently published by Rev. Bishop Meade, of Virginia. Before I read that part in favour of evangelical flogging, let me read a few extracts from another part, relating to the duties of the slave. The sermon, by the way, was published with a view of its being read by *Christian* masters to their slaves....

"Having thus shown you the chief duties you owe to your great Master in Heaven, I now come to lay before you the duties you owe to your masters and mistresses on earth. And for this you have one general rule that you ought always carry in your minds, and that is, to *do all services for them, as if you did it for God himself.* Poor creatures! You little consider when you are idle, and neglectful of your master's business; when you steal, waste, and hurt any of their substance; when you are saucy and impudent; when you are telling them lies and deceiving them; or when you prove stubborn and sullen, and will not do the work you are set about, without stripes and vexation; you do not consider, I say, that what faults you are guilty of towards your masters and mistresses, are faults done against God himself, who hath set your masters and mistresses over you in his own stead, and expects that you will do for them just as you would do for him. And pray, do not think that I want to deceive you, when I tell you that your *masters and mistresses are God's overseers*; and that if you are faulty towards them, God himself will punish you severely for it."

This is some of the Southern religion. Do you not think you would "grow in grace in the knowledge of the truth."

I come now to evangelical flogging. There is nothing said about flogging—that word is not used. It is called correction; and that word as it is understood at the North, is some sort

Frederick Douglass   *Bishop William Meade*

of medicine. Slavery has always sought to hide itself under different names. The mass of the people call it "our peculiar institution." There is no harm in that. Others call it (they are the more pious sort), "our Patriarchal institution." Politicians have called it "our social system"; and people in social life have called it "our domestic institution." Abbot Lawrence has recently discovered a new name for it—he calls it "unenlightened labour." The Methodists in their last General Conference, have invented a new name—"the impediment." To give you some idea of evangelical flogging, under the name of correction, there are laws of this description,— "any white man killing a slave shall be punished as though he shall have killed a white person, unless such a slave die under *moderate* correction." It commences with a plain proposition.

"Now when correction is given to you, you either deserve it, or you do not deserve it..."

The Bishop goes on to say, "Whether you really deserve it or not," (one would think that would make a difference), "it is your duty, and Almighty God requires that you bear it patiently. You may perhaps think that it is a hard doctrine," (and it admits of little doubt), "But if you consider it right you must needs think otherwise of it." (It is clear as mud. I suppose he is now going to reason into them the propriety of being flogged evangelically.) "Suppose you deserve correction; you cannot but see that it is just as right you should meet with it. Suppose you do not, or at least so much or so severe; you perhaps have escaped a great many more, and are at last paid for all. Suppose you are quite innocent; is it not possible you may have done some other bad thing which was never discovered, and Almighty God would not let you escape without punishment one time or another? Ought you not in such cases to give glory to Him?" [209]

The failed white opposition

The national political atmosphere, and the increasingly doctrinaire atmosphere within Virginia and its capital city of Richmond, continued to shape the debate over slavery within the white community and to narrow the alternatives that white opponents to slavery felt they could publicly articulate. In the latter part of the 1830s and the early 1840s, the colonization option continued to be one of the few alternatives that was promoted in public. Sometimes it was pressed by persons opposed to slavery; sometimes by slavery advocates who wanted to remove potentially troublesome free black persons from the city and state.

In the late 1840s, the Colonization Society had its best days in Virginia, under the leadership of a new agent, Rufus W. Bailey. Bailey was a Congregationalist minister from western Massachusetts who had come to Staunton and founded the Augusta Female Academy, now Mary Baldwin College.[210] He joined a group of Presbyterians centered at Washington College in Lexington, now Washington & Lee University, in recruiting black persons to emigrate. One of the professors at Washington College, George E. Dabney, had freed his slaves in 1846 and taken an antislavery stand. William Henry Ruffner, the son of the college's president, had joined the Colonization Society to work as an agent under Bailey. After the war, the younger Ruffner was Virginia's first superintendent of public education.

In 1848 and 1850 Bailey came to Richmond to fight movements in the legislature to force mandatory expulsion of free blacks from the state. Instead, in 1850, he persuaded the legislature to agree to pay the passage of any free black person who wished to emigrate to Liberia. His first group of emigrants was sent out from the Lexington Presbyterian Church by Rev. George Junkin, another Presbyterian minister, who had become president of Washington College and whose daughter married

Stonewall Jackson. The Lexington church had a "colored Sabbath school," in which Jackson taught both free and enslaved children to read.[211]

By 1850, Bailey was stating the goal of sending as emigrants all the free blacks from one county, such as Rockbridge, to set an example of what could be done. As a tool, he sought to use a Virginia law that required free blacks to register with authorities, urging the authorities to deny extension of their permission. Bailey applauded those who had emigrated voluntarily. "The others [free blacks] have no right of residence by law," he said, "& will be required to leave with the offer of assistance to Liberia."[212] No county was willing to accept this draconian plan. Bailey made it clear that, in this policy, he thought he was being a friend to the free black Virginians.

In September 1851, Bailey recruited over a hundred free persons to sail to Liberia and said that he had applications for passage on hand from more than 400 others.[213] Within a year, however, he had received the bad news of the death of one of his leading émigrés. Soon thereafter his largest expedition, comprised of 149 free black Virginians who left Norfolk on the *Morgan Dix* on November 1, 1851, ended in catastrophe. Thirty-seven of the 149 passengers died on shipboard and another twenty-three soon after arrival, forty percent of the total. Bailey's prospective passenger list evaporated. He fell into bad health. He resigned in 1853, and with him went much of the remaining energy of the colonization movement in Virginia.

In February 1847, also in Lexington, Washington College President Henry Ruffner gave an unanticipated address to the Franklin Society that captured the attention and imagination of some of his hearers. The address enumerated various economic and social reasons for the gradual elimination of slavery in the western part of Virginia. Some slaves were to be freed and most sent out of the state. The address was published, and widely read, under the title "Address to the People of West Virginia." Because of the striking interest that the "Ruffner pamphlet" aroused, he and some citizens of Lexington resolved to start an antislavery newspaper in Virginia, to be published weekly, when he retired as president. It did not happen. He retired in 1848. His wife died. After a little travel, he returned to his home in Kanawha County, Virginia—now West Virginia—to the tiny town of Malden. There he had, as a young minister, founded Kanawha Salines Presbyterian Church in 1819. There, several years after his death, his sister-in-law, Viola Knapp Ruffner, became the mentor to a young African-American boy named Booker T. Washington.

Virginia did not have an antislavery newspaper. Another prominent Virginian was hoping to start one in 1847, this time in Richmond. John Hampden Pleasants, son of a former governor of Virginia, had been editing the *Richmond Whig* for several decades. In 1845 he began a series of articles attacking slavery. The beginning of the series was, not surprisingly, "a vitriolic attack on abolitionists."[214] Some of the ensuing articles, which genuinely opposed slavery, were written by Samuel Janney, a well-known Virginia Quaker. On January 9, 1846, Pleasants unexpectedly announced his resignation as editor of the *Whig*. It appeared that his antislavery campaign had run afoul of his publisher. Pleasants revealed that he would be starting a new publication, called the *Richmond Globe,* which it was anticipated would be an even more intentionally antislavery journal.

For years, Pleasants' competition in Richmond journalism had been the *Richmond Enquirer*, edited by Thomas Ritchie, who had become a friend. But Ritchie was now in Washington and his sons Thomas Jr. and William were editing the paper. While Pleasants was working to start his new publication, on January 20, 1846, the *Enquirer* published an article calling him an "abolitionist."

As Judge Robert W. Hughes told the story to the Virginia Press Association in 1897, "There appeared in [the *Enquirer*] a communication over the signature of 'Macon,' stating that Mr. Pleasants was about to found an abolition journal. At that time anti-abolition sentiment in Virginia ran extremely high, and no more mortal insult could have possibly been offered to a public man, than to accuse him of sympathy with a party which was thought to be secretly working to incite a servile insurrection."[215]

Pleasants called the charge an "unqualified falsehood." He believed that "slavery was an evil, and ought to be got rid of, but at our own time, at our own motion, and in our own way." To emphasize his point, he asserted, "I can only say I would go farther to see some of the Abolition leaders hanged than any man in Virginia."[216]

The writer in the *Enquirer,* Thomas Ritchie, Jr., replied that Pleasants' answer "affords strong corroborative evidence of our opinion...that facts within our knowledge prove him to be a coward.... Let it be—we shall not disturb him."[217]

The epithet "coward" would normally have provoked a duel in Pleasants' and Ritchie's world. As Judge Hughes explained the *code duello* to the journalists, "Until comparatively recent years its hold upon the Virginia public was such, that a resort to it in case of a personal attack upon character, was as much a measure of self-defence, as a repulse of a physical assault. No man could retain his influence and standing in the community, who forfeited his character, and no man could retain his character who tamely submitted to insult. Hence the frequency of resort to the duello."[218]

Pleasants, although he was known to be opposed to this code, told Ritchie he would meet him on the morning of February 25 at dawn in Manchester, on the south side of the James.

The duel took place beside the Mayo Mill Canal, "200 yards above the cotton factory," across Mayo's Bridge, in the town of Manchester. Dr. A. L. Warner, a friend, went with Pleasants across the bridge that morning. He testified under questioning by the Prosecutor in the case against Ritchie that was tried in Chesterfield County Superior Court. Ritchie was acquitted by a jury. Here is Warner's account of how that morning began:

> The next morning it was very inclement. A little before daybreak I went to Mr. Deane's room. It was in the gray of the morning, and the guards were just leaving the corner of the street below. We left Mr. Deane's room and went over Mayo's Bridge together.... After passing on the Manchester side of the bridge, I said to Mr. Deane, "The other parties are on the ground." ...I then saw three individuals, of whom I knew Messrs. Ritchie and Greenhow.
>
> ...Mr. Pleasants wrapped his cloak around him and passed Mr. Ritchie. I did not hear him say anything.... I approached, and then shook hands with Greenhow and Ritchie. I heard Mr. Deane use the expression, "you say this can't be adjusted—that you will do nothing." Mr. Greenhow replied "I have had my friend here fifteen minutes after the time appointed. He is here to repel an assault from Mr. Pleasants. I will keep him here fifteen minutes more, and then remove him from the ground.
>
> ...The parties were near the tree. Mr. Pleasants crossed the bridge.... Mr. Archer called to him to arm. He threw off his cloak and commenced arming. ...He put a revolver in the left pocket of his coat; then, he took two dueling pistols, one in his right and the other in his left hand. The next weapon I saw him arm himself with was his sword-cane under his left arm. He had a bowie knife under his vest.... [They were] within a few feet of each other. I heard both Greenhow and Archer's voice calling on Mr. Pleasants to stop.... The cry of

stop lasted about two seconds: everything was done very quickly. Immediately after the cry..., I saw the flash of the first pistol, and heard the first ball passing between myself and Mr. Deane.... I thought Mr. Ritchie fired at a distance of about thirty yards.... I saw the first flash and heard the ball pass. The ball from the second pistol, I think, passed over us. At the time of the third report, there were two flashes; the report of the pistol was almost one. I thought Mr. Pleasants then fired his first and Mr. Ritchie his third pistol. Mr. Pleasants turned his body, so as to make me believe that he was wounded at the third fire in the left breast.... Mr. Pleasants advanced.

At the third fire, Mr. Ritchie's form became obscured; Mr. Pleasants still advancing. I saw him within 6 or 7 feet of Mr. Ritchie.... It was then that Mr. Pleasants fired his second pistol. I saw Mr. Pleasants level his second pistol; I heard the report: I saw Mr. Ritchie staggering back and I remarked to Mr. Deane, "Ritchie is a dead man." ...Then I heard several discharges without knowing who was firing. I saw Mr. Pleasants striking at Mr. Ritchie with some weapon, whether a cane or a pistol I do not know.... He gave several blows and two or three thrusts. I do not know if the sword was sheathed. During this part of the affair, I saw Mr. Ritchie with his sword in hand: I did not see him draw it. I saw him in the attitude of one making a thrust, and did see him make one or two thrusts at Mr. Pleasants. I remarked to Mr. Deane, "let's go up or he'll be stabbed." Two or three times the cry was made "stop, Pleasants; stop, Ritchie." We went up. Mr. Pleasants was tottering; Mr. Ritchie was standing a few feet off, the point of his sword on the ground, and perfectly quiet. Mr. Archer took Mr. Pleasants' arm, and carried him aside and laid him down.... He was on the ground when I reached him. Before I reached Mr. Pleasants, I saw Mr. Ritchie leaving the ground. [219]

Pleasants lay mortally wounded. He died two days later. No one in Virginia started an antislavery newspaper for general circulation in the two final decades of state-sanctioned slavery in Virginia. White opposition to slavery was effectively silenced.

In 1833, William Henry Harrison, from Berkeley Plantation twenty-five miles down the James River from Richmond, openly discussed his views on slavery and his membership in 1790 in an abolitionist society. "I am accused of being friendly to slavery," Harrison said. "From my earliest youth to the present moment, I have been the ardent friend of Human Liberty. At the age of eighteen, I became a member of an Abolition Society established...at Richmond, Virginia; the object of which was to ameliorate the condition of slaves and procure their freedom by every legal means.... I have been the means of liberating many slaves, but never placed one in bondage." But in 1840, when he was running for president, Harrison denied he had been an abolitionist and asserted that the organization he joined in his youth was simply a "humane society."[220]

In 1859, when John Letcher, a Lexington lawyer and Congressman, was running his successful race for governor, he was accused of having endorsed William Ruffner's antislavery pamphlet in 1847. He repudiated the pamphlet.

6

Capital City of Slavery
1780–1861

Richmond's culture of slavery

Richmond became the capital city of Virginia by action of the General Assembly in 1779, and in May 1780 the legislature met in Richmond for the first time. In 1782 the city of Richmond was incorporated within Henrico County.[221] The Common Hall, Richmond's governing body, included Richard Adams, the owner of Richmond Hill. It met for the first time at the Henrico County Court House at 22nd and East Main streets. In 1775 Richmond had a population of about 600, but as soon as it became the capital, the town began to grow. By 1800 its population had swelled to 5,737, of which 49.5 percent were white and 50.5 percent black. One-fifth of that black population was free.[222] The remaining four-fifths was enslaved.

The institution of slavery in Richmond and Virginia had evolved considerably in the eighteenth century. Africans had been enslaved in significant numbers in the colony for four or five generations. The population of Africans in Virginia grew during the eighteenth century from 6,000 in 1700 to 367,164 in 1800. The population of Tidewater Virginia—where white bond servitude and then African slavery were, in sequence, the foundations of the economy—was virtually evenly split between white and black. Most of the white population was by this time free; eighty-five percent of the black population was enslaved. By 1825 the state's African-American community was composed largely of persons born in Virginia.

The tobacco economy deteriorated. African Americans came to Virginia's burgeoning cities, hired out for cash by their rural owners. The new capital city of Richmond became a manufacturing center. Industrial slaves joined their artisan brothers and sisters as persons with some freedom to come and go and some ability to earn their own overtime wages. Taverns and gathering places mixed free and enslaved Africans throughout the town.

Richmond's population remained nearly evenly divided between whites and blacks through 1840, with as many as one-fourth of the black population free. During the last two decades before the war, the white population increased to sixty percent, and the percentage of free blacks began to slip.

Population of Tidewater Virginia 1830-1850			
	Whites	Free blacks	Slaves
1830	167,001	28,920	185,457
1840	170,530	29,252	172,791
1850	189,314	32,790	178,081

Source: Letters from Virginia. *New York Times*, June 20, 1854

Several evangelical churches mixed free and enslaved Africans with white congregants in the Richmond area. Charles Irons calls the first quarter of the nineteenth century—the period between Gabriel's Rebellion and Nat Turner's Rebellion of 1831—the period of "biracial Christianity."[223] White-controlled interracial churches did not present any serious challenge to the institution of slavery in Virginia, however. Whites justified slavery by the opportunity it gave them for evangelizing and encouraging blacks. White preaching took on a decidedly paternalistic cast. White church people in Virginia supported the efforts of the American Colonization Society to free blacks and give them homesteads in Liberia.

After two generations of biracial Christianity and Nat Turner's failed uprising, the leaders of Virginia became more defensive toward black Christianity. They recognized that Turner was involved with a growing "invisible church" of African Americans who met informally outside the formal meetings of evangelicals. The General Assembly

Population of Richmond 1800-1860							
	1800	1810	1820	1830	1840	1850	1860
Whites	2,837	4,808	6,445	7,755	10,718	15,274	23,635
Blacks							
Slave	2,293	3,748	4,387	6,345	7,509	9,927	11,699
Free	607	1,189	1,235	1,960	1,926	2,369	2,576
Total	2,900	4,937	5,622	8,305	9,435	12,296	14,275
% free	21%	24%	22%	24%	20%	19%	18%
Total pop.	5,737	9,745	12,067	16,060	20,153	25,570	37,910
% white	50%	49%	53%	48%	53%	55%	62%

Source: U.S. Census data in Richard C. Wade, Slavery in the Cities: The South 1820-1860 (New York, 1964), 327; and Historical Census Browser, [Retrieved 28 October 2009], from the University of Virginia, Geospatial and Statistical Data Center: http:/fisher.lib.virginia.edu/collections/

First African Baptist Church, East Broad Street, Richmond, with members of the congregation. Library of Congress photo.

required that a white clergyman be in charge of all gatherings of black Christians, and white Christians were motivated to make sure that blacks worshipped at formal times and in prescribed places.

As early as 1822, black Baptists in Richmond had asked the General Assembly "that your honorable body...pass a law authorizing them to cause to be erected within this city, a House of public worship which may be called the Baptist African Church."

The Assembly denied the petition,[224] and later passed a law making such an arrangement illegal. But by 1841 black Christians were in a position to establish churches that were somewhat independent, while still under the oversight of a white minister.[225] The first and best known of these in Richmond was the First African Baptist Church. Under the leadership of the Reverend Robert Ryland of Richmond College, the white congregation of First Baptist Church sold the old church to its black members and moved two blocks up Broad Street to a new building. The black congregation started with a thousand members and doubled quickly.

The predominantly white denominations continued to provide services to both black and white members. Between May, 1853 and May, 1854, for example, the Episcopal clergy of Virginia reported that nearly one-third of the 248 couples they married were black.[226] But the Episcopalians had no success in adding black members to their congregations in that same decade.

With the systematic and near-total absorption of Richmond in a hierarchical culture of race-based slavery, one needs to go to outside observers to gain descriptions of the way the city functioned. During the first half of the nineteenth century, a number of prominent international visitors came to Richmond, and many of them left accounts of their observations. One of the most detailed descriptions comes from Charles Dickens. The great English author and social critic visited America in March 1842 and published an account of his journey entitled *American Notes* in the same year. After visiting Baltimore, he took a steamboat to Potomac Creek and a stagecoach to Fredericksburg, where he boarded a train for Richmond.

[The coach came to] Fredericksburg, whence there is a railway to Richmond. The tract of country through which it takes its course was once productive: but the soil has been exhausted by the system of employing a great amount of slave labour in forcing crops, without strengthening the land: and it is now little better than a sandy desert overgrown with trees. Dreary and uninteresting as its aspect is, I was glad to the heart to find anything on which one of the curses of this horrible institution has fallen; and had greater pleasure in contemplating the withered ground than the richest and most thriving cultivation in the same place could possibly have afforded me.

In this district, as in all others where slavery sits brooding (I have frequently heard this admitted, even by those who are its warmest advocates), there is an air of ruin and decay abroad, which is inseparable from the system. The barns and outhouses are mouldering away; the sheds are patched and half roofless; the log-cabins (built in Virginia with external chimneys made of clay or wood) are squalid in the last degree. There is no look of decent comfort anywhere. The miserable stations by the railway side; the great wild woodyards, whence the engine is supplied with fuel; the negro children rolling on the ground before the cabin doors, with dogs and pigs; the biped beasts of burden slinking past: gloom and dejection are upon them all.

In the negro car belonging to the train in which we made this journey were a mother and her children who had just been purchased; the husband and father being left behind with their old owner. The children cried the whole way, and the mother was misery's picture. The champion of Life, Liberty, and the Pursuit of Happiness, who had bought them, rode in the train; and, every time we stopped, got down to see that they were safe. The black in Sinbad's Travels, with one eye in the middle of his forehead which shone like a burning coal, was nature's aristocrat compared with this white gentleman.

It was between six and seven o'clock in the evening when we drove to the hotel: in front of which, and on the top of the broad flight of steps leading to the door, two or three citizens were balancing themselves on rocking-chairs, and smoking cigars. We found it a very large and elegant establishment, and were as well entertained as travelers need desire to be. The climate being a thirsty one, there was never,

The Exchange Hotel, on the right, was built in 1841 and was Richmond's finest hostelry when Dickens came to Richmond in 1842. It occupied the block between Franklin Street and Main, 14th and 15th. in 1855 the Ballard House hotel was built across Franklin Street; later the hostelries were joined by a bridge. Located next to Richmond's slave market, the Exchange provided a venue where traders negotiated purchase with out-of-town buyers and sellers. Photo courtesy the Pickett Society.

at any hour of the day, a scarcity of loungers in the spacious bar, or a cessation of the mixing of cool liquors: but they were a merrier people here, and had musical instruments playing to them o' nights, which it was a treat to hear again. The next day, and the next, we rode and walked about the town, which is delightfully situated on eight hills overhanging James River; a sparkling stream, studded here and there with bright islands, or brawling over broken rocks. Although it was yet but the middle of March, the weather in this southern temperature was extremely warm; the peach-trees and magnolias were in full bloom; and the trees were green....

The city is the seat of the local Parliament of Virginia; and, in its shady legislative halls, some orators were drowsily holding forth to the hot noonday. By dint of constant repetition, however, these constitutional sights had very little more interest for me than so many parochial vestries; and I was glad to exchange this one for a lounge in a well-arranged public library of some ten thousand volumes, and a visit to a tobacco manufactory, where the workmen were all slaves.

I saw in this place the whole process of picking, rolling,

pressing, drying, packing in casks, and branding. All the tobacco thus dealt with was in course of manufacture for chewing; and one would have supposed there was enough in that one storehouse to have filled even the comprehensive jaws of America. In this form the weed looks like the oil-cake on which we fatten cattle; and, even without reference to its consequences, is sufficiently uninviting.

Many of the working appeared to be strong men, and it is hardly necessary to add that they were all labouring quietly then. After two o'clock in the day they are allowed to sing, a certain number at a time. The hour striking while I was there, some twenty sang a hymn in parts, and sang it by no means ill; pursuing their work meanwhile. A bell rang as I was about to leave, and they all poured forth into a building on the opposite side of the street to dinner. I said several times that I should like to see them at their meal; but, as the gentleman to whom I mentioned this desire appeared to be suddenly taken rather deaf, I did not pursue the request. Of their appearance I shall have something to say presently.

On the following day I visited a plantation or farm, of about twelve hundred acres, on the opposite bank of the river. Here again, although I went down with the owner of the estate, to "the quarter," as that part of it in which the slaves live is called, I was not invited to enter into any of their huts. All I saw of them was that they were very crazy, wretched cabins, near to which groups of half-naked children basked in the sun, or wallowed on the dusty ground. But I believe that this gentleman is a considerate and excellent master, who inherited his fifty slaves, and is neither a buyer nor a seller of human stock; and I am sure, from my own observation and conviction, that he is a kind-hearted, worthy man.

There are two bridges across the river: one belongs to the railroad, and the other, which is a very crazy affair, is the private property of some old lady in the neighbourhood, who levies tolls upon the townspeople. Crossing this bridge on my way back, I saw a notice painted on the gate, cautioning all persons to drive slowly: under a penalty, if the offender were a white man, of five dollars; if a negro, fifteen stripes. The same decay and gloom that overhang the way by which it is approached, hover above the town of Richmond. There are pretty villas and cheerful houses in its streets, and Nature smiles upon the country round; but jostling its handsome residences, like slavery itself going hand-in-hand with many lofty virtues, are deplorable tenements, fences unrepaired, walls crumbling into ruinous heaps. Hinting gloomily at things below the surface, these, and many other tokens of the same description, force themselves upon the notice, and are remembered with depressing influence, when livelier features are forgotten.

To those who are happily unaccustomed to them, the countenances in the streets and labouring-places, too, are shocking. All men who know that there are laws against instructing slaves, of which the pains and penalties greatly exceed in their amount the fines imposed on those who maim and torture them, must be prepared to find their faces very low in the scale of intellectual expression. But the darkness—not of skin, but mind—which meets the stranger's eye at every turn; the brutalising and blotting out of all fairer characters traced by Nature's hand; immeasurably outdo his worst belief.

I left the last of them behind me...and went upon my way with a grateful heart that I was not doomed to live where slavery was, and had never had my senses blunted to its wrongs and horrors in a slave-rocked cradle.[227]

Voyage of the *Creole*

Six months before Dickens' visit, on October 25, 1841, the *Creole,* a brig under the command of Captain Robert Ensor, left Richmond with a cargo of 102 enslaved African Americans and some tobacco, bound for New Orleans. After stopping at Norfolk to take on thirty-three more slaves, the brig sailed on October 30 from Hampton Roads until Sunday, the seventh day of November, at about 9:00 p.m., when the vessel was near the island of Abaco in the Bahamas. At that point, nineteen of the enslaved Africans on the brig, under the leadership of Madison Washington, took charge of the ship. At least one of the slaves and one of the crew were killed in the ensuing battle.

The leaders of the *Creole* uprising had been imprisoned together by Robert Lumpkin in Richmond and were part of a shipment he was making to the slave markets of New Orleans. They had learned of the remarkable emancipation of thirty-eight enslaved Africans only a few months earlier, in October, 1840, when the schooner *Formosa* ran aground on the island of Abaco. British authorities in the Bahamas had rescued the crew and emancipated the slaves. The liberated enslaved Africans from the *Formosa*, like the great majority of those on the *Creole*, had been shipped out by a Richmond trader.[228]

The *Creole* conspirators compelled the ship's crew to take the vessel to the port of Nassau, arriving on November 9, 1841. For four days the United States consul attempted to persuade the British governor to keep the passengers in bondage and prosecute them for mutiny. Finally the governor ordered the nineteen who had participated in the revolt to be imprisoned. Bahamian citizens, filling the harbor with their own boats and encircling the *Creole*, freed all the remaining slaves. Madison Washington and sixteen of the nineteen leaders were finally released on April 16. Two had died in prison.[229] The *Creole* left Nassau and arrived in New Orleans December 2. According to the official Presidential report, "three women, one girl, and a boy concealed themselves on board… and were brought to New Orleans." Attempts to put the conspirators on trial were never successful.[230]

President John Tyler, a slaveowner whose plantation twenty miles down the James River from Richmond had been passed by the *Creole* on its historic journey, reported to the Congress on the matter, and attempted to resolve the "property" issues for the owners of the slaves. The great abolitionist Frederick Douglass helped to make the story of the *Creole* widely known, publishing a short fictional biography of Madison Washington called "The Heroic Slave" in 1852. In 1855 an Anglo-American claims commission finally awarded $110,330 to owners of the liberated slaves, thereby vindicating the Southern position and that of the Tyler administration. The incident resulted in the negotiation by Daniel Webster of the Webster-Ashburton Treaty between the British and American governments, covering issues of extradition. In practice, the treaty was never applied to extradition of former slaves who had found freedom in British territories, a position which would have been impossible for the British government.

The downriver slave trade

The *Creole* Affair opened a window to the world on the massive domestic trade in citizens of African descent that was carried on from 1800, after the importation of slaves from Africa and the West Indies was prohibited in Virginia, until the Civil War finally ended the practice in 1861. During that sixty-year period, between 300,000 and 500,000 enslaved Africans were sold and transported from Virginia to the South and the Caribbean in the domestic slave trade. Richmond was the largest slave market in the New World except for New Orleans, the destination of many of the persons who were sold from Richmond. In 1835 alone, 40,000 slaves were exported from Virginia to points south. The domestic slave trade was thus a major element—by 1850 the largest single piece—of Richmond's economy for the period from the Revolution to the Civil War.[231]

Richmond's Shockoe Bottom, six blocks from the Governor's Mansion and Jefferson's Capitol, had become the center of the downriver slave trade by 1840, having taken over the dubious honor from Alexandria.[232] Because of this massive commerce, the population of enslaved Africans in Virginia remained essentially constant from 1830 through 1860.[233] The Richmond trade is estimated to have reached between $3,500,000 and $4,000,000 in value in 1857, perhaps $100 million a year in present-day dollars.[234] The Richmond *Enquirer* reported in June 1859 that "the best class of slaves" were selling in Richmond from $1,000 to $1,500 per person, depending on age and gender. The value in 2010 dollars would be from $24,000 to $36,000.[235] In 1860, Richmond's white population had a per capita income of $1,593, the third highest of any city in America.[236]

Virginia was shipping its surplus labor at great profit to the new cotton and sugar plantations opening in Louisiana, Mississippi, and Alabama, and after 1845, in Texas. The invention of the cotton gin in 1794 had made the industry possible. The Louisiana Purchase in 1803 added momentum. To see the shape of the new cotton-based slave trade, you only had to follow the money. New York and Boston banks provided much of the capital to develop the cotton trade and the slave trade that went with it. Ships from Liverpool and Bristol, which were no longer allowed to transport imprisoned Africans to Virginia or, after 1808, to any port in the United States, found new opportunity in the transportation of cotton back to England. There, during the first half of the nineteenth century, Manchester, with Liverpool as its port of entry, became the center of the world's cotton manufacture. By 1840, the value of cotton exceeded the total of all other exports from the United States of America, and by 1860, the United States was producing seven-eighths of the world's cotton for export.[237]

Labor was in sudden demand in America, and involuntary servitude was the quick answer. Just as the sudden success of Bermuda tobacco in Virginia had caused a tobacco boom in the 1600s, which in turn motivated planters to purchase thousands of white servants and bring them to an early death in the tobacco fields, the cotton trade exploded the demand for black slave labor in the Lower South in the 1800s. As the locus of nearly fifty percent of the nation's

African slaves at the beginning of the century, Virginia was the market of preference. "Richmond was the best place in the State,"historian Frederic Bancroft says, "to sell nearly all kinds of slaves at good prices without publicity as to ownership." [238] Public knowledge might have been embarassing, Bancroft suggests, because it indicated that a slave owner was no longer able to maintain the social status which owning slaves represented.

Early trade occurred in Alexandria, Fredericksburg, and Richmond, but it shifted steadily downstate. The national financial panic of 1837 sealed the end of Alexandria's primacy. By 1840 prices at Richmond's local slave market came to be dominated by the demand for labor from out of state. "After the explosion of King Cotton in the 1820s," historian Steven Deyle writes, "planters in these new states were willing to pay hundreds of dollars more per slave than were owners in the older states...."[239] The local Richmond price moved up and down in direct proportion to the situation in New Orleans and the cotton states. As the *Richmond Enquirer* put it at the time, "The price of cotton as is well known, pretty much regulates the price of slaves in the South."[240]

What stability had existed in slave life disintegrated. Sales accelerated. Owners and merchants, to satisfy the opportunity for profit, were willing to uproot and split families, display persons naked as objects to be bought, and subject human beings to six- to eight-week journeys, coffled together. Speculators from outside and inside the state came to Richmond to assemble shipments of slaves to take south. Other slave merchants combed the rural areas of the mid-Atlantic to bring slaves to Richmond for sale. The enormous and lucrative trade far exceeded the incoming trade from Africa to Virginia of the previous century—between 300 and 400 percent of the original forced African inmigration. During the twenty years of Richmond's full slave-trading ascendancy, the price of a person categorized as a "prime male hand" sold in Richmond nearly tripled.[241] Prices went so high in the 1850s that South Carolinians and others began to lobby the federal government to reopen the African slave trade.

Three different types of slave merchants set up shop in Shockoe Bottom: auctioneers, speculators, and proprietors of slave jails. The 1860 city directory listed eighteen "Negro Traders," eighteen "Agents, General and Collecting," and thirty-five "Auctioneers." There were at least three and as many as six major slave jails. Eight or ten of the auctioneers counted the slave trade as their primary business. The slave market district lay between 14th and 17th, Cary and Broad streets, just down the hill from the Capitol. At its center was Richmond's finest hostelry, the Exchange Hotel, where five slave agents maintained offices. Across the street, at the southeast corner of Cary and 15th, was one of the largest jails for the interstate trade, belonging to Bacon Tait. The district was surrounded by churches.[242]

The exodus to the South had begun when white Virginians took their own slaves with them to the new southern territories. White exodus from Virginia was so massive that at one point in the early 1800s the United States Congress contained as many as 100 persons who had been born in Virginia. But as demand for labor from the "Cotton Kingdom" multiplied, speculators came north to buy slaves. Steven Deyle says that "during this period coffles of slaves...could be found on every southern highway, waterway, and railroad."[243] Richmond's increasing prominence in the downriver trade was helped by its development as a rail center. By the 1840s, three major rail lines had been developed in the city, and two more began service in the next decade.[244] By the 1850s rail transport was the major form of transportation south for the captives.

Slaves being sold in Richmond were frequently kept in private slave jails. The three best-known jails were owned and operated by Robert Lumpkin, Silas Omohundro, and Bacon Tait. These owners also speculated in enslaved Africans, whom they bought and kept in their jails.[245] Lumpkin's Jail was known by African Americans as "the Devil's Half Acre." His complex consisted of at least four buildings: his house and office, a boarding house for traders, a kitchen and dining facility, and a jail for enslaved persons. All of these buildings surrounded a courtyard. The facility was on the west bank of Shockoe Creek, and the slave jail itself was down the bank next to the water.

In 2008, Richmond's Slave Trail Commission excavated the site of Lumpkin's Jail, uncovering the courtyard and the foundations of three of the four buildings known to have made up the complex.

Lumpkin's Slave Jail

We have a first-person account of what it was like to be in Lumpkin's Jail because in 1854 Anthony Burns was arrested under the Fugitive Slave Act in Boston and returned to Richmond to be interred there for four months. He told his story and it was published in Boston in 1856. With the Burns situation, as in other cases, it appeared that people in the North and in other cities knew more about the events surrounding slavery in Richmond than Richmonders and Virginians knew.

Right: Anthony Burns was captured and incarcerated in Lumpkin's Slave Jail in 1854. Below: Photographer Andrew Russell took this photo from Church Hill in 1865, showing part of the slave-trading district on the hillside below the state Capitol (upper left-hand corner). Lumpkin's Jail is the complex of buildings in the lower right-hand corner, and the roof of the jail building where Burns was kept is just above and beyond the tree at the bottom (arrow). Library of Congress photo.

Burns had been born in Stafford County around 1833. As a young man, he received written permission from his master to be baptized and joined a church in Falmouth, next to Fredericksburg, which was composed of white freedmen and black slaves. He became a preacher. In the early 1850s his owner, Colonel Suttle, sent him to Richmond to earn money. Burns was "hired out," under an increasingly common practice for slave owners in this period. He took charge of the other slaves whom Colonel Suttle sent to Richmond and found jobs for them. He himself went to work at a flour mill where he continued to learn to read and write. He supplemented his income by setting up a school where he taught twelve to fifteen other slaves to read and write.[246] Burns returned most of his earnings to his owner. He was required to report back regularly to his home where his mother and his sister, whom he said was kept by the master as "a breeding-woman," still lived.[247]

After a year in Richmond, Burns went to work for a druggist named Millspaugh. Millspaugh soon realized that he didn't have enough work for him, so he proposed what he told Burns was an illegal arrangement: he suggested that Burns find his own work, pay him fortnightly, and Millspaugh would reimburse Suttle. Burns went ahead with this arrangement. He spent an increasing amount of time unloading ships carrying guano and coal at the Richmond wharves, and got to know sailors who were sympathetic to his plight. In February 1854, one of the sailors helped him stow away on a ship for Boston. After only two months of freedom, Burns was arrested under the Fugitive Slave Law. Charles Henry Dana, an attorney best known for his novel *Two Years Before the Mast*, agreed to represent Burns pro bono. The case attracted great attention in Boston and drew big crowds.

Burns' examination by authorities began in Boston on May 29, 1854, twelve hours after news arrived of the passage of the Kansas-Nebraska Bill by the United States Congress. That bill, which infuriated opponents of slavery, abrogated the Missouri Compromise on slavery, which had determined which states would be slave and which would be free. Under the new terms, white citizens of Kansas and Nebraska could decide by vote whether or not slavery would be permitted in those states.

Boston was in an uproar and, as historian Pat Hickin describes it, "thousands of people surged around the Court House." When the court "ordered that Burns be returned to his master," the government determined to put him on a ship for Virginia "at an expense estimated at between twenty and one hundred thousand dollars."

Twelve hundred troops and one hundred fifty citizens armed with cutlasses conducted Burns to the wharf, marching through Boston streets past stores and offices draped in black, the flags flying at half mast. As Burns boarded the ship for

Virginia, Boston church bells tolled his return to slavery.[248]

He was brought to Richmond and incarcerated in Robert Lumpkin's jail for several months. Then he was auctioned and purchased into freedom by abolitionists. This account was written with him by Charles Emery Stevens the year after his freedom was restored:

[He] was accompanied to the jail by one Robert Lumpkin, a noted trader in slaves. This man belonged to a class of persons by whose society the slaveholders of the South profess to feel disgraced, but with whose services, nevertheless, they cannot dispense. He had formerly been engaged exclusively in the traffic in slaves. Roaming over the country, and picking up a husband here, a wife there, a mother in one place, and an alluring maiden in another, he banded them with iron links into a coffle and sent them to the far southern market. By his ability and success in this remorseless business, he had greatly distinguished himself, and had come to be known as a "bully trader."

At this time, however, he had abandoned the business of an itinerant trader, and was established in Richmond as the proprietor of a Trader's Jail. In this he kept and furnished with board such slaves as were brought into the city for sale, and, generally, all such as their owners wished to punish or to provide with temporary safe keeping. He also kept a boarding-house for the owners themselves. Lumpkin's Jail was one of the prominent and characteristic features of the capital of Virginia. It was a large brick structure, three stories in height, situated in the outskirts of Richmond, and surrounded by an acre of ground. The whole was enclosed by a high, close fence, the top of which was thickly set with iron spikes.

Lumpkin's Jail

Here [Burns] was destined to suffer, for four months, such revolting treatment as the vilest felons never undergo, and

such as only revengeful slaveholders can inflict. The place of his confinement was a room only six or eight feet square, in the upper story of the jail, which was accessible only through a trap-door. He was allowed neither bed nor air; a rude bench fastened against the wall and a single, coarse blanket were the only means of repose. After entering his cell, the handcuffs were not removed, but, in addition, fetters were placed upon his feet. In this manacled condition he was kept during the greater part of his confinement.

The torture which he suffered, in consequence, was excruciating. The gripe of the irons impeded the circulation of his blood, made hot and rapid by the stifling atmosphere, and caused his feet to swell enormously. The flesh was worn from his wrists, and when the wounds had healed, there remained broad scars as perpetual witnesses against his owner. The fetters also prevented him from removing his clothing by day or night, and no one came to help him; the indecency resulting from such a condition is too revolting for description, or even thought. His room became more foul and

Archeologist cleans cobbles in excavated courtyard of Lumpkin's Jail. Burns described this courtyard in the account of his imprisonment. James River Institute of Archeology photo, courtesy Richmond Slave Trail Commission.

noisome than the hovel of a brute; loathsome creeping things multiplied and rioted in the filth. His food consisted of a piece of coarse corn-bread and the parings of bacon or putrid meat. This fare, supplied to him once a day, he was compelled to devour without plate, knife, or fork. Immured, as he was, in a narrow, unventilated room, beneath the heated roof of the jail, a constant supply of fresh water would have been a heavenly boon; but the only means of quenching his thirst was the nauseating contents of a pail that was replenished only once or twice a week. Living under such an accumulation of atrocities, he at length fell seriously ill. This brought about some mitigation of his treatment; his fetters were removed for a time, and he was supplied with broth, which, compared with his previous food, was luxury itself....

His residence in the jail gave him an opportunity of gaining new views of the system of slavery. One day his attention was attracted by a noise in the room beneath him. There was a sound as of a woman entreating and sobbing, and of a man addressing to her commands mingled with oaths. Looking down through a crevice in the floor, Burns beheld a slave woman stark naked in the presence of two men. One of them was an overseer, and the other a person who had come to purchase a slave. The overseer had compelled the woman to disrobe in order that the purchaser might see for himself whether she was well formed and sound in body. Burns was horror-stricken; all his previous experience had not made him aware of such an outrage....

After a while, he found a friend in the family of Lumpkin. The wife of this man was a "yellow woman" whom he had married as much from necessity as from choice, the white women of the South refusing to connect themselves with professed slave traders. This woman manifested her compassion for Burns by giving him a testament and a hymn-book. Upon most slaves these gifts would have been thrown away; fortunately for Burns, he had learned to read, and the books proved a very treasure. Besides the yellow wife, Lumpkin had a black concubine, and she also manifested a friendly spirit toward the prisoner. The house of Lumpkin was separated from the jail only by the yard, and from one of the upper windows the girl contrived to hold conversations with Anthony, whose apartment was directly opposite. Her compassion, it is not unlikely, changed into a warmer feeling; she was discovered one day by her lord and master; what he overheard roused his jealousy, and he took effectual means to break off the intercourse.

After lying in the jail four months, his imprisonment came to an end. It had been determined to sell him, and the occurrence of a fair in Richmond presented a favorable opportunity. Accordingly, his manacles were knocked off, his person was put in decent trim, and he was led forth to the auction room. A large crowd of persons was already assembled.[249]

The slave markets in Richmond attracted international attention in the mid-19ᵗʰ century. Top: Eyre Crowe, "Slave Auction at Richmond, Virginia" (Illustrated London News, 27 September 1856). Below: G. H. Andrews, "A Slave Auction in Virginia – from a sketch by our special artist" (Illustrated London News, 16 February 1861). Courtesy Maurie McInnis.

A visit to Richmond's slave market

In 1852 and 1853, the English artist Eyre Crowe accompanied English novelist William Makepeace Thackeray on a lecture tour in America. In 1893, he published his memoir, *With Thackeray in America*. The volume is filled with his drawings, and includes this account of slave sales he observed on Richmond's Wall Street, which ran north and south from Lumpkin's Jail to a point near present-day 15ᵗʰ and Franklin streets:

The 3rd of March, 1853, is a date well imprinted on my memory. I was sitting at an early *table d/hote* breakfast by myself, reading the ably conducted local newspaper, of which our kind friend was the editor. It was not, however, the leaders or politics which attracted my eye, so much as the advertisement columns, containing the announcements of slave sales, some of which were to take place that morning in Wall Street, close at hand, at eleven o'clock.

Ideas of a possibly dramatic subject for pictorial illustration flitted across my mind; so, with small notepaper and pencil, I went thither, inquiring my way to the auction rooms. They consisted, I soon discovered, of low rooms, roughly white-washed, with worn and dirty flooring, open, as to doors and windows, to the street, which they lined in succession. The buyers clustered first in one dealer's premises, then moved on in a body to the next store, till the whole of the tenants of these separate apartments were disposed of. The sale was announced by hanging out a small red flag on a pole from the doorway. On each of these was pinned a manuscript notice of the lot to be sold. Thus I read: – "Fifteen likely negroes to be disposed of between half-past nine and twelve – five men, six women, two boys, and two girls." Then followed the dealer's signature, which corresponded to that inscribed over the doorway. When I got into the room I noticed, hanging on the wall, a quaintly framed and dirty lithograph, representing two horsemen galloping upon sorry nags, one of the latter casting its shoe, and his companion having a bandaged greasy fetlock; the marginal inscription on the border was to this effect: – "Beware of what you are about." I have often thought since how foolish it was, on my part, not to have obeyed this premonitory injunction to act prudently in such a place as this was. The ordeal gone through by the several negroes began by making a stalwart hand pace up and down the compartment, as would be done with a horse, to note his action. This proving satisfactory, some doubt was expressed as to his ocular soundness. This was met by one gentleman unceremoniously fixing one of his thumbs into the socket of the supposed valid eye, holding a hair by his other hand, and asking the negro to state what was the object held up before him. He was evidently nonplussed, and in pain at

IN THE RICHMOND SLAVE MARKET.

Eyre Crowe published "In the Richmond Slave Market," the original sketch he made on March 3, 1853, in With Thackeray in America *in 1893. He exhibited an oil painting of the sketch in the Royal Academy Exhibition in May 1861 entitled "Slaves Waiting for Sale."*

the operation, and he went down in the bidding at once. More hands were put up; but by this time feeling a wish for fresh air, I walked out, passing intervening stores and the grouped expectant negroes there.

I got to the last and largest end store, and thinking the sales would occupy a certain time, I thought it might be possible to sketch some of the picturesque figures awaiting their turn. I did so. On rough benches were sitting, huddled close together, neatly dressed in grey, young negro girls with white collars fastened by scarlet bows, and in white aprons. The form of a woman clasping her infant, ever touching, seemed the more so here. There was a muscular field-labourer sitting apart; a rusty old stove filled up another space. Having rapidly sketched these features, I had not time to put my outline away before the whole group of buyers and dealers were in the compartment. I thought the best plan was to go on unconcernedly; but, perceiving me so engaged, no one would bid. The auctioneer, who had mounted his table, came down and asked me whether, "if I had a business store, and someone came in and interrupted my trading, I should like it." This was unanswerable; I got up with the intention of leaving quietly, but feeling this would savour of flight, I turned round to the now evidently angry crowd of dealers, and said, "You may turn me away, but I can recollect all I have seen." I lingered in a neighbouring vacated store, to give myself the attitude of leisurely retreat, and I left this stifling atmosphere of human traffic.[250]

Within a year or two of Crowe's adventure, a young man named Otis Bigelow visited the market district from Syracuse, New York, and left a record of his experiences. He related that he had been curious to find out more about the slave trade. Following a man "who had purchased a boy," he went deeper and deeper into the back streets. The man he was following "turned into an entrance, over which was the sign 'Lumpkin's Jail':

> Against one of the posts sat a good natured fat man, with his chair tipped back. It was Mr. Lumpkin. I duly introduced myself as from New York, remarking that I had read what the Abolitionists had to say, and that I had come to Richmond to see for myself. Mr. Lumpkin received me courteously and showed me over to his jail. On one side of the open court was a large tank for washing, or lavatory. Opposite was a long, two-story brick house, the lower part fitted up for men and the second story for women. The place, in fact, was a kind of hotel or boardinghouse for negro-traders and their slaves. I was invited to dine at a large table with perhaps twenty traders, who gave me almost no attention, and there was little conversation. They were probably strangers to one another.[251]

Henry "Box" Brown

One of the most poignant and powerful stories of this time is that of Henry "Box" Brown. Although marriage between slaves was not sanctioned by law in Virginia, Henry and Nancy lived as husband and wife. They had three children and a fourth on the way. Henry had helped Nancy's master with his debts in the past. One day, Nancy's master came to the house and said that he was again in debt, and that Nancy and the children would have to be sold. He sold them for $1,050 to a trader who was taking them south. Henry did everything he could, asking persons he knew to buy Nancy and the children back. Finally, he heard that if he wanted to tell them goodbye, he could find the caravan heading south.

He first saw five wagons go by, in which were the children. Henry recognized his oldest child. Then came the adults, chained together in a coffle and walking. "I went with her for about four miles hand in hand," he wrote, "but both our hearts were so overpowered with feeling that we could say nothing, and when at last we were obliged to part, the look of mutual love which we exchanged was all the token which we could give each other. I was obliged to turn away in silence."[252]

Henry was broken-hearted. Several months later he prevailed upon a friend, Samuel Smith, to pack him in a box three feet by two feet eight inches by two feet and ship him to the Philadelphia Anti-Slavery Society.[253] On March 23, 1849, Smith prepared the package and delivered it to the Adams Express office at the Exchange Hotel, from which it was transported to the Richmond, Fredericksburg, and Potomac train which left from 8th and Broad Street. After a jarring and frightening journey on train, steamboat, and wagon, Brown arrived in Philadelphia. His story became known all over America and in Europe as well. He never saw Nancy or his children again.

The Underground Railroad was very active in Virginia during the last decades before Richmond and the Confederacy fell. William Still, a noted black abolitionist, published his account of hundreds of escapes in Philadelphia in 1872. His book, *The Underground Rail Road*, gives

"The Resurrection of Henry Box Brown at Philadelphia," lithograph by Samuel Rowse, published in Philadelphia c. 1850. Library of Congress photo.

a strong sense of the prominence of Richmond in the slave trade in the nineteenth century. A surprising number of escapes from Richmond and Tidewater seem to have involved a steamship, the *City of Richmond*, which plied the route between Richmond and Philadelphia.[254]

The fruits of denial

The strangest fact about the downriver slave trade, perhaps, is that it was virtually unknown in Virginia or Richmond history until the last decade of the twentieth century. It did not appear in ordinary history books and was not taught in any of the state's required courses in Virginia history. Virtually all the artifacts and locations of the trade itself were buried under parking lots and superhighways. The sale of African Americans as slaves was one of the principal profit-making enterprises in the prewar economy of Richmond. It represented the largest, latest, and most distinctive involvement of Virginia in the slave system in America in the nineteenth century. During the half century of its prominence, an African-American population equivalent to the entire African-American population of the state was shipped across the continent from Tidewater Virginia.

There seems some indication that the trade was kept virtually invisible from all but the men who had to know about it,[255] even during the time it was at its greatest level. But it is certainly clear that the trade was made invisible to the next century of Richmonders and Virginians once the city had burned and slavery was abolished.

In 1993 Hope in the Cities and Richmond Hill sponsored the Richmond Unity Walk, a walk through Richmond's history, in which more than 500 Richmond citizens were introduced to some of the sites where the slave trade had been conducted.[256] Subsequently, the City Council appointed an official Slave Trail Commission, which has developed and marked a trail of historic sites from the Manchester Docks to First African Baptist Church.The Reconciliation Statue was erected along the trail on the site of the Exchange Hotel at 15th and Franklin streets, marking the triangular slave trade between Virginia, Great Britain, and Africa.[257] In a major excavation of the Lumpkin's Jail site in the second half of 2008, archeologists uncovered the intact courtyard and the foundations of most of the buildings. Remarkably, that same jail building which had been the site of Anthony Burns' incarceration became, after the war, the site of the first school for freed slaves in Richmond. Robert Lumpkin's widow, probably the woman who had befriended Anthony Burns during his imprisonment, rented it in 1867 to the Colver Institute, the first predecessor institution of today's Virginia Union University.

In 2011, extensive community action resulted in the purchase of the site of the Burial Ground for Africans by the state and its donation to the city to be preserved as a sacred site. The Slave Trail Commission developed proposals for a formal city heritage district including the Burial Ground, Lumpkin's Slave Jail, and a National Slavery Museum.

The impact of this buried history is difficult to estimate. Clearly, much of the history was psychologically and emotionally hidden from Richmond when it was actually occurring. Both for those who were traumatized, and those profiting from the traumatization, the denial was all but complete. An interstate highway and a parking lot cover the sites, which are buried under fifteen to forty-five feet of fill and rubble. Their hidden secrets represent effectively the collective psyches of many who inhabit the land. Is it possible for healing to take place? How? What are the mechanisms? To what degree is the current disintegration of metropolitan Richmond due to an unconscious flight from trauma, fear, and guilt? To what extent are the presently depressed citizens of the city the unconscious heirs of the trauma and abuse?

What is clear is that Richmond's collective depression did not begin with the defeat of the Confederacy and the burning of the city. Frederick Law Olmsted, the famous American journalist and landscape architect of the nineteenth century, visited a number of American cities, and came twice to Richmond. In 1860, in his book entitled *A Journey in the Back Country*, he published this haunting evaluation of what he saw:

> Richmond...somewhat surprised me by its substance, show, and gardens.... [It] is a metropolis, having some substantial qualities, having a history, and something prepared for a future as well. Compared with northern towns of the same population, there is much that is quaint, [and] provincial.... It is only the mills and warehouses, a few shops and a few private residences and hotels, that show real enterprise or real and permanent wealth....
>
> What a failure there has been in the promises of the past! That, at last, is what impresses one most in Richmond.... [It] is plainly the metropolis of Virginia, of a people who have been dragged along in the grand march of the rest of the world,

but who have had, for a long time and yet have, a disposition within themselves only to step backward.[258]

View of excavation of Lumpkin's Slave Jail next to Main Street Station in Shockoe Valley, Richmond, December, 2008. Upper portion of excavation is the courtyard (upper right triangular patch) and the kitchen building (upper left). Lower portion, where there are pools of water, is foundation of jail building. The lower level was about eight feet below the courtyard, and was next to Shockoe Creek, fourteen feet below the present surface parking lot. The photo is courtesy of the Richmond Slave Trail Commission.

7

Developing Structures of Segregation
1865–1954

Toward the end of the 1850s, the nation's struggles over slavery began to affect Virginia in contradictory ways. On the one hand, Virginians reaffirmed their belief in the Declaration of Independence, the Constitution, and the Union, in whose formation their fathers and grandfathers had played such a predominant role. On the other hand, white Virginians became increasingly protective of their slave system, overtly defending it against Northern critics.

In 1858 Richmond celebrated the relocation of the remains of President James Monroe to a new tomb in Hollywood Cemetery. In the same year, the majestic equestrian statue of George Washington was dedicated on the Capitol grounds. In 1860 a statue of Henry Clay was erected at the Capitol. Richmond was the focus of national attention, and representatives from other cities and states, North and South, attended the celebrations.

In 1859 the city government passed a new ordinance "Concerning Negroes." It required blacks to carry passes or free papers; it prohibited slaves from renting rooms, hiring themselves out, buying liquor or medicine, joining secret societies, owning guns, gathering in groups, riding in carriages, walking in Capitol Square, or walking near the city spring or city hall. It required that "[a] negro meeting or overtaking, or being overtaken by a white person on a sidewalk, shall pass on the outside; and if it be necessary, to enable such white person to pass, shall immediately get off the sidewalk."[259]

In October 1859 Richmond militia units rushed to the front when John Brown attacked Harper's Ferry (then Virginia, now West Virginia) with an armed group of abolitionists and free African Americans. The next year Abraham Lincoln was elected president, an event that was followed closely by the secession of seven Southern states from

View of Richmond in ruins from Manchester. Library of Congress photo.

the Union. In early 1861 Virginians called a convention to consider secession. A majority of the convention was in favor of remaining in the Union until, on April 15, President Lincoln attempted to call up 8,000 soldiers from Virginia to deal with the rebellion that had begun at Fort Sumter in Charleston, South Carolina, two days earlier. Then, with Richmond in an uproar, the convention voted to secede.

The trauma of white Virginia

On July 21, 1861, the Union army engaged the army of the Confederate states at Bull Run, near Manassas, Virginia. Here is how Virginius Dabney, former editor of the *Richmond Times-Dispatch*, tells the story:

It was the first major engagement of the war and a victory for the South. Richmonders rushed to the conclusion that Confederate troops would move swiftly into Washington. Nothing of the sort happened, of course. [Confederate] President [Jefferson] Davis, who had been present on the field of Manassas, gave a huge crowd outside the Spotswood Hotel a report immediately upon his return. He warned that hard fighting lay ahead. Yet it was difficult in the afterglow of the first great Southern victory to suppress the optimism that pervaded the Confederate capital.

But when trains bearing hundreds of seriously wounded chugged into the station at Eighth and Broad in the pouring rain, the city was suddenly made aware of the grim realities. Here were men wrapped in bloody bandages, shot through the body or with an arm or leg missing, men blinded or moaning in pain. Anguished relatives at the station looked in the storm, with the aid of flickering lanterns, for husbands, sons, or brothers. Would they find them there or on one of the trains loaded with the coffins of the dead? ...Coffins bearing the officers were taken to the Capitol as the "Dead March"... sounded through the streets. That mournful dirge would be heard during the ensuing four years as thousands of Virginians went to their deaths on the battlefields and were laid to rest in Hollywood and Oakwood cemeteries.[260]

Over the next four years, even while rows and rows of new markers were added to its cemeteries, Richmond's population more than doubled, from under 50,000 in 1861 to more than 110,000 in 1865. The city was filled with soldiers, prisoners, wounded men, visitors, and individuals from all over the world who had commercial or political agendas. By 1862, more than 10,000 wounded men were being cared for in forty-four hospitals and many private homes. Prisons held another 10,000 or more, including more than 4,500 enlisted men in miserable conditions on Belle Isle in the middle of the James River. Provisions were short for both residents and prisoners. On April 2, 1863, a mob of women broke into stores around 15th and Cary streets—the Richmond Bread Riot. Governor John Letcher called out the Public Guard and Mayor Joseph Mayo read the Riot Act.

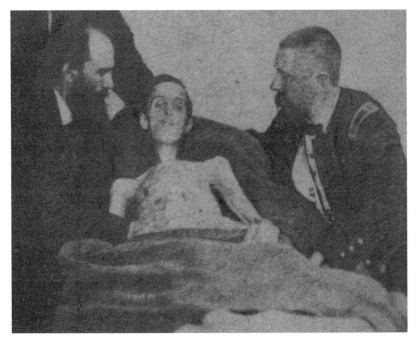

Daniel Trattles of the 19ᵗʰ Michigan Infantry was one of the emaciated Union prisoners finally released from the prison on Belle Isle in Richmond. Photo was provided by his great grandson and is reprinted by permission.

Two years later, on Sunday April 2, 1865, two weeks before Easter, the Union army broke through the Confederate lines at Petersburg. A soldier came into St. Paul's Church on Grace Street, where President Jefferson Davis sat at worship, to tell him that Petersburg had fallen, and that the way to Richmond was open to the Northern armies. By nightfall, the Confederate government and troops had evacuated the city, going west and south, and the city was in flames. A fire lit by departing soldiers to destroy munitions had spread throughout the city south of the Capitol.[261] Liquor from another storehouse was running in the streets, the result of the destruction of casks ordered by officials. People were on their hands and knees drinking from the gutters, and as the fire-lit night progressed, the spirits-filled mob spread out of control.[262]

Early Monday morning, according to the *Richmond Whig,* the city "presented a spectacle that we hope never to witness again....The air was lurid with the smoke and flame of hundreds of houses sweltering in a sea of fire."[263] Mayor Mayo drove his buggy out Main Street, at the foot of Richmond Hill, until he reached the Union troops encamped east of the city around New Market Heights. He invited them into the

128

city to help extinguish the fire and reestablish civic order. Black and white companies both claimed later that they were the first to arrive in the city.

As the Union Army entered the city, Richard Gill Forrester brought from his home at College and Marshall streets the American flag which had last flown over the Capitol on the day, four years earlier, that Virginia seceded from the Union. Forrester, although fair-skinned, was black and Jewish, the son of one of Richmond's wealthiest free, non-white families. At the age of fourteen he was a Capitol page, a very unusual position for a person of color. His daily task was to raise and lower the flags at the Capitol. On April 17, 1861, the day that Virginia seceded and declared war, the American flag had been taken down and thrown on a pile of trash. Forrester had rescued it and kept it hidden under his mattress.

At 7:30 a.m. on April 3, 1865, he raised the flag of the United States of America at the Capitol of Virginia. Lt. Royal B. Prescott of the 13th New Hampshire Volunteers, who had just arrived in Capitol square with his men, asked the seventeen-year-old Forrester, who was descending the Capitol steps, who had raised the flag. Forrester told him the story of the flag's rescue, and wrote on a page in the Yankee soldier's diary, "Richard G. Forrester put the flag on the capitol in Richmond, VA." At 8:15 a.m., at the city hall across the street from the Capitol, Mayor Mayo formally surrendered the city of Richmond to General Godfrey Weitzel.[264]

The next morning, on April 4, 1865, a boat rowed by twelve sailors arrived at Rockett's Landing. President Abraham Lincoln, with his son

USS Malvern *at dock in Norfolk, Virginia. U.S. Naval Historical Center Photograph.*

Left: "Lincoln enters Richmond," by Thomas Nast. This picture, which originally appeared in Harper's Weekly, *was based on a description and sketch by reporter Charles Coffin of the Boston Morning Journal, who witnessed the event. Right: Abraham Lincoln and his son Tad. Statue by sculptor David Frech at the Richmond National Battlefield Park at Tredegar. Dedicated on April 5, 2003, this represented the first public memorial to Lincoln's Walk in Richmond. Some public controversy accompanied the erection of the statue of Lincoln, even though it occurred 138 years after the original event.*

Tad and Rear Admiral David Porter, stepped from the boat. A group of about seventy-five African Americans working at the docks recognized him. They came running to the landing, cheering, weeping, and shouting, and the president greeted them. Then Lincoln and his party walked up Main Street, through the smoldering ruins, amid both black and white onlookers, until they arrived at the White House of the Confederacy. Lincoln sat in the chair of President Davis.

After meeting with city and state authorities and with General Weitzel, Lincoln returned to the dock. By that time USS *Malvern*, the large steam vessel that had brought him from Grant's headquarters at City Point (now part of the city of Hopewell) to Dutch Gap, had broken through the Confederate obstructions in the river and reached Rockett's. After spending the night on the *Malvern*, Lincoln returned to City Point Wednesday morning.[265]

Lincoln continued down the James River to the Chesapeake Bay and up the Potomac. He arrived in Washington in time for the celebration of the surrender at Appomattox on Palm Sunday, April 9. On Wednesday night of Holy Week he had a dream in which he saw himself in a coffin. On Good Friday he was shot. And early in the morning of Holy Saturday, he died. On Easter Sunday, General Robert E. Lee returned from Appomattox to Richmond, to his home on Franklin Street, to find a Union soldier guarding the door. He then learned of Lincoln's assassination.

Four years of trauma had ended. The Virginians of African descent who had not been free were now freed men and women. A new period of Richmond's history would now begin. What would change, and what would remain much the same, was yet to be determined.

The century that followed the burning of Richmond may be divided into two periods. The first is that of Reconstruction and adjustment, an era of social fluidity, as the society reinvented itself on the premise that slavery, as it had been known, was over. The second period, beginning around the turn of the century, was one of highly structured and legislated racial segregation. This period ended with an event as momentous in its own way as the events we have just described: the decision of the U.S. Supreme Court in *Brown v. Board of Education*. Just as the Union army had broken through the Confederate lines defending Petersburg in April of 1865, so the moral force of humanity had on May 17, 1954, finally broken through Richmond's elaborate walls defending racial segregation.

Race and Reconstruction

Before the rubble had been cleared from the devastated business district of the capital city, Richmond's press began to campaign against voting rights for its freed black citizens. "The former masters of the Negroes in Virginia have no feeling of unkindness toward them," editorialized the Richmond *Times*, "and they will give them all the encouragement they deserve, but they will not permit them to exercise the right of suffrage, nor will they treat them as anything but 'free Negroes.' They are laborers who are to be paid for their services...but vote they shall not." [266]

Edward A. Pollard, wartime editor of the Richmond *Examiner*, declared authoritatively that the war had ended slavery and restored the Union, but it "did not decide negro equality; it did not decide negro suffrage." Pollard's monumental Confederate history, *The Lost Cause*, was published in 1866, proclaiming an unrepentant theme for the last half of the century: "(The South's) well-known superiourity in civilization...has been recognized by every foreign observer, and by the intelligent everywhere; for it is the South that in the past produced four-fifths of the political literature of America, and presented in its public men that list of American names best known in the Christian world. That superiourity the war has not conquered or lowered; and the South will do right to claim and cherish it."[267]

The Union army did not initially improve the situation of the formally emancipated black population of Richmond. General Grant ordered all "Negro" troops to leave Richmond by the end of April.[268] Thousands of rural blacks who had come to the city after the surrender were captured in May and June by the Union troops and placed in former slave jails, until they could be sent back to the rural areas to work on the plantations.[269]

General Edward O.C. Ord, the Yankee commander who took initial charge over occupation policy in Richmond, was removed in June 1865 and replaced by General Alfred Terry. Terry abolished the pass laws, which had, even after emancipation, required all black citizens to carry identifying passes in the city.

On January 15, 1866, the Virginia General Assembly passed a severe "vagrancy" law, which essentially made unemployment a crime. Persons judged to be vagrants could be compelled to work "for the best wages that can be procured." If they should "run away" from this compulsory labor, the statute ordered, "said employer shall then have the power...to work said vagrant confined with ball and chain." The bill had been in preparation for some time, and General Terry observed that in many Virginia localities white employers had already made agreements not to hire freedmen at normal wages, thus forcing wages to be depressed and providing an opportunity for the enforcement of the vagrancy statute. "The ultimate effect of the statute will be to reduce the freedmen to a condition of servitude worse than that from which they have been emancipated," Terry wrote, "a condition which will be slavery in all but its name." Nine days later he prohibited the law from being applied "to any colored person" in the territory under his authority.[270]

On April 2, 1866, a year after Richmond burned, black citizens of Richmond celebrated Liberation Day. "An immense cavalcade of black horsemen organized by fraternal orders walking together in ceremonial garb," paraded to the Capitol. The Patriarch leading the procession carried a staff on which was a gourd covered with ribands. His apron was black and gold. There was a gold stripe down his legs and a chapeau on his head, gracefully embellished with a black feather. The parade's organizers published a notice for the white citizenry:

After the War the Freedmen's Bureau/U.S. Christian Commission was at the Southeast Corner of Broad and 10ᵗʰ Streets, the current site of the General Assembly office building. In the print above, note the spire of St. Paul's Church on the right and the equestrian statue of George Washington in Capitol Square on the left. Library of Congress photo.

"The Coloured people of the City of Richmond would most respectfully inform the public that they do not intend to celebrate the failure of the Southern Confederacy, as it has been stated in the papers of this City, but simply as the day on which GOD was pleased to Liberate their long-oppressed race."[271]

Under the first Reconstruction Act passed by Congress in March 1867, blacks were allowed to vote. For a brief period, from 1867-1869, they comprised a majority of Richmond's registered voters, a situation not to prevail again until a century later. In the Virginia constitutional convention of 1867-1868, blacks comprised one-third of the Republican majority, and nearly one-fourth of the total delegates. Two black delegates were from Richmond.[272]

The city maintained a fundamental policy of racial segregation, including separate voting places, separate insane asylums, separate cemeteries, separate public schools, and separate seating on streetcars. Blacks were not permitted in the theatre, the YMCA, or the Virginia State Library. Blacks who had organized at First African Church attempted to integrate the streetcars in April 1867, but eventually had to settle for racially segregated cars, except for black mammies accompanying white children and for white men—who could ride anywhere they wanted. Black citizens were subject to public whipping. The state penitentiary's chain gang, which worked around the city, was composed almost solely of black prisoners.

In 1867 Richmond annexed two and a half square miles of Henrico County, doubling the size of the city. The council added two new voting wards for the new territory, raising the number of wards to five. In 1870 Richmond's voting population was almost evenly split between the two races—6,868 whites and 6,220 blacks—and these were almost evenly divided in all of the five wards, with blacks having a majority in one. Black voting strength ranged from a low of 44 percent in Madison Ward to a high of 52 percent in Monroe Ward.[273]

In 1871 the Conservatives gained control of the city government. Almost immediately they created a new sixth ward, whose boundaries were carefully drawn to include the majority of the black population. From this point forward, blacks were able to elect representatives to the Common Council only from the new Jackson Ward. The black vote was further reduced—eventually by 2,000—by a law disqualifying from voting anyone who had been convicted of petty larceny.

Although Virginia's public school system was founded in 1869, its beginnings were slow. Throughout the latter half of the nineteenth century, whites criticized the Richmond public school system and those with means sought to send their children to private school. The criticism resulted in significant shortfalls in funding. In the great Funder/Readjuster controversy that racked postwar Richmond, the Conservative Party took the "Funder" position, seeking to repay $45,000,000 in prewar debt to investors rather than to fund public education fully.

The Readjusters, putting together a coalition of Republicans and black citizens, won both houses of the legislature in 1879 and the governorship in 1881. Governor Mahone abolished the poll tax as a precondition for voting, established Virginia State University, readjusted the debt, and freed money for development of schools. In 1888 the only African American to be sent to Washington by Virginia before the last decade of the twentieth century,

John Mercer Langston

John Mercer Langston, was elected to Congress from Petersburg.[274] But the Democrats took over in 1888, and by the late 1890s, there were no blacks left in statewide office. There would be none anywhere in the commonwealth for the next fifty years.[275]

As reaction set in, constantly fueled by racial issues, Conservatives in Richmond were able to make an electoral issue in 1883 out of the appointment of two black men to the Richmond School Board. They pointed out "that most teachers were women and that the black members of the board therefore exercised direct control over white women."[276]

In 1885 the school board chair told the city council that the schools were overcrowded and underfunded, with many students able to attend only half a day. Hundreds of whites and over 1,000 blacks were, he said, "denied admission," for lack of resources.[277] Even in 1902, the Virginia constitution mandated only four months of public education for blacks but nine for whites. In 1892 a white group sought to remove eighty-four African-American public school teachers in Richmond and replace them with whites. Another movement sought to require that only the tax revenue from black citizens be used to support the public schools of blacks.

The 1890s brought the revival of Confederate sentiment for the

"Lost Cause." Monuments in Richmond show the power of Confederate themes in that time. The first and largest of these, the Lee Monument, was unveiled on May 29, 1890. The ceremony began with a procession of 15,000 Confederate veterans leading a crowd which eventually totaled more than 100,000 from the Market at 17th and Main streets to the site on the city's western edge, accompanied by Generals Fitzhugh Lee, Joseph Johnston, James Longstreet, and Jubal Early. The *New York Times* said the statue was unveiled "in the presence of the largest and

Unveiling of the Lee Statue on Monument Avenue on May 29, 1890.

most distinguished gathering assembled here in a quarter of a century." Addressing the crowd, Governor Philip McKinney opened the ceremony. According to the *Times* reporter, he said "that the love of the Southern people for those who fell in battle in their behalf was unconquerable, and that while there were no more loyal people to the Government under which they lived, the people of the South would never forget its gallant dead." [278]

The Lee Monument was the focus of a new real estate development, which moved the center of the city west. By 1907, statues to General J.E.B. Stuart and President Jefferson Davis had been added on Richmond's Monument Avenue. In the east, a tall column honoring Confederate soldiers and sailors was erected in 1894, facing the river at Libby Park. The new housing developments also spread out the population of the city and hastened both racial and class segregation.

The Knights of Labor attempted to organize workers in Richmond during the postwar period. But the organizational strategies of the Knights ran headlong into the racial issues of Richmond. The Knights had a nondiscriminatory policy, and sought to be true to that policy in Richmond. The white establishment opposed the Knights and made it difficult for integrated groups to meet in town. White laborers apparently supported the white investors and owners. The situation came to a head when, in October 1886, the Knights held their national convention in Richmond. The union's top black leader was Frank J. Ferrell, a resident of New York who was a Virginia native. After several of the meetings of the organization had run into conflict because of segregated facilities in Richmond, Ferrell addressed the major plenary session. He was supposed to introduce the governor of Virginia, Fitzhugh Lee, to the gathering.[279] Lee refused to let him do so. Ferrell then introduced Terrence V. Powderly, General Master Workman of the Knights, who introduced Lee. The Knights had little success after that in Richmond.[280]

During the 1880s the white leadership of Richmond continued to restrict black voting power, although blacks were able to muster a majority in the one gerrymandered district, Jackson Ward. During the period from 1865 to 1895, a total of twenty-five black citizens served on the city council, eighteen of them from 1880 to 1890. The city council was a larger body from which the mayor, registrar, and seven aldermen were chosen. The last term of the last black member of the city council ended in 1896. From then on, there were no black members until after the Second World War. One of the regular tactics to diminish black voting strength was to delay voters by interrogating them. Thus, thousands of black voters were still standing in line in Jackson Ward when the polls closed.[281]

Gov. Fitzhugh Lee

A new state constitution passed in 1902 was immensely effective in reducing Richmond's black vote. To illustrate its effectiveness: in 1896 there were 2,983 black voters and 789 white voters in Jackson Ward; after the new constitution was adopted, only thirty-three black voters were able to register, a reduction of ninety-nine percent. According to the constitution, sons of Confederate veterans were given the right to vote without further requirement, but a court ruled that black sons of Confederate veterans were illegitimate by definition and therefore could not vote. In 1903 Richmond abolished Jackson Ward as a separate voting district, distributing its population among several majority-white wards.[282]

During the latter part of the nineteenth century, with the increasing concentration of the black population in Jackson Ward, the African-American community grew significantly in its ability to support itself through its own institutions and businesses. As segregation increased, blacks increased their self-sufficiency, pooling their limited resources to build and educate.

One incident in 1890 illustrates the level of disregard for the African-American community that was exhibited by Richmond's white power structure. The city decided to extend 7th Street across Bacon's Quarter Branch to the Northside, in order to support a new suburb. Michael Chesson reports that "the street and viaduct cut through and tore up Richmond's historic black cemetery, in which many of the city's most famous slaves and free Negroes had been buried. Where the displaced remains were reinterred is still uncertain."[283]

Managing segregation

The 1880s were the last time, until the period following the Second World War, in which a significant black voting populace had a major impact on elections in Virginia. In the last decade of the nineteenth century, the state came under the control of the Democratic Party, representing a coalition of the white elite and white working class, with the specific exclusion of blacks. For the next three-quarters of a century the party controlled the Commonwealth of Virginia and most of its localities through an increasingly sophisticated series of strategies that maintained white power, white economic control, and racial segregation.

Harry F. Byrd

Racial segregation was both the purpose of the control and the means of control. Potentially dissident groups of whites were kept in check through the threat that a divided white electorate in the general election might enable blacks to have electoral influence.

The Virginia Machine retained its power under two leaders. The first was Thomas S. Martin, who as patriarch of the Democratic Party served in the United States Senate from 1893. When he died in 1919, his place in the party was taken by Harry Flood Byrd, who became governor in 1925 and then was elected to the U.S. Senate, where he served until 1965.

The first task was the restriction of the electorate, a process known as disenfranchisement. Virginia's white Democratic political leaders, and some white Republicans, decided that they would do whatever they could do to take away the right to vote from black citizens. This would be done despite the U.S. Constitution's Fifteenth Amendment, passed in 1870, which declared that "the right of citizens of the United States to vote shall not be denied or abridged by the United States or by any State on account of race, color, or previous condition of servitude." In many subsequent actions, Virginia's leaders became adept at developing strategies for racial segregation that would have the intended effect but be deniable, that is, could be represented as having some other lawful purpose.

a. Disenfranchisement

At the beginning, in Virginia's Constitutional Convention of 1901-1902, the goal of black disenfranchisement was openly stated to anyone who cared to listen. Carter Glass of Lynchburg, who later served as Woodrow Wilson's Secretary of the Treasury and subsequently as senator from Virginia until his death in 1946, was one of the leaders of the convention and suggested the eventual compromise legislation. The convention, he said, intended to produce

> discrimination...within the letter of the law, and not in violation of the law.... Discrimination...is precisely what we propose; that, exactly is what this Convention was elected for—to discriminate to the very extremity of permissible action under the limitations of the federal Constitution, with a view to the elimination of every negro voter who can be gotten rid of.[284]

The amended state constitution provided three major mechanisms for restricting the vote. First was a literacy requirement: a prospective voter could be required to be "able to read any section of this Constitution submitted to him by the officers of registration and to give a reasonable explanation of the same" or simply to give the explanation if the officer read it. In addition, he would have to be able to give written answers to "any and all questions affecting his qualifications as an elector, submitted to him by the officers of registration." He could not be guilty of any crime, including petty larceny—which had been an effective means of excluding black voters for the previous three decades. And he must have paid the poll tax for the three years preceding, and to have paid it in full at least six months before the election.

The 1902 constitution had the effect of severely restricting the electorate. Not only were blacks effectively excluded, but a significant percentage of the white population also found the process for registration too cumbersome. In the first half of the twentieth century, about ten percent of Virginia's eligible voters elected its governor every four years. One-third of these voters were either state employees or officeholders.[285]

A study of black voting patterns in Virginia in 1930 revealed the long-term success of Virginia's disenfranchisement strategies. Black voter participation in that period ranged from a low of two percent in Petersburg to a high of fourteen percent in Danville. The typical registrar would require potential black registrants to memorize required answers to questions in advance and deliver them without prompting. Whites, on the other hand, would be given a piece of paper and a pencil and led through the necessary questions. Even when the obvious discrimination of this method began to wane in the '30s, the poll tax, which required three years' back payment six months before an election, remained an effective disincentive to voting.[286]

Virginia's leaders were unabashed in their racial discrimination. The state's junior senator, Claude Swanson, addressed the United States Senate in defense of Virginia's voting restrictions. Virginia, he said, "has exercised her constitutional right to eliminate a class of ignorant, shiftless, and corrupt voters who for many years were in charge of her local, municipal, and State affairs, with the result of unspeakable impoverishment and disgrace."[287] The acknowledged head of the party, Harry F. Byrd, had in his 1925 campaign for governor charged an ineffectual Republican opponent with wanting to restore the franchise of 700,000 black citizens, an idea which the white Republican could not have put forward. The patriarch solemnly promised to anyone who would hear that Virginians "will never again enthrone the negro as the arbiter of our political destiny by giving him the balance of power."[288]

b. One-party rule

Fortified by the restriction of the electorate, in 1905 the Democratic Party instituted a primary election process. This Democratic primary was essentially a private election; no blacks were permitted to vote in it. The process allowed the white community to work out any differences it might have before facing any enemy that might put together a coalition of white dissenters and African Americans.

The party developed its power through the appointment of various officers at the courthouse of every county, a power that gave it control over patronage, school boards, judges, taxation, and law enforcement.

When in 1927 the U.S. Supreme Court ruled against racially segregated party primaries, 500 black citizens of Richmond petitioned the court to take part in a primary election for mayor. By the time all appeals were exhausted, the election was long past. Blacks had won the point, but their ability to participate in party primaries was severely restricted for another twenty-five years through other strategies.

The one-party system of the Democrats, managed first by Thomas Martin and later by Harry Byrd, was so successful that the machine essentially picked the governor of Virginia for seventy-two years, from 1893 until 1965. Finally, in 1969, A. Linwood Holton, a moderate Republican, was elected governor.

By the first decade of the twentieth century, Richmond's white community had invested in a panoply of segregationist legislation and practice that isolated African Americans from the major public institutions. But the process did not end there. It continued, in more and more sophisticated form, through the next four decades until, following the Second World War, new situations pointed to new methodologies. J. Douglas Smith, whose book *Managing White Supremacy* is the most comprehensive study available, states simply, "The most significant of Virginia's Jim Crow statutes were adopted not in the 1900s and 1910s but in the 1920s and 1930s."[289]

c. Transportation

The first classic Jim Crow law in Virginia, passed in 1900, required that there be separate cars for blacks and whites on railroads. The U.S. Supreme Court's 1896 decision in *Plessy v. Ferguson* had legitimized the concept of separate but equal, and Virginians seized upon the opportunity. The General Assembly followed up with a 1904 law permitting the segregation of streetcars.

Richmond's Virginia Passenger and Power Company decided to enforce segregated seating on its cars. Richmond's black community reacted with a streetcar boycott that lasted almost a year before giving out. John Mitchell, editor of the *Richmond Planet*, said, "Let us walk. A people who willingly accept discrimination...are not sufficiently advanced to be entitled to the liberties of a free people."[290] In 1906 the General Assembly made streetcar segregation mandatory.

The 1919 Code of Virginia stated the prohibition explicitly and comprehensively: "There shall be a complete separation of white and colored passengers upon all urban, interurban and suburban electric railways, and...the conductor or other person in charge of an electric street car shall have the right to require any passenger to change his or

On February 2, 1888, Richmond became the first city in the world to have a functioning electric-powered streetcar system, designed by Frank Sprague. In 1906 the Virginia General Assembly required that Richmond's streetcars be segregated by race. Picture of Sprague's streetcar courtesy Shore Line Trolley Museum, East Haven, Conn.

her seat as often as it may be necessary or proper." A 1930 amendment added buses to the list, although the practice was already firmly established. No specific law required that whites sit in the front and blacks in the back; it was, however, a firm custom that was enforced by the courts.

d. Residential segregation

For many freed black persons, the issue was not where they would live, but whether or not they would have a place to live. At no point in the entire period following the Civil War did Richmond, Virginia, or the United States of America attempt to deal with the lack of property or land in the hands of freed African Americans. No compensation or back wages were provided by persons who had used their labor for free, no credit given for years served. Freed slaves were free to fend for themselves, and if possible, to avoid arrest or conviction for vagrancy.

Residential neighborhoods were segregated by custom and cost long before there was any specific legislation requiring it; but as the twentieth century began, white leaders began to write down these codes. In 1911 Richmond City Council passed what a Richmond historian calls "the most elaborate and comprehensive racial zoning code in the nation, the first major attempt to control property values using government power to separate racial groups."[291]

142

The law was declared unconstitutional by the U.S. Supreme Court in 1917,[292] but this did not daunt Richmond's white leaders. During the 1920s various schemes were used to encourage segregation of neighborhoods, and in 1929 the city passed an ordinance that required it. At the suggestion of undertaker and alderman Henry W. Woody, the new ordinance said that persons whom the state prohibited from marrying could not live next to each other, and Virginia's miscegenation law prohibited marriage between black and white individuals. The ordinance was passed unanimously by the council and aldermen, and by Mayor J. Fulmer Bright. The U.S. Supreme Court voided it in 1930. Segregated housing determined housing quality; a federal official called housing for Richmond blacks "disgraceful, inhuman, pestilential, and in a civic sense entirely too costly to be tolerated by the people of this city."[293]

When the Federal Housing Administration (FHA) began in the mid 1930s to establish mechanisms to prevent widespread foreclosures and facilitate home mortgages, the federal Home Owners' Loan Corporation (HOLC) was asked to grade the neighborhoods of more than two hundred American cities for their creditworthiness. The neighborhoods were graded from A to D, and each letter was assigned a color. D neighborhoods were colored red, having "detrimental influences in a pronounced degree." The FHA and HOLC severely discouraged mortgage lending in these "redlined" neighborhoods. Race was one of the major criteria used to delineate between neighborhoods, so it was hardly surprising that every single African-American neighborhood in Richmond was given a D rating and redlined for mortgages.[294] The Federal Home Mortgage Disclosure Act (1975) and Community Reinvestment Act (1977) officially reversed the discriminatory policies, but they persisted locally. In 1980, the Richmond Urban Institute published a detailed study on bank and mortgage redlining in Richmond, indicating a severe disparity in mortgage activity between black and white neighborhoods. All of the major Richmond banks appeared to be guilty of redlining. On the strength of the study, a community group, Richmond United Neighborhoods, officially challenged federal approval of the proposed merger of First & Merchants Bank of Richmond and Virginia National Bank. The challenge was dropped when the new bank entered a consent agreement with federal regulators to remedy the situation.[295]

Covenants restricting sale by race were common; one of the best-known examples was that of the town of Colonial Heights, south of Richmond, which was established as an all-white enclave on the edge of Petersburg. "Racial steering" and "blockbusting," a process under which housing values in a "white neighborhood" were artificially depressed by real estate speculators who moved a black family in, were common until the 1970s in Richmond, and probably still continue today. In 1968 the Federal Fair Housing Act was passed, making racially restrictive covenants illegal in real estate, and in 1971 Richmonders founded Housing Opportunities Made Equal (HOME) of Virginia, which began challenging segregated sale and rental policies.[296]

e. Miscegenation and Marriage

One of the most insidious weapons in Virginia's arsenal of segregation was that of the state Bureau of Vital Statistics. Armed with the Racial Integrity Act passed by the General Assembly in 1924, W.A. Plecker, registrar of the bureau, functioned as an advocate of the eugenics movement. Criticized by the National Association for the Advancement of Colored People (NAACP), he defended the new state anti-miscegenation law and his pamphlet entitled "Eugenics in Relation to the New Family." "We shall continue to educate against miscegenation and the mixture of negro blood with the white race in Virginia and elsewhere," he told the *Richmond Times-Dispatch* in 1925.[297]

The Racial Integrity Act required the state registrar of vital statistics to "prepare a form [listing] the racial composition of any individual, as Caucasian, negro, Mongolian, American Indian, Asiatic Indian, Malay, or any mixture thereof, or any other non-Caucasic strains, and if there be any mixture, then the racial composition of the parents and other ancestors, in so far as ascertainable, so as to show in what generation such mixture occurred."

The form would be used for all persons who were born after the passage of the law, for anyone who wished to correct their own form with the state, and for anyone who wished to be married. "It shall hereafter be unlawful," the act continued,

> for any white person in this State to marry any save a white person, or a person with no other admixture of blood than white and American Indian. For the purpose of this act, the term "white person" shall apply only to the person who has no trace whatsoever of any blood other than Caucasian; but persons who have one-sixteenth or less of the blood of the American Indian and have no other non-Caucasic blood shall be deemed to be white persons.

Intermarriage was a felony. The exception for Indian blood was made specifically for any white Virginians who claimed descent from

Thomas Rolfe, the son of Pocahontas and John Rolfe.

In 1930 the revised Racial Integrity Act made another exception: if a person were one-fourth Indian and less than one-sixteenth black, he or she could be classified as an Indian if living on a reservation. This meant that a brother and sister of the same parents who lived in different places could be classified as different races.

Plecker insisted throughout his tenure that Virginia Indians should not be considered a separate race, but that they were all partly, and therefore legally, black. He and his fellow zealots also worked with the Virginia state Board of Censors to censor movies that dealt with racial themes.

Another adjunct of the movement was involuntary sterilization. Beginning in 1924, "for nearly 50 years, the Commonwealth of Virginia sterilized thousands of individuals, white and black, deemed feebleminded, insane, or prone to criminal behavior."[298]

f. Education

Although Virginia had committed itself to public education in 1870, the schools were always segregated by race and there was neither public policy nor intention that the black and white schools would be equal in quality. Richard Gustavus Forrester, one of Richmond's most prominent non-white citizens in the postwar period, served on the city council from 1871-1882, and from 1881-2 was also allowed to serve on the school board. During that year he was able to help to hire some black teachers and improve some of the black schools.[299] Still, a 1919 study documented significant instances of inequality in the black schools, among which were overcrowding, inadequate facilities, low teacher pay, and abbreviated school years. In 1925, the average total expenditure in a public school in Virginia was $40.27 for a white student and $10.47 for a black student.[300]

Often, there was not enough space in the cramped Negro schools. One year, Richmond simply did not enroll two hundred black students because there was no room. Before 1933 the Richmond School Board refused to hire black principals in black schools.

Black teachers had some success in the 1930s toward equalizing teachers' salaries. In 1930 state superintendent of schools Harris Hart declared a new pay scale: white teachers would receive $60 per month plus up to $50 extra based on their qualifications; black teachers would receive $45 per month and up to $25 extra based on their qualifications. In 1938 a black Norfolk school teacher, Aline Black, sued for equalization of her salary. The court ruled against her and, although

Norfolk students protest the firing of Aline Black, June 1939.

she was a twelve-year veteran teacher, the school system fired her.

Segregated education also produced a fertile opportunity for the teaching of fantasy history to Virginia's segregated white students. In the 1920s tenth graders were required to read a volume entitled *Slavery and Secession*, written in 1909 by Beverley Bland Munford. Through this volume, as historian Douglas Smith observes, Virginia's high school history students were taught that since colonial times "the institution of slavery was regarded with disfavor by a majority" of Virginians who "tolerated its existence as a *modus vivendi* to meet the dangers and difficulties of the hour" but hoped to "render feasible its abolition, with a maximum of benefit to the slaves and their owners, and a minimum of danger to society and the state."

Virginians would have freed their slaves, Munford said, if it had not been for Nat Turner's Rebellion and the hostility of Northern abolitionists. These latter "not only attacked the institution of slavery but the morality of slaveowners," thereby "alienating the good people who wanted to free their slaves."[301] The social studies textbook required to be used by every fourth-grade student in Virginia in 1965 devoted only three of its 328 pages to African Americans. The story of Booker T. Washington was told in six paragraphs. Two paragraphs discussing the causes of the War Between the States were devoted to the topic of slavery:

Northern and Southern people did not think alike about slavery. The Northern people did not need much help to work their small farms. The planters in Virginia and in the South needed many men to work for them. They had slaves to do their work.

By this time many people knew that slavery was wrong. But the planters did not know how they could free their slaves and keep their plantations going. Some people in the North said that the Southern people had to free their slaves no matter what happened to their plantations. The South said that the North had no right to tell them what to do. They believed that each state had the right to decide how the people were to live in that state. So the North and the South quarreled about the rights that each state had.... Virginians loved the United States and did not want to leave it. But Virginians wanted people in every state to have their rights.[302]

The next chapter, entitled "Lee Surrenders," allowed the institution of slavery to die without conflict in a final benign paragraph:

While men fought and died on the battlefields, women and children and old men at home were doing all they could to help in the war. Some of the Negro servants left the plantations because they heard that President Lincoln was going to set them free. But most of the Negroes stayed on the plantations and went on with their work. Some of them risked their lives to protect the white people they loved.[303]

By control of public school textbooks and strict control of its state university system, the General Assembly virtually assured that this ethnocentric version of Virginia history would be regarded as undisputed fact by the great majority of white Virginians, and by a large number of nonwhite citizens, well into the last decades of the twentieth century.

g. Employment

Employment remained segregated in a number of ways in Virginia until after the Second World War. Blacks and whites received different salaries for the same work, and many positions were open only to white people. Black people were not allowed to supervise white people. One observer noted that "white officials in Richmond worked harder than those in any other [Virginia] city to deny the benefits of citizenship to blacks." Mayor J. Fulmer Bright was elected in 1924 on a platform that specified that there would be "no Negroes on the city payrolls—city jobs for hard working white men." The only blacks employed by the city would be black teachers in black schools.[304]

h. Public assemblages

After a white woman attending a dance performance at Hampton University was not given a seat separated from black persons in the audience, she complained to her newspaper editor husband, and the fracas eventuated in 1926 in a specific law about public gatherings in Virginia. The bill required "the separation of white and colored persons at public halls, theaters, opera houses, motion picture shows and places of public entertainment and public assemblages."

i. Public facilities

Recreational facilities were segregated, but Richmond refused to provide adequate recreational facilities for blacks. Some alleviation of the problem was provided in the 1920s by private contributions from white people. When it was suggested that Clark Springs Playground, in the black West End, be turned over to blacks, the Hollywood Memorial Association complained because they felt it would dishonor the Confederate dead in neighboring Hollywood Cemetery.[305]

In 1939 Samuel Tucker, an African-American attorney, later of the pioneering Richmond firm Hill, Tucker and Marsh, filed a suit in his native Alexandria on behalf of black students who were not allowed into the city public library. Tucker had gone to high school in Washington, because Alexandria had not provided a high school for black students. On August 21, 1939, five students held a sit-down strike at the library and were arrested. The young white city attorney upholding segregation was Armistead Boothe, later a Tucker ally in Virginia's civil rights battles. The judge eventually held in favor of the students. Two days later the city announced it would open a separate library for blacks.[306]

j. Anti-lynching

The Byrd machine boasted of its anti-lynching law as an example of its progressive racial stance. It was the strongest anti-lynching law in the South, making lynching a state crime, and was passed in 1928. Fewer African Americans had been killed by mobs in Virginia than any other Southern state—about seventy or more from 1880 to 1930. The horrible event usually had to do with some allegation about a black man and a white woman. The law seems to have had some effect in discouraging lynching, but it was never invoked in a case involving the murder of a black person.

k. Racial invective

The first three decades of the twentieth century saw the full development in Virginia of rhetoric by white politicians seeking to use race to defeat their opponent. The Virginia version of the 1928 presidential election featured race as a major theme. Each side called the other a "threat to white supremacy." One well-known white leader, who had become a progressive force by midcentury, entered politics in Virginia talking race in a congressional campaign in a 1936 Tidewater election. His printed circular called his opponent "a nigger lover." "If you vote for [him], niggers will be teaching your children soon." Paradoxically—or perhaps not—he also bought black votes. Despite the rhetoric and insults, these developments meant that blacks in Virginia were beginning to be a political force.

l. Higher education

Virginia did not provide graduate school for African Americans in the first half of the twentieth century. In 1935 Alice Jackson, whose father was a druggist in Richmond, wanted to study French at the University of Virginia (UVA). Ms. Jackson was a graduate of Virginia Union University and a graduate student at Smith College in Northampton, Massachusetts. However, UVA denied her admission. Fearing a court ruling that would abolish the racial segregation of their graduate schools, state officials developed a two-part alternative strategy. First, they started a graduate program at all-black Virginia State College (now University). Second, in March 1936, they passed the Educational Equality Act, offering tuition grants to black persons to pursue graduate study out of state. In 1936 Ms. Jackson was one of the first thirty students to participate in the out-of-state program.

The issue of opening graduate schools to blacks in Virginia was a sensitive one for Virginia's leaders. Virginius Dabney, editor of the *Richmond Times-Dispatch,* warned of the danger that loomed before them: "Any effort to force the abolition of segregation, over the protest of a strongly hostile white South, is bound to do far more harm than good to the Negro. If I were a Negro, I should wish the system done away with, but I hope I should have the intelligence to realize that no lasting benefit would result, so long as the great majority of white southerners were ranged in opposition."[307] The issue, he wrote, was "whether the South's system of segregated education is to be destroyed from top to bottom, and both races mingled indiscriminately all the way from the elementary grades to the graduate and professional schools."[308]

Virginia's segregation of graduate schools lasted into the second half of the twentieth century. Both Henry L. Marsh, Richmond's first African-American mayor, and L. Douglas Wilder, who when he was elected Governor of Virginia was the first African American ever elected governor of a state, attended Howard University Law School in Washington, D.C., because they were not allowed to be admitted to a law school operated by the Commonwealth of Virginia. Both graduated from Howard in 1959.

The segregationist edifice erected in the first half of the twentieth century did not ultimately survive the social and economic explosions that followed the Second World War. Richmond and Virginia changed rapidly in the period from 1950 to 2000. But the shape of the changes in the second half of the century was deeply affected by the segregated foundation laid in the first half of the century. The troubles that still afflict the culture of metropolitan Richmond have their roots in problems long denied, changes not attempted, prophecy unheeded, injustice unacknowledged.

8

Massive Resistance and Resegregation
1955–1972

The twenty-five years following the Second World War were in many ways as momentous for Richmond as the period of the American Revolution and the time of the Civil War. By 1971 the city of Richmond had become just one of eight jurisdictions in a growing multijurisdictional city.[309] Over two decades, more by disingenuousness and default than by design, the Virginia General Assembly had developed an urban policy that created fragmented metropolitan cities separated into nonrelated segments, without any common land use control, zoning, taxation, or transportation. In the case of several of the new metropolitan cities—most notably Richmond, Petersburg, Norfolk, Charlottesville, Fredericksburg, and Roanoke—the fragmentation masked a very sophisticated form of racial and class segregation.

Richmond was the oldest jurisdiction in its growing metropolitan city. Its infrastructure was decaying, its bonding capacity was exhausted, and there was no new land for development or expansion. The metropolitan city sprawled outward until this small, oldest jurisdiction (the "city of Richmond") had less than three percent of the land. Alone among the major jurisdictions, it had a majority black voting population and African-American leadership, but it also had all the public housing and nearly fifty percent of the poverty, an unemployment rate probably over twenty percent,[310] a median household income half that of the remainder of the metropolitan city, and a public school system in which seventy-five percent of the students qualified for free or reduced price lunch. Alone among the major fragments of the metropolitan city, Richmond was subject to special state controls not exercised over the surrounding counties, and special funding relationships which diminished state responsibility for both capital and operating expenses.

The story of Richmond's evolution is intertwined inexorably with three dramatic developments that occurred in Richmond after the Second World War. The developments were urban renewal, racial integration of public schools, and the realignment of the structures of government. They occurred against the backdrop of massive suburban expansion driven in every American city by postwar affluence, technological development, and freeway construction.

Urban renewal

The urban renewal movement in America was in its infancy when the Second World War began. In 1940, with the authorization of the General Assembly of Virginia, the city created the Richmond Housing Authority as a quasi-governmental agency, with the right to condemn property and issue bonds to construct housing.

From the very beginning, urban renewal focused on "blighted Negro housing." By this was meant the black neighborhoods of town. The white leaders began with the group of neighborhoods into which Richmond blacks had been forced in the decade immediately following the Civil War. Those neighborhoods, including those in Jackson Ward, had begun as the place of refuge and had become the center of the independent black economy that had grown up in Richmond in the first half of the twentieth century. Beginning with the establishment of the housing authority, white Richmond tore down Jackson Ward block by block until, by 1980, only a small portion of the original sanctuary remained.

Housing in Richmond was segregated by race and by neighborhood until well after the Second World War. Until 1964 the housing authority designated public housing projects by race. After 1964 the designation was effectively enforced by custom. Prior to that year, the Federal Housing Administration would not insure any mortgages or loans for housing that was not racially homogeneous.

In 1941, the housing authority took its first bite out of Jackson Ward. In a section on the north side, adjacent to the St. Luke Penny Savings Bank which pioneering black entrepreneur Maggie Walker had founded in 1903, the city demolished the neighborhood called Apostle Town, nearly 200 houses, and built 297 units of public housing. Only twenty-five of the 576 applications for the new project, called Gilpin Court, were from families that had formerly lived in Apostle Town.[311]

In 1946 the city adopted its first master plan, drawn up by the national consulting firm of Harland Bartholomew & Associates. In 1948 voters approved a new city charter, which was in turn approved by the General Assembly, establishing a nine-member city council elected at large, and a city manager to run the city. These two decisions gave the white majority the ability to prosecute what was known as a "progressive" urban agenda that focused heavily on urban renewal.[312]

Over the next thirty-five years, in the name of urban renewal, the city council pursued a plan that destroyed or invaded every major black neighborhood in the city. The neighborhoods included Apostle Town, Jackson Ward, and Navy Hill in the north; 17th Street, portions of Church Hill, and Fulton in the east; Oak Grove and Blackwell in the south; and the black West End ("Randolph"), Penitentiary Bottom, and Carver in the west. The preferred method was "clearance" of entire areas and the construction of new public housing projects. "Detailed studies will be made of city records to determine areas of tax delinquency, lowest assessment and revenue production, areas where normal growth is impeded by slum conditions, and finally those slum areas most attractive to private developers," the *Richmond Times Dispatch* stated prophetically in 1950. [313]

Residents displaced by the process were given several hundred dollars to help them move, but no other support for relocation. They were given priority for application to the new projects, but many found these unattractive or socially demeaning. The result of the massive clearance was the destruction of most major black neighborhoods. In the decade of the '50s, the city destroyed 4,700 units of housing in black neighborhoods and replaced them with 1,736 units of public housing.[314] Those who could pushed outward from the destruction into formerly all-white neighborhoods. White and black realtors collaborated either overtly or coincidentally in "blockbusting" and turning these neighborhoods from white to black. Many displaced white residents were then sold housing being developed in the newly adjacent, racially segregated suburbs in adjoining counties.

A tacit, but identifiable, record of these social movements can be found in the histories of the location of dozens of white and black churches in Richmond. First African Baptist Church, for example, which began in 1841 at Broad and East 13th streets, followed its congregation to Northside, where it purchased a building formerly owned by a white congregation. Overbrook Presbyterian Church, a white congregation located on Overbrook Road in Northside, followed its members to a new church building on Lakeside Avenue in adjacent Henrico County, and a new interracial Presbyterian congregation, All Souls', took the old building. In 1959 St. Philip's Episcopal Church, an African-American congregation, moved from St. James' and Leigh in Jackson Ward to 2900 Hanes Avenue in Northside, displacing Epiphany, a white congregation, which moved to suburban Lakeside. Between 1950 and 1960, the population of the city of Richmond actually decreased by 10,000 persons. During that decade, the population immediately across the city line in Henrico County doubled, from 57,340 in 1950 to 117,339 in 1960.[315]

The "clearance areas" were not used solely, or even primarily, for housing, however. The new public housing projects compressed residents into a much smaller area. Newly cleared land was used to construct broad, divided urban boulevards to provide rapid access from the new suburbs in the counties; new civic projects such as the Richmond Coliseum; and, in the case of the 17th Street bottom and Fulton bottom, new industrial sites for economic development.

It was the building of the Richmond-Petersburg Turnpike, now part of I-95, which inaugurated the wholesale destruction of Richmond's largest, most historic, and most prestigious black community, Jackson Ward. Initially proposed immediately after the war in 1946 by the consulting firm R. Stuart Royer and Associates, the turnpike was endorsed by two other consultants but rejected in two public referenda. The city council and business leadership turned to the Virginia General Assembly, in which there was no black representation, to override citizen opposition. In April, 1954 the General Assembly obliged by creating the Richmond-Petersburg Turnpike Authority and giving it the power of eminent domain. Four months later the new Authority announced the highway would be built through Jackson Ward.[316]

For eight years the consultants had insisted that the highway must be built next to the Central Business District, presumably to keep middle and upper-middle income whites engaged in the central city economy. Royer's report said that the housing for hundreds of families which would be destroyed in Jackson Ward "offers no serious obstacle to a highway location." In fact, the expressway would be "a great improvement to the surrounding area...upon which to face needed rebuilding projects." The consultants continued, "An incentive is needed...in these districts to encourage repair and rebuilding activities."[317]

As many as 1,000 homes of African Americans lay in the path of the proposed expressway. Residents of Jackson Ward, who were not represented in the City Council or on the Richmond-Petersburg Turnpike Authority, were powerless to stop the destruction of their historic neighborhood. The expressway cut a barrier canyon the width of a city block through the middle of the neighborhood, from east to west, separating half of it from the center city, eliminating pedestrian pathways, and blocking thirty-one streets.

When the project began, the *Richmond Times-Dispatch* gushed with civic enthusiasm. "The project will change the city's appearance," the white-owned and -staffed newspaper crowed, "as bulldozers and wrecking crews push aside scores of dwellings and businesses to make way for the ribbons of concrete to follow.... Unfortunately, the demolition of scores of dwellings and business places will create difficult problems for some of the persons involved. This is not the first time, nor will it be the last, when individual citizens must be inconvenienced for the good of the community."[318] Property records archived in the basement of City

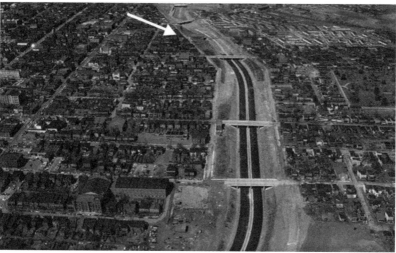

The Richmond-Petersburg Turnpike cut a trench one block wide and eighteen blocks long through Jackson Ward, destroying nearly 1000 homes in the historic center of Richmond's African American community. The highway avoided Sixth Mount Zion Church (top picture and arrow in bottom picture), the only surviving building on the north side of Duval Street. Top picture, taken November 3, 1957, is reprinted from the Richmond Times-Dispatch *by permission.*

Crowd gathers at the Broad Street interchange for opening ceremonies of the Richmond Petersburg Turnpike, now I-95, in Shockoe Valley on June 30, 1958. Richmond Times-Dispatch *photo reprinted by permission.*

Hall, searched in preparation for seizure and demolition by the state, bore a detailed history of Richmond's black community, the names of many of Richmond's most prominent black families.

The neighborhood's only victory was the rescue of historic Sixth Mount Zion Baptist Church, established on that site in 1867 when Rev. John Jasper and the congregation purchased a building from white Presbyterians. Renovated in 1887 at the direction of black architect George Boyd, the church held 1,400 worshipers. Highway authorities suggested to the congregation that the church could be moved, or that it could be demolished and reconstructed. But eventually the church was preserved, the only building remaining on the north side of Duval Street. A retaining wall held the steep bank below as the turnpike broke its straight line to miss the church's foundation by a few yards.

Jackson Ward was cut in half, effectively destroyed as the center of the black community in Richmond. Sixth Mount Zion lost one thousand members. Other churches and businesses left the neighborhood. But church members and others still recall the solid and constant pressure of the entire black community to save the church; and they smile at the story of church secretary Cerelia Johnson working dutifully as an elevator operator at city hall, reporting daily to the Pastor, Dr. A. W. Brown, about the latest plans being discussed in the halls of power.[319]

The turnpike opened in 1958. The Bartholomew plan was not finished with Jackson Ward, however. Through the 1960s, further condemnation proceedings were carried out by the Richmond Housing Authority to provide land for the Richmond Coliseum, completed in 1971, and for the expansion of the Medical College of Virginia (VCU). What remained of the historic neighborhood of Navy Hill, where one of the earliest black schools in Richmond had flourished and community leader Maggie Lena Walker had taught, was seized upon by planners as the ideal site for the new Interstate 64 to enter the new north core development around the coliseum. Remaining portions of that seizure have become the Virginia BioTechnology Park and, in 2008, the new research facility for Altria/ Philip Morris. No building from the Navy Hill neighborhood remains.

New public housing was built for blacks in the Near West End and south of the river, in Manchester. But the great majority of the new public housing was concentrated in the East End of Richmond, in Church Hill. Five projects—Creighton Court (1952), Fairfield Court (1958), Whitcomb Court (1958), Mosby Court East (1962), and Mosby Court West (1962)— were built within one mile of each other. Not coincidentally, most of these projects were built during the period of court-ordered desegregation, when a major strategy of Southern resistance was the attempt to promote neighborhood schools as a way of maintaining racial segregation.

To serve the five new projects, in September 1964, Richmond opened its newest and largest school. Located in the center of Mosby Court, on a 30-acre site made available by extensive neighborhood clearance, the new Mosby School was designed to hold 1,500 junior high school students and 1,000 elementary school students. All of metropolitan Richmond's public housing projects were built within three miles of the center of Richmond. Richmond developed what is now the sixth highest concentration of public housing among cities over 200,000 in population. [*Color chart 1, see page 189*]

In the mid-1970's, the Church Hill Area Revitalization Team (CHART), a community group in Church Hill, uncovered a long-standing joint city-state plan to demolish the remaining center of Jackson Ward and the center of Church Hill for a new, six-lane divided highway which would connect Eastern Henrico with the western portion of the city. The city had announced that it was involving Church Hill residents in the design of a new bridge across Shockoe Valley to replace the two-lane Marshall Street viaduct, used extensively by pedestrians, and connect Church Hill to Jackson Ward. Residents were surprised when they discovered that the neighborhood bridge they had thought they helped to plan was actually a six-lane facility designed for higher speed traffic. Strangely, the bridge ended in Church Hill in a confused network of narrow cobblestone streets. On the other end, once it passed the coliseum in a six-lane, bi-level configuration, it ended suddenly in the relatively narrow passage of Leigh Street through what had been the center of black life in Richmond: the hotels, the churches, funeral homes, schools, and Maggie Walker's House.

CHART, led by community activist James Elam, discovered the bridge was actually the centerpiece of yet another downtown by-pass planned by state legislators and the Virginia Department of Highways. On its west end, the road was designed to travel through the Leigh Street Corridor, demolishing the historic buildings on at least one side of the street and dissecting the fragment that remained of the once-vital center of Jackson Ward. On the other end, it would cut through a neighborhood of single family homes in the center of Church Hill, creating a wide barrier of traffic and concrete separating all of the newly erected public housing projects from the revitalizing historic district to the south. Richmond's five major public housing projects would thus be completely fenced in by limited access superhighways.

An artifact of white control and the supremacy of the state government over the city, the plan received no support from the new black-majority City Council, and the identification of the Maggie Walker House in Jackson Ward as a national landmark brought federal involvement to the preservation of the Leigh Street corridor. The project was officially abandoned.

In 1966, the Richmond Metropolitan Authority was formed. It was given the power of eminent domain to build a toll road for commuters from the white West End of Richmond and the new western suburbs of Chesterfield County. This "downtown expressway" was driven through a lower-income white neighborhood and through the established black West End of Richmond, displacing more than 1,000 households. Over the next twenty years, the housing authority built homes for purchase by low- and moderate-income persons on some of the cleared land not used by the expressway. In the center of the city, the expressway completely obliterated the historic Penitentiary Bottom neighborhood.

The last clearance and "neighborhood revitalization" project undertaken in Richmond under federal urban renewal policy was in Fulton Bottom. The total demolition of Fulton's 2,800-person multigenerational neighborhood began in 1970 and was completed in 1973. By this time, the federal government required relocation payments to persons whose houses were bulldozed, and many members of the community found housing elsewhere. Funding for rebuilding Fulton was delayed for a decade, and rebuilding was still not completed in 2011. Although many hearings were held before the final Fulton plan was announced, the citizens of Fulton had little effect upon its basic shape.

The plan reserved a majority of Fulton's 370 acres for industrial sites, an industrial boulevard, and flood control; called for the demolition of every single building; and relocated most of the major streets. Although residents had been promised that their community would be rebuilt, by the time housing began to reappear in Fulton the community had been dispersed so fully that it could not be reconvened.

Richmond's urban renewal policy was carried out by the white establishment with little participation or input from the African-American community. Among the major public reasons given for the policy were these:

- It would clear "slums" and provide poor citizens with new housing. The city thereby claimed to be accepting responsibility to help alleviate the poor housing of the black community.
- It would build modern roadways, giving Richmond a proper transportation network for the growing automobile-centered culture.
- It would make available a significant number of sites for public facilities and upgraded economic development.
- It would remove unsightly and dilapidated structures to "improve" the quality of the city.
- In the case of Fulton bottom, it would provide flood control.

Whether or not they were intentional, the results of the policy were these:

- Virtually all the long-term black neighborhoods were destroyed or mutilated.
- Low-income persons, all black, were crowded together in eight concentrated public housing "courts," which rapidly became problems in themselves.[320]
- The white establishment took the land of African Americans to build its new highways, its new public facilities, its new professional employment centers, and its new industrial sites.
- The displacement of black citizens caused by the clearance projects hastened white and middle-class flight from the city's inner suburbs, and contributed to the building up of new white suburbs in bordering jurisdictions.
- The new expressways became commuter roads enabling suburbanites, who no longer contributed to the tax base of the city, to live and educate their children in one jurisdiction and work in another.

Harland Bartholomew produced three plans for Richmond, in 1941, 1956, and 1961. The plans, carried out over a forty-year period, had the effect of clustering low-income persons, who because of slavery and segregation were mostly black, in the central jurisdiction of metropolitan Richmond, while at the same time severely disintegrating the social structure of the African-American community.

In virtually every instance the plans and their projects were carried out by leaders of the white power structure of the Richmond community without the agreement of the affected population, which was largely African American, and often without the consent of working-class white citizens as well. In at least two situations when the majority of the population would not give permission, the ruling group got the Virginia General Assembly, which was controlled by the state's white power structure, to override the citizens.

Massive Resistance

On April 23, 1951, sixteen-year-old Barbara Johns led 450 students at Moton High School in Farmville, Virginia, out of school to begin a two-week protest of the school board's refusal to provide separate but equal facilities for education in Prince Edward County. Within several weeks, Richmond civil rights attorney Oliver W. Hill had entered a suit, *Davis v. Prince Edward*, on behalf of the Farmville students. That suit became one of the five cases consolidated into the Supreme Court's 1954 decision in *Brown v. Board of Education* that "separate but equal" educational facilities were "inherently unequal."[321]

In the two years after the Farmville students' suit was filed, Virginia made efforts to improve educational facilities for black children, at least in appearance. The state Board of Education asked the General Assembly to appropriate $40 million in August 1953 for this purpose,[322] but the improvements within the city of Richmond were mostly cosmetic.

Richmond had just appointed its first black member to its school board, after a three-year fight. When a member of the board died in 1950, citizens had petitioned the mayor and council to appoint attorney Oliver Hill, who was African American, to the vacancy. They refused, and instead appointed Lewis F. Powell, a white lawyer who subsequently served as school board chair from 1952 to 1961. In 1953 Booker Bradshaw was chosen by the council as the board's first black member.

Richmond and Virginia responded to the U.S. Supreme Court's decision in *Brown v. Board of Education* on May 17, 1954, with what soon became near-hysterical opposition. From that time until jurisdictional segregation was achieved in the early 1970s, the state legislature was almost totally preoccupied with strategies to retain a society in which schoolchildren remained segregated by race. Legislative policies affecting every aspect of life were tested for their effect on the single goal of preserving racial segregation. In 1954 public facilities, employment, housing, and commerce were still largely segregated in Richmond. Redlining by banks and insurance companies had not been challenged, nor had the major open housing efforts begun.

Virginia Governor Thomas Stanley's immediate response to *Brown* was to appoint, in August 1954, a commission chaired by state Senator Garland Gray to make recommendations. In November 1955, the Gray Commission recommended three strategies to prevent or delay racial integration of the public schools:

- Repeal of the state's compulsory attendance law, so that no one would be forced to attend a racially integrated school;
- Provision for state tuition grants to private schools for any child, presumably white, who might otherwise have to go to a racially integrated school; and
- Establishment of a state Pupil Placement Board to review the application of any black student requesting to go to a school other than the one to which he or she was assigned.

Meanwhile, on May 31, 1955, the Supreme Court had handed down the second part of its decision in *Brown*, saying that integration of the schools must proceed with "all deliberate speed." The mood of opposition in Virginia and the rest of the South escalated. On February 24, 1956, the patriarch of Virginia's political machine, Senator Harry F. Byrd, proclaimed what became the mantra of Virginia's fight against racial integration of the schools: "If we can organize the Southern States for *massive resistance* to this order," Byrd said, "I think that in time the rest of the country will realize that racial integration is not going to be accepted in the South."[323]

James J. Kilpatrick, editor of the *Richmond News Leader,* became the journalistic leader of the movement for Massive Resistance, and called for "Interposition" of the power of the state between the localities and the federal government. The Virginia General Assembly passed a resolution proclaiming its right to reject federal law.

On August 27, 1956, Governor Stanley convened a special session of the General Assembly. This session passed thirteen bills. The most significant of those required that the state close any public school to which a child of another race was ordered admitted by the court. "Such school is closed and removed from the public school system," the legislation declared.[324] Seven of the bills were aimed at making the NAACP illegal in Virginia. The legislation created a state Pupil Placement Board, which was to oversee any applications for individuals to attend a school other than the one to which they were assigned.

"Leading the extremist majority," recalled journalist Benjamin Muse, "and riding on top of the emotional wave, were some of the most potent figures" in the political organization of Virginia's Senator Harry F. Byrd, which controlled state politics. Byrd's chief lieutenant was state senator Mills E. Godwin, whom Muse called "chairman of the massive resistance team."[325]

"Integration is the key which opens the door to the inevitable destruction of our free public schools," Godwin proclaimed. "Integration, however slight, anywhere in Virginia would be a cancer eating at the very life blood of our public school system."[326] Godwin was later elected governor of Virginia twice, helping to lead a significant portion of the remnant of the Byrd machine into Virginia's Republican Party when he ran for a second term.[327]

The Assembly, under Godwin's leadership, resolved that racial integration should not take place anywhere in the state, even where localities desired it, and decided to take immediate disciplinary action against Arlington County. Arlington had obtained special permission from the legislature in 1948 to elect its own five-member school board, becoming the first locality in Virginia to do so. All other school boards were appointed by "school trustee electoral boards," which were in turn appointed by judges, who were in turn appointed by the Byrd machine's General Assembly. But when, in January 1956, Arlington's elected school board announced a plan to integrate its schools in voluntary compliance with the Supreme Court decision, the Assembly eliminated the county's elected school board and passed a law authorizing the county Board of Supervisors, controlled at the time by opponents of integration, to appoint a new and compliant school board.[328]

In November 1957, J. Lindsay Almond, who had secured the approval of Senator Byrd to be the next Democratic governor, was elected on a platform of defiance to racial integration. "We will oppose with every facility at our command, and with every ounce of our energy, the attempt being made to mix the white and Negro races in our classrooms," Almond intoned. "Let there be no misunderstanding, no weasel words, on this point: we dedicate our every capacity to preserve segregation in the schools."[329]

As 1958 began, the confrontation between Virginia and its localities and the integration orders from federal courts was coming to a head. Governor Almond proclaimed the policy of Virginia's white leadership in his inaugural address on January 11: "Against these massive attacks we must mount a massive resistance," he said.

Because public schools in Front Royal, Charlottesville, and Norfolk were under federal court order to integrate, they were closed by the state. By the end of September 1958, 12,700 Virginia children were out of school. Arlington was due to integrate in February. Six

Attorneys Oliver W. Hill (center), Martin A. Martin (left), and Roland W. Ealey (right) appear at federal court September 10, 1958, to protest state order to close public schools where racial integration is federally mandated. Richmond Times-Dispatch *photo reprinted by permission.*

black children had applied to previously all-white schools in Richmond—Nathaniel Bacon in the East End and Westhampton in the West End—but no firm court order had yet been issued. The *Richmond News Leader* called on its editorial page for support of private education to counter what it called the "evils of race mixing."

Meanwhile, the law closing the public schools in four Virginia localities had been challenged in both the U.S. District Court for the Eastern District of Virginia (in Norfolk) and the Supreme Court of Virginia.[330] The Norfolk case was the only case in the South where the plaintiffs asking the court to order racial integration were white. The judges of the state and federal courts consulted privately after they had reached their decisions and agreed that they would issue them on the same day, with the first announcement coming from the state court. The judges hoped that this strategy would make the decisions more likely to be respected by the agitated white citizenry.

On January 19, 1959, the birthday of Robert E. Lee and a state holiday, the Supreme Court of Virginia and the federal district court joined in declaring the state's closure of the schools illegal. The next day Governor Almond spoke on television:

> To those in high place or elsewhere who advocate integration
> for your children and send their own to private or public
> segregated schools; to those who defend or close their eyes to the
> livid stench of sadism, sex, immorality and juvenile pregnancy
> infesting the mixed schools of the District of Columbia and
> elsewhere; to those who would overthrow the customs, morals
> and traditions of a way of life which has endured in honor and
> decency for centuries and embrace a new moral code prepared
> by nine men in Washington whose moral concepts they know
> nothing about; ... to all of these and their confederates, comrades
> and allies, let me make it abundantly clear for the record now
> and hereafter, as governor of this state, I will not yield to that
> which I know to be wrong and will destroy every semblance of
> education for thousands of the children of Virginia.[331]

Segregationist forces in Virginia frantically discussed ways of
preventing the integration ordered by the courts. Senator Byrd made
no secret of his desire to continue the conflict. Almond called a special
session of the General Assembly for January 28. In that session he
announced, to the surprise of many, that he could do nothing further to
prevent the integration of the schools in Arlington and Norfolk:

> It is not enough for gentlemen to cry unto you and me, "Don't
> give up the ship!" "Stop them!" "It must not happen," or "It can
> be prevented." If any of them knows the way through the dark
> maze of judicial aberration and constitutional exploitation,
> I call upon them to shed the light for which Virginia stands
> in dire need in this her dark and agonizing hour. No fair-
> minded person would be so unreasonable as to seek to hold
> me responsible for failure to exercise powers which the state is
> powerless to bestow.[332]

On February 2, 1959, twenty-one black students—four in Arlington
and seventeen in Norfolk—entered previously all-white Virginia public
schools for the first time, without incident. The General Assembly, at
Almond's urging, passed three pieces of legislation in lieu of further
attempts to prevent integration completely. They established a tuition
grant plan, passed a law against bombing threats, and repealed the state's
compulsory attendance law. Almond's refusal to fight the court decision

Demonstrators were arrested and charged with trespassing at Thalhimers department store February 22, 1960. Those arrested would not leave after being refused service at a tearoom and a lunch counter. Richmond Times-Dispatch *caption and photo reprinted by permission.*

ended his political career. Almond later revealed that he had been visited by a delegation of white businessmen, including railroad executive Stuart Saunders, banker J. Harvie Wilkinson, and attorney and future U. S. Supreme Court Justice Lewis Powell, who had told him that Virginia could not hope to attract any national corporations and businesses to the state if it lost its public schools.

The momentum for racial integration in Richmond increased. On February 22, 1960, thirty-four students from Virginia Union University were arrested for seeking to be served food and drink at the fabled Richmond Room restaurant in Thalhimer's department store in downtown Richmond. They were taken to police headquarters in six patrol wagons, booked, and released. The Richmond 34's sit-in spurred boycotts, which eventually brought about the full desegregation of Richmond's core retail district.

Six months later, after three years of litigation, on September 6, 1960, Gloria Jean Mead and Carol Irene Swann entered previously all-white Chandler Junior High School in Richmond. The *Richmond News Leader* proclaimed in a banner headline that "Integration is Quiet in City," and reported that "there were no racial problems at Chandler" caused by the integration of the two girls into the formerly all-white school.[333] That fall, some six years after the U.S. Supreme Court decision, out of 204,000 black students in the schools of Virginia, only 170 were attending racially integrated schools.[334]

The next decade saw a complicated series of maneuvers in Richmond, mirroring similar efforts throughout Virginia, in which the city school board, aided by city and state leaders, attempted to minimize the racial integration of the schools. In 1961, thirty-one black students were attending formerly all-white schools in Richmond. By 1963, of Richmond's 26,000 black students, 312 (1.2 percent) were attending racially integrated schools.

In 1964 the progress of racial integration in the nation was increased by the passage of the Civil Rights Act, which prohibited racial segregation in public

Gloria Jean Mead (left), 13, and Carol Irene Swann, 12, are followed by a Richmond plainclothesman as they walk toward Chandler Junior High School, to become the first Negro pupils to enter formerly all-white Richmond public schools. Photo and caption: Richmond Times-Dispatch. *Used by permission.*

Richmond students leave Mosby Junior High School after first day of classes August 31, 1970. Richmond Times-Dispatch *photo, by permission.*

accommodations and employment.

By 1966, as required by the state, Richmond adopted what it called a "freedom of choice" policy, under which students could apply to the school of their choice. In practice, however, assignment of students to racially integrated schools lagged. The racially segregated housing in Richmond meant that blacks seldom lived near all-white schools, and no bus transportation was provided. Faculties were not racially integrated.

In 1968 the United States Supreme Court, ruling in *Green v. New Kent*, said that freedom of choice could not be a legitimate response to *Brown* so long as the effect of it was to maintain a dual school system. This had been its effect throughout Virginia and was clearly its purpose. The court held that Richmond's neighboring New Kent County should "convert promptly to a system without a 'white school' and a 'Negro school' but just schools."[335] Richmonders brought a case to the federal court under the New Kent decision, calling for the rejection of Richmond's freedom of choice plan.

In response, on May 1, 1970, the Richmond School Board proposed pairing black and white schools. Under this plan, schools in certain neighborhoods might have been integrated. But in the newly annexed area of Chesterfield County, there were 8,017 white students and only 206 blacks; and in Richmond's East End there were 13,743 black students and only 374 whites. Richmond's segregation policies in housing had been very effective. Significant racial integration was not possible without busing. On June 26, 1970, federal Judge Robert Merhige rejected the pairing plan. When the schools opened that fall, 5,000 of the 8,000 white students from the annexed area were not present in the Richmond Public Schools.

By April 1971 Judge Merhige had concluded that Richmond could not or would not integrate its schools without a more drastic solution. He ordered what became known as "cross-town busing." Under court order, Richmond purchased school buses to help the school system achieve its court-mandated goal: that every individual school reflect in its integrated attendance the racial proportions of the city's school population, about seventy percent black and thirty percent white. The program began in September with the total integration of the middle and high schools. Virginia's white Republican governor Linwood Holton sent his three children to the newly integrated schools.

Merhige and others recognized that the Richmond system's integrated status was fragile. Black plaintiffs requested immediately that Richmond's 43,000-student system be merged with the school systems of Henrico and Chesterfield counties. Both suburban counties had schools that were more than ninety percent white. The integrated system would have had a total of

104,000 students, a third of them black. The attorney general of Virginia and the state board of education joined the suburban counties in opposing the merger. In January 1972 Judge Merhige ordered the consolidation.

Again, hysteria erupted. The *Richmond Times-Dispatch* said that the merger would destroy the "quality" of the schools and "fail to give children the best possible academic education." The order was stayed pending appeal, and in June 1972 the U.S. Court of Appeals for the Fourth Circuit overturned it. A year later, in May 1973, the Supreme Court, by a 4-4 vote, upheld the Fourth Circuit's decision to reject consolidation. Justice

Three-jurisdiction population 1950-1980

	Richmond	Henrico	Chesterfield	TOTAL
1950	230,310	51,560	31,970	315,790
1960	219,958	111,269	61,762	394,949
1970	249,621	143,812	68,012	461,445
1980	219,214	177,000	140,000	536,214

Table: Moeser and Dennis, *The Politics of Annexation*, p. 30.

Lewis Powell, at one time chair of the Richmond School Board and now a member of the court, had recused himself.[336]

By 1976, 12,000 white students had left the Richmond Public School System, and black enrollment had reached eighty percent. Blacks had gone to the suburbs, too, creating what Robert Pratt calls "discernible class divisions."[337] In 1987 Henrico's system was twenty-six percent African American and Chesterfield's, fourteen percent.[338]

State policies for jurisdictional segregation

During the 1950s Richmond remained the largest jurisdiction in its metropolitan area, but by 1960 the majority of the white population in the metropolitan city lived in suburban Henrico and Chesterfield counties. By 1980 the total population of Henrico and Chesterfield had come to exceed that of the center city of Richmond.

School integration in Virginia set the stage for a massive retooling of the jurisdictional lines in Virginia and of the laws governing metropolitan areas. During the 1960s the Virginia General Assembly was preoccupied with issues of racial integration and urban boundaries.

The constitution of Virginia had provided for cities that were independent of counties. These cities had special rights of taxation and annexation, but were also subject to approval by the General Assembly for any change in their charter. Richmond had annexed territory eleven times from 1782 to 1942.[339]

When racial integration threatened the white leadership of the commonwealth, and the General Assembly saw it could not legally segregate public schools in a single jurisdiction by race, white leaders seized upon the independent city provisions of the constitution as a way to maintain substantial white majorities in jurisdictions. The constitution provided that while cities could annex portions of counties, cities could not annex other cities.

The first time these strategies were employed was in the Tidewater area. There, suburban and rural whites were threatened by the city of Norfolk, which had a substantial black population. Norfolk had only fifty-three square miles of land, and was in need of new territory. To prevent this annexation, in 1963 the small oceanfront city of Virginia Beach joined with rural Princess Anne County, which adjoined Norfolk, to form the new "city" of Virginia Beach—250 square miles of land and an equal area of water. Virginia Beach city was still rural and mostly white, but now it was immune from annexation by Norfolk. At the same time, the small city of South Norfolk joined with the much larger Norfolk County to form the new "city" of Chesapeake. This area comprised 350 square miles of land, including the vast Dismal Swamp of Virginia, and a largely rural, white-majority population. Ten years later the town of Suffolk completed a merger with rural Nansemond County to make the "city" of Suffolk—429 mostly rural square miles. Norfolk remained fifty-three square miles, unable to annex any land.

Throughout the 1960s, the city of Richmond was attempting to grow. Public statements by advocates of annexation focused on the need to maintain Richmond as a stable and healthy economic entity, representing with its political boundaries the major economic and population growth of the expanding metropolitan city.

Richmond and Henrico leaders proposed a merger of the two localities in 1961. Submitted to referendum, the proposal passed voters in Richmond but failed in Henrico.[340] The next day, December 13, 1961, the city entered into the prescribed annexation proceeding in state court, seeking to annex portions of Henrico and Chesterfield. Richmond proposed to annex 152 square miles of Henrico, with 115,000 in population, and 51 square miles of Chesterfield, with 40,000 in population. This would have caused the city to grow from 40 to 312 square miles. It would have left Henrico with only 90 square miles and 2,000 people.

The annexation court dealt first with the proposal to annex Henrico. In 1965 the court rejected the city's proposal and awarded only 17 square miles of Henrico County with 45,000 people to Richmond. There was little vacant land to grow, and the award would have cost the city a $55 million payment to Henrico. The city rejected the award.[341]

Richmond then turned to its suit against Chesterfield County. Privately, and without the presence of black members of the city council, representatives of Chesterfield and Richmond negotiated over the annexation, with the court's deliberations pending and threatening. The emphasis seemed to have shifted decisively away from acquiring land to grow to preserving a white majority in the city of Richmond. John Moeser and Rutledge Dennis, in their remarkable book *The Politics of Annexation,* detail the progress of this conversation as it was later revealed in a suit challenging the annexation after it was awarded.

Richmond city's population in 1964 was estimated to be 46 percent black. In 1966, just two years later, it was estimated to be 48 percent

Attorney and City Council member Henry L. Marsh addresses special session of Virginia General Assembly on March 19, 1969. Governor Mills E. Godwin had called the special session to consider amending the state constitution to give the legislature power to enlarge the boundaries of the state's capital city unilaterally. The bill passed on first reading, but was abandoned before its final reading when, on July 1, 1969, the state court allowed Richmond to annex a portion of Chesterfield County containing 44,000 citizens, 97 percent of whom were white. The General Assembly then prohibited any further annexation by Richmond. Richmond Times-Dispatch *photo, by permission.*

black. More dramatically, in 1964 only 18,161 African Americans were registered to vote in Richmond, but by 1966, this number had climbed to almost 30,000. Black registrations had increased 65 percent in only two years, while white registrations, now totaling 58,827, had increased only 13 percent. In 1966 city voters elected three blacks to the nine-member city council. More significant politically, however, was that one of the black candidates, Henry Marsh, had not been endorsed by Richmond Forward, the white-majority political machine that controlled the city.

The 1968 session of Virginia's General Assembly was preoccupied with the capital city of Richmond and the possibility of a takeover of the government by blacks for the first time in its history. Richmond had not had a majority of black voters since 1868, a century earlier. For 100 years the city and General Assembly had kept whites in control of the capital city. The assembly set up a special commission, the Aldhizer Commission, to study annexation, and specifically to study Richmond. They approved the issuing of state bonds to enable Richmond to annex a portion of Chesterfield County.[342] James Wheat, the investment magnate who headed the white political establishment, warned in the 1968 councilmanic election that Richmond could become "a permanent black ghetto, a happy hunting ground for ambitious political opportunists."[343]

In 1969 the Aldhizer Commission proposed an amendment to the constitution that would give the General Assembly, acting on its own, the authority to enlarge the boundaries of Richmond every ten years. The amendment passed the General Assembly on first reading, to be brought back the next year. Race was not the topic openly discussed—a classic strategy in the sophisticated world of Virginia racial politics—but the language of the debate left little question about the fundamental issue bothering the legislators: "What is truly before us today, gentlemen?" asked Senator Leslie D. Campbell, Jr., of Hanover. "Is it a question of finance? Is it a question of financing the city of Richmond's government? ...I say to you that it is not a financial problem. It is a problem of imbalance; all of you down deep know exactly what the problem is."[344]

Finally, Mayor Phil Bagley of Richmond and Irwin Horner of the Chesterfield Board of Supervisors reached an agreement that the city could annex 23 square miles of Chesterfield County. The area had a population of over 44,000 persons, and was 97 percent white. That would make Richmond's black population drop to 42 percent and voting age black population drop from 45 percent to 37 percent. Richmond got no vacant land in the deal, and no industry. The boundary of the annexed area was drawn directly in front of the valuable Spruance plant of E. I. DuPont de Nemours, Chesterfield's largest taxpayer, which employed over 2,500 people, and was about to expand to employ another 1,700.[345] Rumors circulated that DuPont would be closed if it were annexed into the city. On July 1, 1969, the court, in an unprecedented procedure, approved the agreement privately reached by Horner and Bagley, and the General Assembly killed the Aldhizer Amendment in its next session.

The annexation of twenty-three square miles of Chesterfield County was the last annexation permitted under law for the city of Richmond. The General Assembly was in the process of changing annexation laws all over the commonwealth, in order to protect suburban counties against inner cities. The progressive elements of the constitution that had been used to keep cities healthy and their boundaries realistic were abandoned in the face of panicked attempts to replace legalized segregation with a new jurisdictionally established separation of race and class.

On February 24, 1971, Curtis Holt, a resident of Creighton Court in Richmond's Church Hill neighborhood, represented by Cabell Venable, a white attorney, filed suit in federal court to seek invalidation of the Chesterfield annexation, alleging that it had been designed primarily to reduce black voting strength. Soon thereafter the U. S. Justice Department joined in opposition to the annexation. A complicated series of court actions followed. Richmond was enjoined from holding elections to City Council until the matter was resolved. The resulting hiatus in elections, from 1970 until 1977, was the longest period in which any American city had been prevented by federal courts from holding elections.[346]

Holt sought the deannexation of the Chesterfield citizens and territory, a position that was supported by the various citizens' associations in the annexed area. The city sought to retain the annexed area, and to solve the civil rights objections by changing its electoral system from the at-large election of council persons to either single-member districts or a mixed system of some at-large and some single-member districts.

The United States Supreme Court finally ruled on June 24, 1975, that the annexation as constituted was illegal under the Voting Rights Act, but that it could be remedied either by deannexation or by changing the electoral system to one which "fairly recognizes the minority's political potential."[347] It left it to a magistrate to work out the electoral solution. In May, 1976, the magistrate determined that the city could keep the annexed area but would have to change to a nine district single-member ward system to elect its city council, one which had been drawn to make it possible for a black majority to be elected.

The Supreme Court had been definite in its evaluation of Richmond's annexation attempts. In the majority opinion, Justice Byron White wrote that the annexation "was infected by the impermissible purpose of denying the right to vote based on race through perpetuating white majority power to exclude Negroes from office through at-large elections."

Justice William J. Brennan, joined by Justices William O. Douglas and Thurgood Marshall in a supporting minority opinion, was even more direct in his indictment of the racial intent: "The record is replete with statements by Richmond officials," Brennan observed, "which prove beyond question that the predominant (if not sole) motive and desire of the negotiators of the 1969 settlement was to acquire 44,000 additional white citizens for Richmond in order to avert a transfer of political control to what was fast becoming a black population majority."[348]

While Holt was filing his suit at the beginning of 1971, the Virginia General Assembly was continuing to intervene in the situation. The counties of Henrico and Chesterfield applied for the same kind of legislative protection that had been granted to the counties surrounding the city of Norfolk—that is, they applied for city charters to protect them against annexation by the city of Richmond. The General Assembly decided instead to specifically prohibit Richmond from annexing any more territory. In March the General Assembly passed legislation ending the right of annexation for cities of 125,000 or more, which "as a practical matter...applied only to the Richmond metropolitan area."[349]

The Legacy of 1971

Three events which occurred in the first few months of 1971 established the fundamental fiscal, sociological, racial, and political realities of the city of metropolitan Richmond which have endured for four decades:

1. On February 24, 1971, Curtis Holt challenged the annexation by Richmond of 44,000 Chesterfield County citizens and 23 square miles of Chesterfield County, and was joined in the challenge by the U.S. Department of Justice.
2. In March 1971 the Virginia General Assembly prohibited Richmond from seeking to annex any more land from the surrounding counties.
3. In April 1971 Judge Robert Merhige ordered the Richmond Public Schools to bus children throughout the system so that

the racial percentages in each individual school would be equal. At the time, about seventy percent of the students were black and thirty percent were white.

The city boundaries, which had been allowed to expand to reflect the physical and economic city's expansion in eleven annexations since 1742, were made permanent. The newly permanent boundaries separated the majority of the white population, which now resided in Henrico and Chesterfield counties, from the majority of the black population, which resided in the historic city called Richmond. The city's public schools, which had been effectively segregated by race since they were established a century before, were totally integrated. And Holt's suit began the final fall from power of the white leadership which had ruled the city since its beginning and established the foundation for black governance of the central city, surrounded by majority white suburbs.

Richmond held no elections for City Council and mayor from 1971 until 1977. The courts had enjoined the election because the case was pending in federal court under the Voting Rights Act, contending that Richmond had annexed 44,000 white citizens of Chesterfield County for racial reasons.

On March 8, 1977, in their first elections for nearly seven years, the citizens of Richmond elected nine members to the City Council, five of them black and four of them white. The Council then elected Henry L. Marsh, an African-American attorney, the first black mayor of Richmond.[350]

African Americans had taken leadership in Richmond, but in some ways the city was regarded by the state and the surrounding jurisdictions as Jackson Ward had been in the century after the Civil War. Its boundaries were drawn by the General Assembly, its tax base restricted, its charter subject to state approval, and its public services supported at a disproportionately low level by the state. Its schools were again racially separate and in many ways, as they had been described in the *Brown* decision, "inherently unequal."

9

A Metropolitan City without
Legalized Segregation
1970-2010

U nder firm pressure from the federal courts, metropolitan
Richmond and Virginia dismantled the legal edifice of
mandatory racial segregation in the early 1970s, with the
support of African-American citizens, anti-Byrd white politicians,
and some of the more moderate business community. In March
1977, Henry L. Marsh became the first African-American mayor in
the former capital of the Confederacy. Thirteen years later Virginians
chose his fellow student at Howard Law School, L. Douglas Wilder, to
be the first African-American elected governor of an American state.

From the point of view of racial history, the developments were
momentous. Since 1607, the government of Virginia had considered
persons of at least one race or class to be ineligible for full economic
rights, full citizenship, or elected office. In its colonial policy, the
English Crown had reserved servile status first for Indians and English
servants, and subsequently for African slaves, for imported prisoners,
and for indentured servants. Having achieved freedom for themselves,
Virginians of European descent retained a policy of slavery for most
persons of African descent and diminished rights for those African-
Americans who were not enslaved. When this policy was no longer
permitted by the victors in the Civil War, the Virginians of European
descent replaced it with systematic policies of social restriction,
disenfranchisement, and economic exploitation known as "racial
segregation." These segregation policies continued in Virginia and in
Virginia's capital city through the 1950s and 1960s. The established
white majority, urged to Massive Resistance by political and editorial
leaders, was able to salvage segregation for almost fifteen years after
Brown v. Board of Education, but finally the overt policies of racial

Members of Richmond City Council take oath of office. Left to right, William I. Golding Sr., Walter T. Kenney, Willie J. Dell (just visible behind Mr. Golding's hand), Wayland W. Rennie, Claudette Black McDaniel, H.W. "Chuck" Richardson, Mayor Henry L. Marsh, Aubrey H. Thompson, and George Stevenson Kemp, Jr. The picture was taken on July 1, 1978, after the new members had served for 16 months. Richmond Times-Dispatch *photo, by permission.*

discrimination and segregation were beaten down.

Three hundred fifty-eight years after the first Africans arrived in Virginia and were sold as slaves, the white legislature of the Commonwealth grudgingly handed over the leadership of its capital city, the former capital of the Confederacy, to the descendants of enslaved Africans.

The black majority

The dramatic change in Richmond's government was celebrated nationally by African-American citizens. The June 1980 issue of *Ebony*, a leading publication of the nation's black community, featured Richmond in its cover story: "Richmond: The Confederate Capital Finally Falls to Blacks."

A city whose foremost tourist attraction is a street lined with monuments to the men who battled the U.S. government in order to maintain White supremacy now has a Black mayor, a Black city manager, a predominantly Black city council, a Black school superintendent, a Black fire chief, a Black treasurer, a

Black personnel director, a Black assistant city manager, and a Black assistant to the mayor. Out in Hollywood Cemetery, President Jefferson Davis must be turning over in his grave.

Unlike Black officials in other cities that have undergone the political power shift from White to Black—like Gary and Newark—Marsh and his colleagues did not inherit a dying city. Richmond, just 500 miles from nearly 50 percent of the nation's population, is financially sound.

...Relinquishing control of such a city did not sit well with the grandsons and daughters of slave owners and aristocrats. First off, the business community balked. "They were used to having their friends in the driver's seat," explains Robert Martin, Richmond Chamber of Commerce vice president in charge of urban affairs. "Then suddenly those positions were filled with people from a different background. Naturally there was going to be some question in their minds."

The political forces in [the] aristocratic West End, an area that had long dominated Richmond politics, pushed forth a referendum to cut city taxes and limit city government, thus sabotaging the effectiveness of the city's new Black leadership. Then, there were (and still are) the death threats that poured into Marsh's office.

"Every day has been a battle," says Councilman [Chuck] Richardson. "It's sticky and difficult, and sometimes just downright cut-throat."

But the city's Black leadership has resolved to make the new government work. "The problem that some folks have is that the complexion of the council has changed," says [Black city manager Manuel] Deese. "People in Virginia have never seen any Black people in an executive level. We're showing that Blacks can do the job. This city, with a sharing of power between Blacks and Whites, can serve as a role model for the rest of the nation."

Undaunted by a vituperative press and hostile foes, the Black leadership has pushed ahead with a $90 million downtown redevelopment program.

The business community appears a little more at ease. Philip Morris, the city's largest private employer, has begun a $42 million expansion of its present facility and is vigorously promoting the city in a national advertisement campaign. Last year, 13 new businesses moved to the city, and 43 expanded present operations, dumping another 1,800 jobs into the market, and the disastrous proposition to cut taxes and hinder city services was soundly defeated. Still, there are problems ahead.

Richmond is almost evenly divided racially, but its school system is 90 percent Black. Helping school superintendent Richard Hunter reverse the trend is a coalition of Whites who are trying to convince their neighbors to return their children to the public schools....

Then there is the problem of White flight. Richmond is losing residents at a rate of 3,000 a year, and although Blacks have broken through politically, they have yet to make meaningful inroads in the business arena....

The eyes of the nation are on the Black leadership in Richmond. "They inherited a solvent organization and they have an obligation to keep it that way," says Martin. "Everybody is watching us," says Marsh. "I know it, but it doesn't bother me. We're going to make this work."[351]

Richmond's new City Council picked up where the white majority council left off. They continued to support the redevelopment of the downtown, a strategy known as "Project One." It had been developed by the white business community under the leadership of Mayor Thomas Bliley, who stayed in office for seven years while courts deliberated over the legality of the Chesterfield annexation. The project called for development of the coliseum area and retail core, the relocation of the downtown Greyhound and Trailways bus stations, and the construction of a new hotel and convention center on Broad Street. "If we don't build the center, we're talking about a loss of seven million dollars a year," Bliley opined.[352]

Mayor Marsh hired a full-time executive assistant in City Hall, an action that was attacked by members of the white establishment. Before long, the majority fired city manager William J. Leidinger, claiming that he was taking his cues not from the Mayor and Council but from the white leaders on Main Street. He was replaced by his African-American assistant, Manuel Deese. Leidinger responded by successfully seeking election to City Council from his Northside neighborhood.

In 1981 the black majority's attempt to carry out the establishment's plans for downtown development ran into a serious snag. The Hilton Corporation announced plans to build a new 350-room downtown

Governor of Virginia Charles Robb joined the city celebration opening the Sixth Street Marketplace and its bridge across Broad Street on September 21, 1985. Richmond Times-Dispatch *photo, by permission.*

hotel closer to the river than the Project One proposal. The Mayor and Council majority perceived that the market would not support both the new Hilton and the proposed Project One hotel. There was also a suspicion that the competitive, potentially budget-breaking Hilton proposal would not have come forward if the white business establishment were still in control. Council passed a special ordinance denying zoning to the Hilton, eventuating in a court suit that the city finally settled at significant cost. Leidinger, the Richmond Newspapers and even the *Wall Street Journal* levied strong and potentially shaming criticism against the mayor and Council majority. Prospects for the black leadership to carry forward an effective public-private development policy were damaged.[353]

Nonetheless, in 1982 Marsh and T. Justin Moore, the President of Virginia Electric Power Corp., collaborated to form Richmond Renaissance,[354] an expressly interracial public-private partnership of businessmen and other citizens organized to coordinate downtown revitalization. Richmond Renaissance worked with nationally known urban developer James Rouse to design a new Sixth Street Marketplace to support the work already done at Project One and anchor the retail center of the city. The central feature of the Marketplace was a bridge spanning Broad Street, connecting the formerly "white" side of the street to the south with the "black" side of the street—Jackson Ward— to the north. Governor Charles Robb opened the Marketplace before a large crowd at the bridge across Broad on September 19, 1985.

The downtown retail revival never materialized. The two anchor department stores of the Marketplace—Richmond's flagship stores that had been locally owned late into the twentieth century—were sold and resold, stripped of their assets. Miller & Rhoads closed in January 1990. Thalhimer's closed January 22, 1992. Sixth Street Marketplace was all but dead just six years after it opened.[355]

The new African-American leadership in City Hall took seriously the quality of public education, neighborhood development and conservation, and issues of affirmative action in hiring, under constant scrutiny from a white establishment that had fought for three centuries to prevent this from happening. The Richmond Newspapers were influential in the new metropolitan situation and particularly threatening to the new black majority. Both daily papers—the morning *Times-Dispatch* and the evening *News Leader*—were owned by a single corporation. Both had avidly supported massive resistance and opposed black leadership. Although the newspaper management claimed repeatedly that its news coverage was independent of its often passionately critical editorial positions, the reporters found it safer and easier to explore stories of alleged misdeeds among black leadership and in black-led public education than to investigate, chronicle, or criticize the momentous movements within the white business community that were dramatically altering the metropolitan city and building new cities in the suburbs.

Even while black leaders sought to provide responsible and effective continuity of government to Virginia's capital city, their efforts were being subverted. Some of the forces were the direct result of the actions of Virginia's last segregationist General Assembly and its successors. Some were the result of national economic forces that were operating in every American metropolitan area. And some were the result of an accelerating, largely white flight of citizens, businessmen, and investors to the adjacent suburban counties.

In the 1960s, Richmond's black leadership had been determined to press its case for control of the capital city, and had opposed efforts to expand into the surrounding counties, which would dilute the black vote. Some of Richmond's white leaders had tried to promote various schemes for annexation of county land and citizenry, but they had been opposed in these efforts not only by Richmond's black citizens but by the majority of the white constituencies in the suburban counties. The General Assembly, which by the state constitution was given special authority over the Commonwealth's independent cities, vigorously opposed the prospect of black leadership in the capital. The result was that the city over which black leaders received stewardship in 1977 was a severely damaged entity—suffering from legal restrictions, financial burdens, and state policies that would make it almost impossible to compete against the swirling forces of disinvestment, sprawl, and middle class flight already upon it.

Inherited and legislated burdens

The actions of the General Assembly in 1971 kept the central jurisdiction of Richmond as a no-growth zone during America's three crucial decades of economic growth at the end of the twentieth century.

The most critical decision of the General Assembly was to enact, in March 1971, a moratorium on annexation of any territory by the city of Richmond. Although styled as temporary, the moratorium was effectively permanent, due to the underlying racial politics of the action. It is still in effect. Although it was couched in terms that made it seem general—it applied to independent cities of 125,000 or more in population—in practice it applied only to Richmond, a fact of which legislators were fully cognizant.[356] While the General Assembly during the ensuing decade altered laws affecting annexation in other, smaller cities in a way that gave them negotiating power to strike financial or territorial deals with surrounding counties, they gave no such right to the city of Richmond. Whereas the Assembly pledged that it would supply a new source of state funding to its capital city to make up for its inability to expand with the growth of economic and population development, that funding was never delivered.

The Old Dominion, alone among the nation's fifty states, had a system of independent cities that were completely separate from surrounding counties. [357] When the system was devised, special revenues and privileges were reserved to cities, on the premise that they carried responsibilities not assisted by the state. But by 1971, nearly all of these special privileges and revenue resources had been made available as well to the urban counties that surrounded the historic independent cities.

The Assembly's 1971 surgery on Richmond resulted in the creation of a specially crafted jurisdictional entity that was severely hampered in its ability to function economically. Virginia had developed for its capital city a second-class status under policy and law. The "city" that black citizens now led had been stripped of its ability to expand—an ability that was essential to the concept of an independent city and that had been exercised by Richmond eleven times. It had no vacant land for industrial, commercial, or residential development. Its boundaries were now permanently fixed at sixty square miles.

Stripping the powers of annexation and failing to replace them with other revenue or negotiating power was a particularly violent legislative blow in the boom environment of the 1970s. National economic trends and superhighway construction were causing cities all over the nation to rebuild in a sprawling, disintegrated fashion. Only those cities that could expand their boundaries or whose central districts had inherent economic advantages could hold their own in the runaway expansion of the period.

At the time when the General Assembly prohibited Richmond from further annexation, the central city was already under severe economic stress. Containing most of the governmental, educational, non-profit, and religious institutions of the metropolitan city, it was unable to collect taxes on more than twenty percent of its property. The tax rate on real property was already extremely high—nearly

Division of land mass in metropolitan Richmond's eight jurisdictions

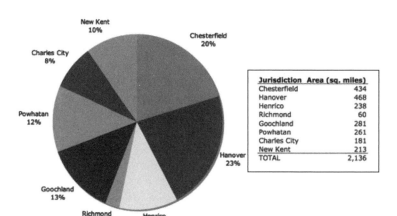

Jurisdiction	Area (sq. miles)
Chesterfield	434
Hanover	468
Henrico	238
Richmond	60
Goochland	281
Powhatan	261
Charles City	181
New Kent	213
TOTAL	2,136

twice that of some surrounding jurisdictions. The city already carried more capital debt than the other three major jurisdictions combined, and the per capita debt was more than twice that of Henrico County. The median household income was forty percent less than that of the surrounding jurisdictions. Richmond banks systematically practiced red-lining—denying mortgages to persons who lived or wished to buy houses in large portions of the city.[358] The clearance policies of the previous two decades had already caused a significant middle class exodus. Meanwhile, Richmond contained most of the metropolitan city's poorest citizens, concentrated in the eight public housing projects that had been built in the city. No public housing existed in the surrounding counties.

Disinvestment and sprawl

The disinvestment of the independent city of Richmond, as the core jurisdiction of metropolitan Richmond, was well underway when the legislature and courts went through the final dramas that ended state-sanctioned racial segregation and ushered in black majority government in Richmond city. Its economic power was effectively dissipated by preventing its ability to expand its borders.

The city of Richmond still contained about half the metropolitan area's population in 1960 and the ill-fated annexation of more than 40,000 citizens of Chesterfield County kept the city's population near fifty percent in the 1970 census. Between 1970 and 1990, however, the central city lost population. Twenty percent of the citizens left, while the suburbs continued to grow. The city's population stabilized by 1990 at about 200,000. In the forty years following racial integration and the General Assembly's decision to terminate Richmond's ability to expand, the total population of the metropolitan city doubled to nearly one million. The central city's share of metropolitan population—the population that lived in the jurisdiction called the city of Richmond— dropped from fifty percent to twenty percent.

From 1970 to 2010 the expanding metropolitan city sprawled across formerly rural portions of Henrico, Chesterfield, and Hanover, consuming land faster than either the Tidewater or Northern Virginia metropolitan areas. The Richmond Regional Planning District Commission estimated that between 1992 and 1997 the growth patterns of metropolitan Richmond were consuming 1.18 acres for every new citizen. At this rate, the 300,000 new citizens predicted in the next decade would necessitate the development of 354 square miles of land, an area larger than Henrico County. **[Color chart 2, see page 190]**

Development reached the outer borders of Chesterfield and Henrico counties, and began to spread into the exurban counties of Amelia, Powhatan, Goochland, Charles City, and New Kent, but the suburban and exurban development was not dense. In 2009, the three major jurisdictions of Northern Virginia (Arlington, Alexandria, and Fairfax) had three times the population density and twice the population of metropolitan Richmond on less than half the land.

Transportation policies played a major role in the disinvestment of Richmond and the sprawling development of its surrounding counties in the period from 1970 to 2010. In 1975, while no elections were being held and anticipating a possible takeover of the city government by a black majority, the lame duck white majority City Council agreed to allow the city's Amtrak station to be moved from downtown Richmond to suburban Henrico, even though the enabling federal legislation for Amtrak had grandfathered train service in Richmond. Also in 1975, the city handed over Byrd International Airport to a new Capital Regional Airport Commission. The city donated the airport, valued at $55 million and located in Henrico County, to the commission, bestowing to Henrico and Chesterfield counties equal ownership and equal status on the commission at no cost.

In the same period metro business leaders committed the city of Richmond to build and cover any future deficits on the Downtown

Expressway, a commuter toll road for Henrico and Chesterfield counties being built through Richmond neighborhoods by the state-chartered Richmond Metropolitan Authority. The effect of this agreement was to saddle the city budget, already bonded up to capacity, with more than $50 million in additional expense, with no legal obligation upon RMA to return the money. In June, 2011, the RMA Board committed itself to repay the city $60.3 million in capital and interest by November, 2011.

Between 1984 and 2004, the state and federal governments spent more than one billion dollars on new superhighways to spur development in the suburban counties surrounding Richmond. Requiring no funding from the local jurisdictions involved, these infrastructure investments served to increase land values and create the major new commercial and industrial areas to which the retail, manufacturing, office, and warehousing operations of the metropolitan city were drawn. Some of these businesses were drawn from locations in the city, and others represented new industry drawn to the area.

Metro Richmond Non-Toll Superhighway Construction, 1984-2004

I-295. **From I-64 West to I-95 South**
Henrico, Hanover, Chesterfield, &
Prince George Counties
53 miles, 1984-1992 $500,000,000

Rt. 288. **From I-95 South to Rt 60 West**
Chesterfield County, 16.1 miles, 1990 $143,000,000

From Rt 60 West to I-64 West
Chesterfield, Goochland, &
Henrico Counties
17.5 miles, 2004 $434,000,000

    TOTALS: 76.6 miles, $1,077,000,000

Two of the major interchanges became the locus of the two newest and largest retail areas—Short Pump and Virginia Center Commons— both in Henrico County. During the same period of time, the General Assembly chose the tax on retail sales to be the major new revenue source for both local and state purposes. This tax supported the growth of the suburban counties and further impoverished the center city.

While expending major amounts of taxpayer capital to develop the sprawling suburbs, the state and federal governments declined to spend comparable amounts to modernize transportation in the central city. Several studies of light rail suggested that a central circulator system, as well as lines along one or more of the major thoroughfares leading into suburban counties, would spur development, encourage urban land use, and make transportation accessible to persons of modest incomes. $200 million, less than one fifth of the cost of the new suburban ring highways, would have built both the circulator and light rail from downtown Richmond to Short Pump. $600 million would have built a full light rail system for metropolitan Richmond, including Midlothian Turnpike, Hull Street to Brandermill, Mechanicsville Turnpike, and the Airport. But state and federal funds for light rail were restricted and demanded significant matching funds from the local jurisdiction – unlike the massive superhighways. And the state, which claimed the right to condemn land to build highways where it wished, continued to give the suburban counties veto power over public transportation on highways built with state and federal money.

Although the city of Richmond invited Chesterfield County to become half owner of the Greater Richmond Transit System in 1989, the county steadfastly refused to permit local bus service on its highways. Henrico allowed, and subsidized, a few local bus routes. Meanwhile, studies showed that by 2010 a large number of the entry level jobs of metropolitan Richmond had moved outside the perimeter of the bus lines, and thus beyond accessibility to lower income citizens, at least half of whom lived in the inner city. A Brookings Institution study published in May 2011 ranked metropolitan Richmond 92nd among the nation's 100 major metropolitan cities in access to jobs by public transportation for working age residents. A bus rapid transit (BRT) route proposed on Broad Street by the Greater Richmond Transit Company (GRTC) in 2010 from downtown Richmond was stopped abruptly at the city line, halfway to the other downtown center of Short Pump, in Henrico County. The county showed no public interest in completing the route or enabling it successfully to link the two primary business and employment centers of the metropolitan city.
[*Color chart 3, see page 191*]

The disintegration of Richmond's political and economic energies into three or four separate jurisdictions, together with continual racial and economic bickering, weakened the city's ability to compete with other growing cities in its region. Charlotte, North Carolina, which had dealt with school integration and metropolitan financial issues in the

1970s by merging services with Mecklenburg County, had also secured progressive banking laws from its state legislature. In the 1990s, Richmond, a banking center since before the Civil War and home of one of the nation's twelve Federal Reserve Banks, lost control over all four of its Virginia-owned banks, three of them to Charlotte. In 1990 and 1991, what had been Richmond's First & Merchants Bank and then Sovran Bank was purchased by the North Carolina National Bank of Charlotte, becoming first NationsBank and later the Bank of America. In 1997 First Union Bank of Charlotte forced Richmond's Signet Bank, formerly Bank of Virginia, to sell out and closed many of its operations. In the same year Wachovia Bank of Winston-Salem, soon to move to Charlotte, bought Richmond's Central Fidelity Bank. United Virginia Bank, named Crestar for a brief period, merged with SunTrust Banks in 1998. Richmond's largest financial services operation, Wheat First Butcher Singer, was purchased by First Union in 1997, and in 2007 the surviving company moved its headquarters to St. Louis. In just seventeen years, after more than a century of prominence, Richmond had ceased to be a headquarters financial center.

The extent of metropolitan Richmond's decentralization can be seen in the increase in value of real property in the surrounding counties. In 1981 the assessed value of real property in Richmond was twenty percent less than that in Henrico. By 2008 Henrico had twice as much real property value as Richmond, Chesterfield had sixty percent

Metro Richmond Property Values in $Billions - 2007

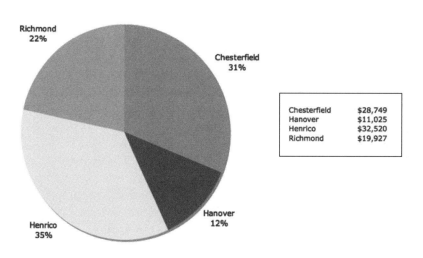

Chesterfield	$28,749
Hanover	$11,025
Henrico	$32,520
Richmond	$19,927

more, and Hanover's property value was growing rapidly. Richmond had only twenty percent of the property value in the four-jurisdiction metropolitan city.

White population in Richmond city diminished steadily through 2000, before reversing in the first decade of the twenty-first century. The concentration of blacks in the city that was present during the battles over segregation and annexation continued through the decade of the seventies; but in the 1980s, an increasing number of African Americans sought the new middle-class housing and the more middle-class school populations of suburban counties, and open housing enforcement made their outmigration possible. Henrico County, whose population had been ninety-three percent white in 1970, was sixty-five percent white in 2009. [*Color chart 4, see page 192*]

Imprisoned in the center

At the core of the metropolitan city of Richmond, whose eight major jurisdictions totaled one million citizens in 2010, was a cluster of 100,000 citizens whose lives were restricted in ways not unlike those of the underprivileged classes of Virginia's past. These citizens, nearly all black, lived in the eastern half of the historic city, and represented fifty percent of its population.

The median household income was below the poverty line, the

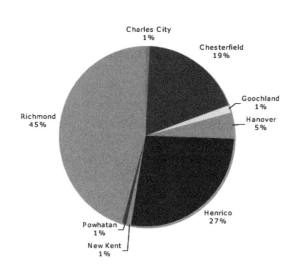

Distribution of Metropolitan Richmond's Poverty by Jurisdiction, 2005-2009

Chart 1: Richmond's Church Hill Plan

Richmond's Church Hill Plan: 1950-1970

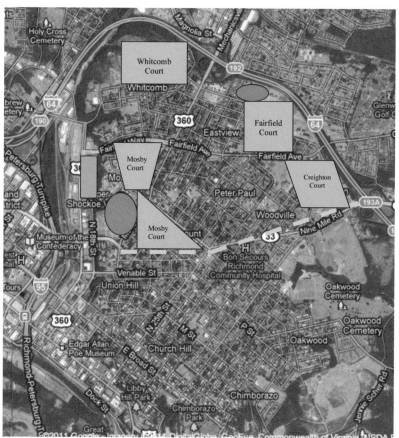

The five Church Hill housing courts are in blue. Schools, in red are Mosby (now Martin Luther King), left, and John F. Kennedy (now Armstrong High School), upper right. Richmond City Jail, in green, is on the left. The secretly planned limited access Leigh Street Expressway bisecting Church Hill, is the yellow broken line across the center of Church Hill.

Chart 2: Four Jurisdiction Population

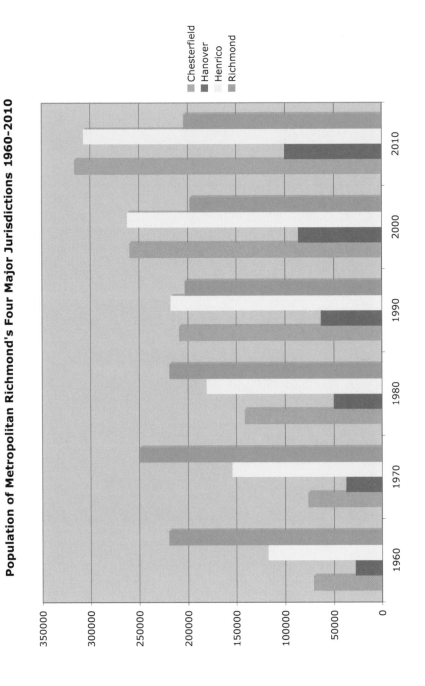

Chart 3: Public Transportation and Jobs

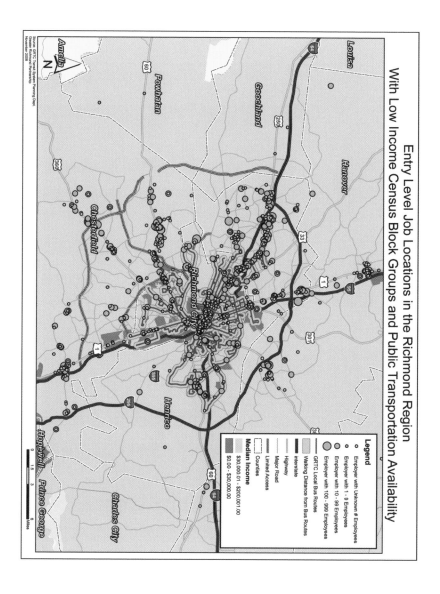

Chart 4: Four Jurisdiction Population by Race

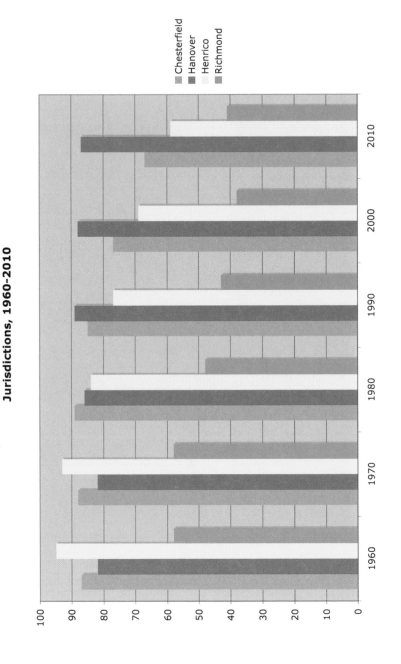

Chart 5: Vehicles per Household

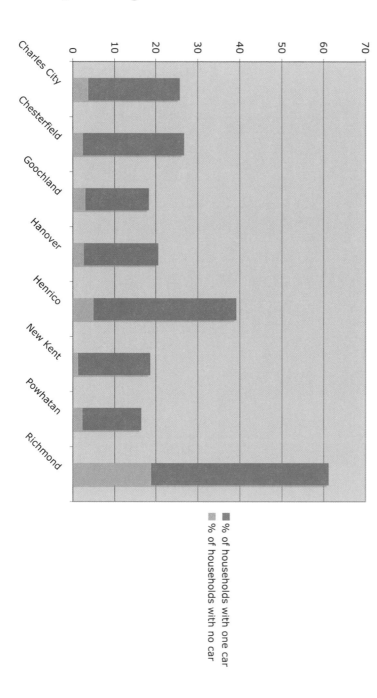

Percentage of Households with no car or one car in metropolitan Richmond 2009

% of households with one car
% of households with no car

Chart 6: Local Government Debt

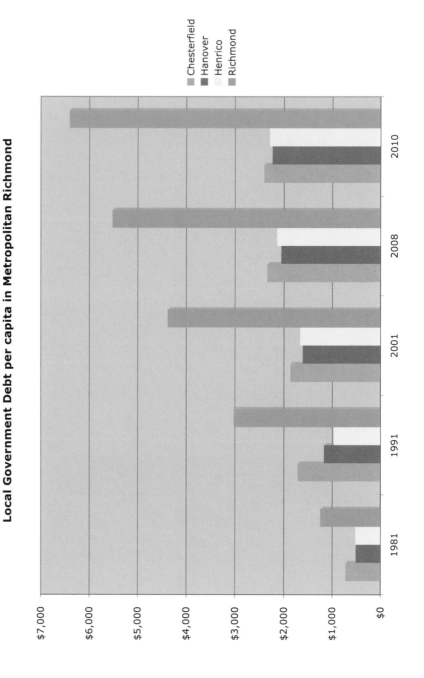

Chart 7: Richmond structural unemployment zone

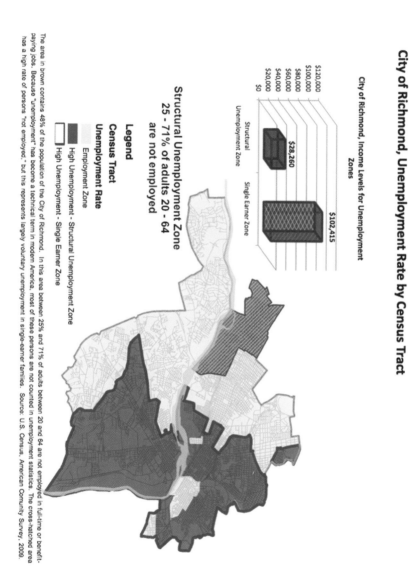

City of Richmond, Unemployment Rate by Census Tract

City of Richmond, Income Levels for Unemployment Zones

$120,000
$100,000
$80,000
$60,000
$40,000
$20,000
$0

Structural Unemployment Zone — $28,260

Single Earner Zone — $102,415

Structural Unemployment Zone
25 - 71% of adults 20 - 64 are not employed

Legend

Census Tract

Unemployment Rate

Employment Zone

High Unemployment - Structural Unemployment Zone

High Unemployment - Single Earner Zone

The area in brown contains 48% of the population of the City of Richmond. In this area between 25% and 71% of adults between 20 and 64 are not employed in full-time or benefit-paying jobs. Because "unemployment" has become a technical term in modern America, most of these persons are not counted in unemployment statistics. The cross-hatched area has a high rate of persons "not employed," but this represents largely voluntary unemployment in single-earner families. Source: U.S. Census, American Comunity Survey, 2009.

*Calculations reflect the State Composite Index formula, and were proposed in the Governor's budget. The formula represents the locality's imputed ability to pay. A higher index entitles a locality to a lower level of support. For FY 2010-2012 the Richmond delegation sought to influence the General Assembly to offset the reduction in support by special appropriation.

Chart 8: Basic state education aid by locality*

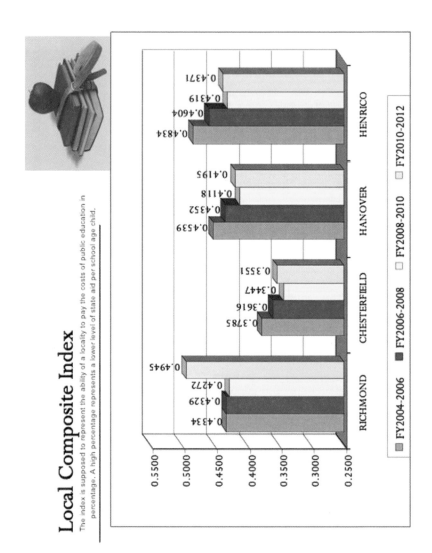

Local Composite Index

The index is supposed to represent the ability of a locality to pay the costs of public education in percentage. A high percentage represents a lower level of state aid and per school age child.

FY2004-2006   ■ FY2006-2008   □ FY2008-2010   □ FY2010-2012

RICHMOND
0.4945
0.4272
0.4329
0.4334

CHESTERFIELD
0.3551
0.3447
0.3616
0.3785

HANOVER
0.4195
0.4118
0.4352
0.4539

HENRICO
0.4371
0.4319
0.4604
0.4834

unemployment rate ranged from twenty-two percent to sixty percent, the high school on-time graduation rate was seventy-five percent, the annual incarceration rate approached ten percent, and the percentage of out-of-wedlock births was in excess of eighty percent. Nineteen percent of the households did not own a car. [*Color chart 5, see page 193*] The children went to schools that were more racially segregated than they had been in 1970, and which were now segregated not only by race but also by income. Within this district lay every unit of public housing constructed in metropolitan Richmond. Few licensed day care centers were available for the children.

The area represented all of Northside Richmond except Ginter Park, all of the East End except the Historic Districts, and all of Southside from Midlothian Turnpike to the James River. Because these citizens were confined to the jurisdiction still called the "city" of Richmond, they were directly affected by the strictures placed on that city during the sessions of the last overtly segregationist General Assembly in 1971.

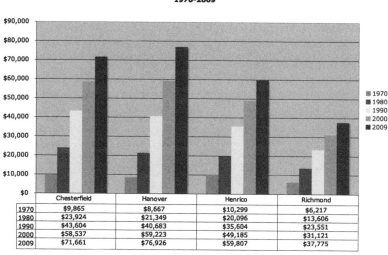

Median Household Income of Metropolitan Richmond's Four Major Jurisdictions, 1970-2009

	Chesterfield	Hanover	Henrico	Richmond
1970	$9,865	$8,667	$10,299	$6,217
1980	$23,924	$21,349	$20,096	$13,606
1990	$43,604	$40,683	$35,604	$23,551
2000	$58,537	$59,223	$49,185	$31,121
2009	$71,661	$76,926	$59,807	$37,775

The city could not annex any further territory, and therefore had no new land for development since 1970. Its population was static. The city had lost its major retail centers to suburban malls and therefore received diminishing income from the local sales tax. The city's base of taxable property was static, but its expenses were higher because its citizenry had a median income half that of the surrounding counties.

Its real estate tax rate was twenty-six percent higher than Chesterfield, thirty-eight percent higher than Henrico, and forty-eight percent higher than Hanover.

Metropolitan Richmond Real Estate taxes per $100 2011	
Charles City	$0.68
Chesterfield	$0.95
Goochland	$0.53
Hanover	$0.81
Henrico	$0.87
New Kent	$0.70
Powhatan	$0.77
Richmond	$1.20

The city's bonded indebtedness per capita was more than twice as high as the three surrounding counties, and since the end of annexation the city had only been able to issue bonds to replace those which fell due. Deferred capital expenditures exceeded $1 billion. [*Color chart 6, see page 194*]

In as many as eighty percent of the city's schools, ninety percent of the students were eligible for free and reduced price lunch, and more than ninety percent were African American. In the three most distressed high schools, one quarter of the student body did not graduate on time.

While the state, through road-building and repair, provided much of the cost of transportation for the suburban counties, it provided only a small subsidy for the bus line of the city and did not require

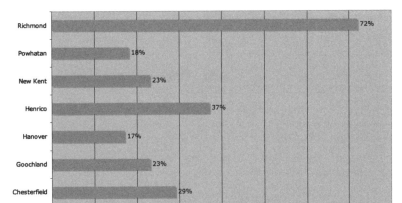

Free and reduced lunch eligibility Metro Richmond Public School systems
2010-2011

counties to allow buses to go to places of employment or retail shopping. Although unemployment in the city of Richmond was at least three times as high as that in the surrounding counties, the Virginia Employment Commission did not maintain an office in the center city. [*Color chart 7, see page 195*]

As many as one-fifth of the households had a member incarcerated or under court supervision every year, and persons were incarcerated in a jail that was overcrowded to nearly two hundred percent of its capacity. The General Assembly provided fifty percent funding for regional jails, that is, jails built by two or more jurisdictions, but only twenty-five percent funding for jails built by one jurisdiction. The state approved funding for fifty percent of the cost of three new regional jails, which the jurisdictions of Henrico, Hanover, and Chesterfield built to share with exurban counties. But when no contiguous locality was willing to join with Richmond to build a facility, state authorities declined to alter or reinterpret the funding criteria in order to replace Richmond's disheveled, overcrowded jail. Rather, they continued to require that the city further overcrowd its jail with as many as three hundred additional state prisoners a day. The state paid the city $4

Richmond City Jail Commitments Fiscal years 2000-2006

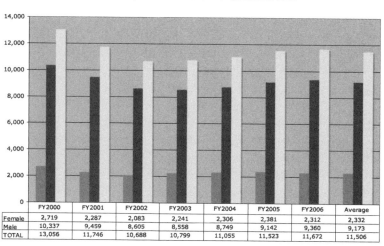

	FY2000	FY2001	FY2002	FY2003	FY2004	FY2005	FY2006	Average
Female	2,719	2,287	2,083	2,241	2,306	2,381	2,312	2,332
Male	10,337	9,459	8,605	8,558	8,749	9,142	9,360	9,173
TOTAL	13,056	11,746	10,688	10,799	11,055	11,523	11,672	11,506

to offset a cost to the city of $42 per day—a deficit of perhaps $3.5 million per year. The jail had no air conditioning, a situation which some persons believed caused the death of a prisoner in the summer of 2010.

Mayor Dwight Jones and City Council were able, in a five-year Capital Improvement Plan for fiscal year 2010-2014, to find a significant bubble in available capital funding capacity. The mayor declared his intention to spend $134.6 million over the five years to replace the city jail and as much as $175 million toward the schools' capital needs. Richmond qualified for 25 percent state funding for the jail, but state authorities indicated the money might not be available.

In 2009 the city created a "stormwater utility," a way of funding capital improvements for drainage by a "service fee" on real estate. The funding mechanism enabled the city to bypass capital budget limitations by using the fee to back as much as $100 million in deferred drainage projects. Unlike conventional real estate taxes, the "stormwater utility fee" was levied against churches, schools, universities, government buildings, and non-profit agencies.

Resegregation of the schools

Beginning in the mid-1950s, metropolitan Richmond's struggle over racial segregation focused on the public schools. The decision of the U. S. Supreme Court in *Brown v. Board of Education* had thrown the state's political leadership into fifteen years of frantic efforts at obstruction, promoted to the public as "Massive Resistance" to the federal courts. It was the decision of Judge Robert Merhige to integrate all of Richmond's schools through "cross-town busing" that precipitated the most severe reactions surrounding the annexation of Chesterfield citizens in 1969 and caused 5,000 of the 8,000 annexed children not to show up for school in the fall.

White leaders frequently used code words to refer to the dangers of racial integration. One of the most frequent was that integration of schools would diminish the "quality" of the education of white children. Once the schools had become completely integrated and the city's suit asking consolidation of schools with the counties had been rejected, editorials and news stories continued for several decades to criticize the "quality" of the Richmond Public Schools.

Long after the deliberate racial positions of the segregationists had been silenced, the habit of attacking the public schools of Richmond stayed in place in the media. In the first decade of the twenty-first century, the theme was even adopted by Richmond's newly elected mayor. Mayor Wilder sought to take control of the schools and to replace the superintendent. He locked the school administration out of City Hall and secretly summoned moving trucks on a weekend to move their offices—an action subsequently enjoined by the local court.

Several months before, twenty-six metropolitan Richmond business leaders, supported by the mayor, had called on the city of Richmond, alone among the jurisdictions in metropolitan Richmond, to surrender the right to elect its own school board.

The Richmond Newspapers, whose editorial pages had led the charge toward Massive Resistance and the prevention of racial integration in schools, continued consistently to provide ammunition for attacks on the public schools on both their front pages and editorial pages through the first decade of the twenty-first century. Hardly a month went by in a forty-year period when there was not either an editorial criticizing the system or a front-page news article on the Richmond city schools that had a critical or controversial cast. Long after Massive Resistance, when journalists would have been appalled to realize they were continuing a pattern begun in anger at racial integration, the unusual habit continued. The coverage stood in stark contrast to the media's absence of critical coverage of county schools, businesses, or governments. In terms of column inches, and often in terms of approach, the coverage of the Richmond Public Schools was remarkable. Several other metro Richmond media, stepping into the well-worn path, picked up the archetypal narrative alleging failure due to incompetence.[359]

Absent from the public narrative was an effective chronicle of the funding disparities of the metropolitan school systems or the challenges of Richmond's unprecedentedly hazardous educational enterprise following more than a century of segregated and unequal education.

In the forty years following Judge Merhige's crosstown-busing decision, the metropolitan school system had been resegregated, and the resegregation carried with it many of the inherent injustices that the court had sought to remedy in its decision in *Brown v. Board of Education.*

The General Assembly of Virginia had crafted a system of de facto jurisdictional racial segregation of schools to replace the prior system of separate segregated school systems within a single jurisdiction. In Richmond and Petersburg,[360] and in several other historic independent cities of the commonwealth, the state cancelled annexation statutes and maintained what were essentially separate public school systems for children who were African American and lower income. School systems in the surrounding counties, with white students in the majority, had varying levels of racial and economic integration in particular schools. Economic disparity was limited by the lack of low income housing in most suburban neighborhoods and by the absence of public transportation. Eastern Henrico had a much higher African-American population than the county's West End, and it was reflected in racial proportions in East End schools. A similar demographic occurred in Chesterfield, but less dramatically.

Richmond City Council had made public education one of its top priorities ever since 1977, and provided the highest level of local expenditure for education in the metropolitan area, despite a population with half the household income of the surrounding counties. As the decades progressed and the system refocused to deal with the intense issues of a highly impoverished school population, test scores and other indicators put the Richmond system in the higher ranks of inner city systems nationwide. The lower graduation rates and higher rates of stress in the

High school	Jurisdiction	% on time
Open	Richmond	100%
Deep Run	Henrico	99.1%
Hanover	Hanover	98.5%
Community	Richmond	97.6%
Cosby	Chesterfield	96.5%
Midlothian	Chesterfield	96.3%
Mills E. Godwin	Henrico	95.7%
Lee Davis	Hanover	95.4%
Atlee	Hanover	95.3%
Douglas Freeman	Henrico	94.3%
Franklin Military	Richmond	93.8%
Matoaca	Chesterfield	92.6%
Thomas Dale	Chesterfield	91.9%
Clover Hill	Chesterfield	91.9%
Patrick Henry	Hanover	91.1%
James River	Chesterfield	91.1%
Charles City	Charles City	89.1%
Monacan	Chesterfield	88.9%
New Kent	New Kent	88.4%
Thomas Jefferson	Richmond	88.1%
Henrico	Henrico	86.1%
Goochland	Goochland	85.8%
Powhatan	Powhatan	85.6%
Manchester	Chesterfield	85.1%
Varina	Henrico	85.0%
Huguenot	Richmond	84.6%
Lloyd C. Bird	Chesterfield	84.0%
Highland Springs	Henrico	83.6%
Hermitage	Henrico	81.9%
J. R. Tucker	Henrico	81.8%
George Wythe	Richmond	81.5%
Meadowbrook	Chesterfield	80.2%
John Marshall	Richmond	75.4%
Armstrong	Richmond	69.3%

On-time graduation rate, Class of 2010 Metropolitan Richmond high schools. Source: Virginia Department of Education

center city schools were consistent with the experience of a segregated low-income population in other cities.

But the costs of segregation were everywhere apparent, and the state of Virginia seemed oblivious and even punitive in its attitude to the situation it had legislated. The Richmond city schools were educating the most impoverished twenty percent of the school age population in the metropolitan city. The most effective tool for this education was racial and social integration in schools where middle class parents, students, resources, and opportunities predominated. But except in special, in-system charter schools such as Richmond Community

High School, Open High School, and in several elementary and middle schools where attendance zones took in a significant number of middle class parents, race and class integration was not a possible strategy for Richmond city. Fifty years after *Brown v. Board of Education* most of the schools were totally segregated by race. A major difference from the previous century was that they were also segregated by income.

Years of experience in urban education had taught Richmond educators strategies necessary to provide equal education to children concentrated in single-race schools with a concentration of low-income students; but these strategies were costly—they involved smaller school units, smaller classes, individual tutoring, and a significant amount of careful individual attention through Individual Education Plans, counseling, and social service support. By 2010 Richmond Public Schools had demonstrated this success in several in-system charter programs, such as the Performance Learning Centers, Franklin Military School, and the specialized high schools, and in a number of elementary schools where the non-profit Communities in Schools, the Micah Association of faith communities, and supportive area corporations had brought in supplementary and volunteer resources to augment school funds.

The finances of metropolitan Richmond's segregated education, however, were hauntingly familiar, and worsened by the economic disparity that had joined racial segregation as an issue. In order to be truly effective across the board with the most stressed twenty percent of the metropolitan school population, the cost of an excellent Richmond system would be from twenty-five to fifty percent more per child than the surrounding counties.

Although Richmond city taxpayers contributed more per child than other area taxpayers were required to do, and although Richmond's level of fiscal distress was already among the highest of any locality in Virginia, the state actually gave the city less basic school aid per child than it gave the surrounding counties. The state funding of local school districts in Virginia was based on a complicated statistical formula called the "local composite index." It purported to compute a locality's "ability to pay" for public education. Regardless of the complex statistical justifications, the index simply resulted in economic discrimination nearly as destructive as the deliberately discriminatory funding of Richmond's segregated black schools in the first half of the twentieth century.[361] ***[Color chart 8, see page 196]***

For example, in January 2011, Governor Robert McDonnell proposed to take an additional $57.6 million away from public education for fiscal year 2012. Of this, fully $5.6 million would come from Richmond's public schools. That is, nearly ten percent of the governor's proposed cuts in funding in Virginia public education were levied against the Richmond Public Schools, who had 1.7% of the commonwealth's public school students.[362] The city's students had the third highest level of poverty among Virginia localities.[363]

State budget calculations also provided for levels of staffing that were frequently unrealistic for a central city school system dealing with high levels of truancy and concentrated poverty. A school system dealing with these issues at this level needs higher numbers of out-of-classroom personnel—assistant principals, counselors, behavioral specialists, security personnel. Thus, an inner city high school in metro Richmond might be calculated to need the same number of these personnel per student as an affluent suburban high school. For many inner city children, the results could only be catastrophic.

Other cost discrimination was even subtler. The isolation of Richmond by the 1971 General Assembly came at a time when the bonded indebtedness of the city was high. By the 1980s Richmond's debt had reached the point where the city could only issue bonds to replace those that retired each year. The resulting austerity plan virtually halted school construction. Meanwhile, many of the schools had reached the limit of their physical lives, especially the "new schools" which had been built hastily and cheaply during the days before integration to "demonstrate" that the segregated system really did intend to be "separate but equal." The normal jurisdictional process in Virginia, where a county decides to sponsor a "bond referendum" for school construction or other purposes, was not available in Richmond. Richmond voters could not approve bonds that the city could not sell on Wall Street. The result of this situation was that many of the city's schools were hopelessly deteriorated, with an average age of 60 years in 2010, and the deferred capital needs of the system approached one billion dollars.

The inner city of Richmond was the major place in which persons lived without private cars available to their household. Whereas seventy percent of the households in the three major suburban counties had two or more cars, sixty-one percent of the households in the city had one car or less. Nineteen percent of the households in the city of Richmond had no car. Thus, school bus transportation was essential, not only for classes, but also for after-school activities and other opportunities that might make the difference of success or failure for inner city children. But additional transportation funds were not available, and Richmond parents did not have the discretionary funds to pay personal money for field trips and other school activities.

In the first decade of the twenty-first century, the "standards" movement came both to Virginia education and to a federal government that had become newly engaged with education. In the ideology of this movement, the answer to segregated inner city education was no longer to be understood as either integration or more resources, but rather the imposition of higher "standards" and, failing a nominally equal performance, firing of personnel, partial privatization, and other draconian measures. Schools that had been resegregated and economically abandoned by the state were now to be labeled "failing schools," with the implication that it was the local teachers and the system leaders who had failed. The state was not held accountable and bore no responsibility. The fault lay not with the legislators and officials who had segregated the systems and then failed to provide remedial resources and support, but with those professionals and leaders who had taken up the challenge of bringing high achievement to students in need.

The Richmond Public Schools were in some ways inured to the new negativity of the national standards movement. The sense of being under attack from state officials and legislators, and from the press, was not new. They had been under public attack for forty years. City superintendents used the standards challenge to stimulate and, as much as possible, to strengthen their program. But the true nature of Richmond's drama was as invisible to the media and the suburban white population as the struggle of the citizens of Jackson Ward had been to the white population of Richmond in the latter half of the nineteenth century, or the emerging civil rights movement had been to the white majority in the 1940s and 50s.

The de facto segregation of the schools continued to be the single most powerful element keeping the jurisdictions of metropolitan Richmond separate from one another. Public education remained the screen upon which the unresolved racial issues of the metropolitan city's history were projected. The General Assembly and state government perpetuated some of the historic inequalities. Although leaders of the metropolitan city's school systems were in frequent contact, metropolitan political leaders had not yet made a collective and concerted plea on behalf of equity for the city schools. There was no effective public vehicle for the collaborative nurture of the metropolitan area's children.

Epilogue:

The healing of metropolitan Richmond

The history of Richmond is the founding history of the nation. There are other founding histories, to be sure. But here at the falls of the James, in a unique way, you can trace the seeds of the nation from its very beginning. Without moving from the spot, you can identify each layer of the nation's physical, social, racial, class, and religious development. The original sins, the great ideals, the failures, and the achievements are here to be seen in a single classroom.

Before 1970, many people in the city at the falls may have believed in racial equality, but it had never been practiced on a widespread basis, and it was actually prohibited by law.

Since 1970 metropolitan Richmond has had the opportunity to practice racial equality. The initial changes were dramatic. A black man became mayor of the former Capital of the Confederacy, and thirteen years later, another African American became governor of the Commonwealth of Virginia. The racial transitions are still going on throughout the metropolitan city. Nearly every school, every major place of employment, every place of public accommodation, and even many faith communities are now at least slightly integrated by race.

Many of the institutions of the metropolitan city, however, may still be viewed as either black-culture or white-culture. This is true of almost all the churches; it is true of most schools and universities; it is true of neighborhoods and many places of employment or job categories within places of employment; and it is true of the jurisdictional governing bodies, political leadership, and administrations.

The city of Richmond's political leadership culture is more black than white, and its administration's leadership is nearly all black. The political leadership culture of the three major surrounding counties is mostly white, as is a significant portion of their administrative leadership. To make observations of this sort is to invite reaction, criticism, anger, or guilt—and therein lies much of metropolitan

Richmond's current problem. There are significant issues still to be dealt with from the metropolitan city's strange history, but they are difficult to talk about. We suspect one another's motives, we are certain of one another's blindness, and we doubt the commitment of anyone, including ourselves, to work toward the best ideals of our best ancestors. White people are uncomfortable with the issue of racism, and black people are wary of racism. White and black persons—all of us—are congenitally blind to the experience of the other. The years of close association have brought us familiarity, but not understanding. We have been in one another's territory, but for different reasons, under different conditions, and with different experiences. The differences are vast.

Forty years of mandatory desegregation have not only brought integration to metropolitan Richmond—they have also brought disintegration. The great, comprehensive mixing of black and white that the white supremacists feared was averted not by massive resistance, but by urban sprawl. Laws permitting racial segregation were struck down. But laws establishing jurisdictional boundaries were firmly reinforced. The result was an explosion of the city across the landscape of central Virginia. The city's first 200,000 people needed sixty square miles. Its next 800,000 people needed an additional 1,000 square miles. The population density of the three newly urban jurisdictions is only twenty-five percent as great as the original jurisdiction.

During the first forty years after full integration of Richmond's public schools, and the thirty-three years after the establishment of a black majority government in Richmond, metro Richmonders erected massive new retail centers in Henrico and Chesterfield counties and constructed more than one billion dollars worth of highways to circumvent the central city. Major office and industrial development located on the new roads capitalized on the booming economic development of the nation, and bled the economic base of the older, central city. Sprawling development of new subdivisions, whose housing cost excluded modest wage earners, reconfigured the population map.

The new suburban development specifically segregated citizens by income category and by physical distance to a degree never before present in metro Richmond. Suburban development followed road construction, paid for by the state and federal governments, and was based on the assumption that households could afford two or more automobiles. The dominant vision assumed no public transportation would be available. None was provided. Economic encapsulation of the "independent city" of Richmond by the General Assembly relieved the new suburban citizens of any responsibility for the massive capital debt of the previous century. It excluded much of the cost burden of the center city's government offices, universities, churches, public housing, and non-profit headquarters that were exempt from real estate tax. Lower real estate tax rates established the suburban counties as virtual "enterprise zones," subsidizing sprawling economic development.

Racial integration was present throughout the new suburban development, in the sense that there was no absolute segregation. But most housing, and most suburban schools, were highly concentrated in one racial group or another. Other minority ethnic groups began to concentrate in the older parts of the suburban counties.

By 2010, with the completion of the circumferential highway around metropolitan Richmond, development was increasing on the periphery of the four-jurisdiction city, involving the exurban counties of Powhatan, Goochland, Charles City, and New Kent. The pace of sprawl was greater than in any other metropolitan area in Virginia.

The four jurisdictions making up the central portion of metropolitan Richmond reported they were spending $2.8 billion each year to provide governmental operations and services for 900,000 citizens who were spread across 1,200 square miles, an expenditure of $3,234 per citizen. The population was nearly the same as the population of Virginia's most populous single jurisdiction, Fairfax County, but the population density was less than one-third of that jurisdiction. Metropolitan Richmond's governments were dependent on the Commonwealth of Virginia for thirty-five percent of their income, while Fairfax County was receiving less than eighteen percent of its income from the state.[364]

Many commuting patterns, and nearly all retail shopping patterns, bypassed the central city of Richmond. The core industries of government, finance, tobacco, medicine, law, and education still drew workers downtown, but an increasing number of citizens of metropolitan Richmond had no knowledge of the central city. They knew nothing of the tumultuous years from 1607 to 1970, either because they were born afterward or because they had just moved from another city to a Richmond suburb. The paved parking lot covering Lumpkin's Slave Jail and the Burial Ground for Africans in Shockoe Valley meant little to them. Racial integration had already occurred so far as they were concerned. The struggles of Richmonders with their history seemed quaint and inexplicable. If the new generations and newcomers were submerged in the history of the place, they did not know it.

The Law and the prophets

Beneath the economic and political development of any society is a spiritual reality. It represents the complex of motivations and dreams that a people have developed or that have called them together. On a daily basis, however, leaders of the government, business, and education do not treat these spiritual issues as influential in economic or social development. Neither, surprisingly, do most religious leaders. So there are few scholars or leaders who would consider or admit publicly that the present state of metropolitan Richmond is related to unhealed history or spiritual illness.

This is not the position of the major prophets and religious leaders who are honored by the majority of the citizens of metropolitan Richmond, however. The great Hebrew prophets and Jesus attributed the health, and the ultimate survival, of a city to its spiritual vision and moral practice. There are parallel texts in the other great religions and in the secular political thinkers who helped to inspire the American Revolution. Significant portions of the prophetic writings in the Hebrew scriptures and the teaching of Jesus in the Gospels are directed toward this topic. Jesus' haunting words about the city of Jerusalem forty years before its destruction are well known: "Jerusalem, Jerusalem, the city that kills the prophets and stones those who are sent to it! How often have I desired to gather your children together as a hen gathers her brood under her wings, and you were not willing!"[365]

Richmond, the city at the falls of the James, a settlement going back thousands of years into the history of the native peoples, is locked in the most important battle of its history. This is a battle against its own denial, against its own fatigue, against its own disintegrated vision, against its own futility, against its own unhealed history. It is a struggle with the dull debilitation of inherited hypocrisy and infidelity. It is a battle against surrender, not to an external enemy, but to an internal one—a renunciation of the dream of the city itself.

Richmond faces its greatest opportunity—an opportunity sensed by Powhatan when he thought, however fleetingly, that the English settlers might be a part of his confederation; an opportunity sensed in the Great Awakening and the Declaration of Independence by many people of central Virginia; an opportunity proclaimed after 363 years by African Americans in the last half of the twentieth century—the opportunity to live its religious faith and its ideals as one people united in a metropolitan city which includes different races and economic levels and is organized for the common good.

America, Virginia, and metropolitan Richmond are nothing without these ideals. They were stated here, and if they are forsaken, the failure will be lived here. Like all the nations and cities of the past, Richmond may someday pass away. But here, for this moment in time, we have the potential to be who it was our ancestors of all races, in their best selves, wanted us to be—a city of hope and justice for all its citizens.

All that is missing is the will to succeed. The people and resources are present. The history of the city at the falls provides a foundation either for success or failure. But the vision and the will must be unashamedly kindled and revived. Here, at the beginning of Richmond's fifth century as a multiracial settlement, the choice can be made to seek a great future, or to surrender to an inner enemy far more destructive than any race or class or nation.

Richmond's unhealed history is not irrelevant. It is the key to metropolitan Richmond's ultimate success, because it reveals to us more clearly than anything else the unconscious forces that bind us.

The common wealth

What makes a great city is its common wealth. A city is a concentration of human beings of different races and professions, religions and occupations, which provides an integrated economy and enables excellence. The city can develop culture at a higher level, because of the specialization and the concentration of interest that is present, as well as the ability to pool resources for different purposes. Every city is a laboratory for human justice as well. It provides opportunity for evil and destruction; and it provides opportunity for persons of faith and vision.

Metropolitan Richmond is a wealthy city. It is wealthy in experience, history, culture, diversity, and idealism. Some of the greatest leaders of our nation—Native American, European, and African American—have been born here, lived here, and led here. Metropolitan Richmond is also financially wealthy. If it were not wealthy, it could not have supported the extraordinarily expensive and sprawling capital investment of the past forty years.

The great cities of the world accumulate a common wealth, however, and this wealth is ultimately built not by sprawl but by complementary investment. By investing together in the same physical area, and addressing an inclusive body of citizens, people increase the quality of life for all. The investment and effort of each citizen benefits not only himself or herself, but also those who live in the same city with them.

Unquestionably, Chesterfield, Henrico, Hanover, and Richmond— the central metropolitan city of Richmond—will never again see greatness without full economic and political cooperation with each other. Under increasing pressure from many diverse geographic sections, the state will do nothing to help Richmond city without the unanimous advocacy of the surrounding counties. It is also unlikely that it will continue to fund four jurisdictions in metropolitan Richmond with twice the funding it gives Fairfax County. But the resources of the four-jurisdiction city of metropolitan Richmond are sufficient for its needs, even for innovative strategies to help those who have been locked in an economic prison by Richmond's unhealed history. And the greatness metropolitan Richmond has longed for is available, perhaps for both the first and last time, by facing its original sin.

The next decades will not permit the level of unrestrained sprawling development that occurred in the last four, if for no other reason than that the Virginia Department of Transportation is out of money. Metropolitan Richmond has already built a basic infrastructure that can support three times its present population. In the coming decades, the task of focused leadership will be to fill in, restore, and strengthen the communities around that basic infrastructure. The result of such policies would be to increase the common wealth, while maximizing individual opportunities. The increase in common wealth is then a bonus to all citizens.

Substantial economies are available to metropolitan Richmond by taking advantage of the infrastructure already built both in the older city and the newer suburbs. Substantial economies are also available in government. No corporation in the American economy would have survived the last forty years if it had insisted on retaining eight separate and identical headquarters operations for one million people living adjacent to one another. But that is what metropolitan Richmond has done. The economies available from consolidation of governmental services are obvious, and the cost of separation is a luxury—or a liability—no longer affordable.

But the penalty for divided jurisdictions and governments is vastly greater than the bill for maintaining separate operations. While metropolitan Richmond's leaders were busy over the last forty years fighting among their fragmented jurisdictions, vying for businesses, abandoning and opening massive shopping centers, trying to keep poor people in other jurisdictions, struggling to build four identical balanced sub-economies, and worrying about race and income levels of citizens, other middle-sized cities in our region stole our entire banking industry, built light rail systems, renewed their downtown areas, acquired major league sports teams, and developed public education systems far more competitive than either metropolitan Richmond's suburban or urban systems. They built the same highways, suburbs, and shopping centers as metro Richmond, but the resulting common wealth was much greater and the larger city prospered.

For the poor, the common wealth is not peripheral but essential. It may be a matter of choice or convenience for a middle-class person to have access to a bus or light rail system; but to a person earning minimum wage, public transportation is life and death. It may be a matter of preference for some people to locate near a public school of their choice or to send their children to private school; but for many wage earners and single parents, there is no choice. The education that is at hand is all that is available.

The economic and political isolation of central Richmond from the healthy, growing economies of the surrounding counties is a recipe for moral and economic disaster. It has the effect of deliberately excluding the poor from the benefits of economic development, locking them up in a no-growth, no-job zone. It forces the creation of special systems of transportation and education exclusively for the poor, systems that are costly and which are never fully funded—systems that increase isolation and contribute to the repetition of poverty over generations. When low-income persons are primarily African American—as they are, due to Richmond's racial history—the economic segregation is de facto racial segregation as well.

The moral vision of metropolitan Richmond must be inclusive. We cannot discriminate by race or family of origin—unless we want to lose our own moral core. If we give up the struggle for our moral core, no matter how conflicted we have been in our history, we will disintegrate and ultimately destroy the metropolitan city of Richmond, Henrico, Chesterfield, Hanover, and surrounding jurisdictions.

The economic vision of metropolitan Richmond must be inclusive. Only a healthy, integrated economy, without artificial boundaries of jurisdiction and tax district, can efficiently allocate resources, create good public systems, and make it possible for all to have mobility within the system. Moral necessity and economic necessity reinforce each other. Deliberate discrimination and division will destroy us. These truths are self-evident.

Metropolitan Richmond needs an effective vehicle for good citizenship. It needs a way in which people who care about healing the past and care about the common wealth of the metropolitan city can seek both their own welfare and the welfare of the entire community. Our committed citizens should not be forced to choose between responsibility for the needs of the city and the energy of urban life on the one hand, and sociological balance and a good child-rearing neighborhood on the other. It is tragically destructive. Metropolitan Richmond needs vision, and the vision needs a vehicle for greatness.

For 370 years the leaders of Richmond skillfully manipulated the structures of government—sometimes for good and sometimes for evil. Great visionaries who established the United States of America met, and many of them lived, here in this metropolitan city. Because they believed in liberty and democracy, and a combination of local government and collective strength, they fashioned governmental structures to carry these ideals out. Having formed a collective vision, they rallied one another to make it happen. They also fashioned and maintained, in most ingenious fashion, a demonic culture of slavery and segregation that took nearly four centuries to begin to dismantle. Central Virginia's leaders have been some of the greatest governmental innovators of the world for four centuries.

But the silence of the present moment is deafening. The frantic suburban sprawl and the despair of the central core of metropolitan Richmond mirror one another in a macabre dance. The common wealth of centuries is allowed to drain away, squandered in denial of common vision, duplication of resources, multiplication of uncoordinated efforts, and professions of helplessness by powerful people.

The economic crisis of the twenty-first century's second decade provides great opportunity for timely innovation. Metropolitan Richmond is in an ideal position to step forward. But there must be vision, desire, determination, a sense of greatness, and for those who can do so, a commitment to prayer. The time is short, but the rewards can be magnificent. The big picture—a dynamic metropolitan city able to direct its energies to its collective moral and economic strength—is the commanding vision.

Metropolitan Richmond must have a political structure that will reflect the reality of the metropolitan city. The specifics of the structure can be worked out by persons who share the goal. Without that shared desire among people from the entire metropolitan city, nothing can happen. With it, the particular strategies will emerge.

To stimulate the thinking, it may be helpful to make certain suggestions:

- A university or civic organization should immediately commission a study of the realistic fiscal savings available from consolidation of some or all services of the multiple governments.
- Metropolitan leaders should develop strategies to address the impossible burden of capital debt faced by the city of Richmond so that the ability to maintain a common public infrastructure can be restored.
- Discussion needs to focus immediately on structural changes, not simply cooperation between jurisdictions. The jurisdictions often cooperate very well within the limits assured by the current structure.
- A common and urgent planning effort, based on a single economy rather than multiple parallel jurisdictional economies, should be inaugurated.
- The jurisdictions should commit themselves to common advocacy and a common program in the General Assembly.
- Spiritual and religious leaders must take responsibility for the conversation along with economic, non-profit, and political leaders.
- Common projects—rapid rail from Washington to Virginia's capital, a light rail or bus rapid transit system along major corridors, a full-scale, university-based, professional training institute for all public school systems, a strategic and honest job training and preparation program for chronically unemployed—need to be identified and designed immediately.

A single elected leadership is essential to a dynamic metropolitan city. The underlying framework will probably be some form of metropolitan "federalism"—that is, the initial consolidation of some major services together with the maintenance of separation in others. Such a structure would permit pragmatic development and negotiation during the years to come as situations change, limitations appear, and benefits become apparent.

Time is short. The economic woes of the next decade have already begun. The metropolitan Richmond jurisdictions are more dependent upon the state government than other jurisdictions, and cuts in state funding will have significant impact. The economic reformation of the nation forced by global movements will reward metropolitan cities that have their act together and fiercely penalize those who don't.

Here in metropolitan Richmond, black and white and Indian people and others, urban and suburban people, people from north and south of the river, church people and people in synagogues and mosques, can revive the vision of a great city at the falls of the James— or perhaps make it honest and true for the first time.

There was, after all, a heresy being acted out at the falls on May 26, 1607. John Smith and Christopher Newport said they intended to create a nation of mutual respect among races, where all would benefit. But they did not mean it. They said they believed in a God of justice and equality, but they practiced a policy of conquest and privilege. For nearly four centuries, many churches and other religious groups in Richmond tacitly accepted that heresy, allowing political leaders to practice oppression, racism, and systemic injustice while acting as if religion were about something else "more spiritual."

At the time of the American Revolution, church leaders backed away and handed over the question of slavery to secular assemblies. There, the architects of the new nation betrayed their own political and religious ideals at the same time they proclaimed them. Some of the world's greatest proponents of freedom and equality shamefully perpetuated a slave republic in their own state and in its capital city.

But ironically, the ultimate seeds of redemption may have come from those very same architects of the new secular state. They established a context for religious faith that would no longer be captive either to the English crown or to the new American government elected by white male property owners. In Richmond in 1786, barely two hundred yards from the island on the James River where Smith and Newport planted King James' cross, Virginia's General Assembly enacted the Statute for Religious Freedom. It forbade, on theological grounds, establishment of religion by the state.

That statute became the basis for the religious freedom clause in the Bill of Rights. Some saw in it the denial of religion. But its result has been a spiritual environment far more dynamic than that of any Western nation where religion has been established by the government. The established religions of Europe had been subverted by political and economic power, and used to justify imperial ambitions. Their integrity had been compromised and their prophetic energy, dissipated.

But disestablishment made available to Virginians the surprising energies of free religion, genuine faith, uncompromising prophecy, and true patriotism. We are free to practice true religion as we discern it and to seek to carry it out in our daily affairs, with a freedom denied to our ancestors. We neither suffer the restrictions under which they operated, nor can we use their same excuses.

True religion seeks justice, not exploitation—proper behavior, not domination of others. True worship of God begins with straightforward respect of other people. The men who planted the cross at the falls on May 24, 1607 promised justice, but did not give it. Now, more than four hundred years later, we can, if we will, renounce that original heresy and claim for this settlement the integrity that was absent at the beginning.

Many in metropolitan Richmond—patriots, citizens, and persons of faith—want to complete now—here at the falls of the James—the establishment of a great city based on our original principles, making possible a genuine citizenship that serves the common wealth. It is the most realistic aspiration for metropolitan Richmond, and it is the most moral as well. It is the ultimate redemption of Richmond's unhealed history.

The Virginia Civil Rights Memorial in Capitol Square in Richmond honors and quotes Virginian Barbara Rose Johns. Johns, aged 16 at the time, organized fellow students to walk out of R.R. Moton High School in Farmville on April 23, 1951, an action which would help to spark the U. S. Supreme Court decision that racially segregated schools are inherently unequal. The memorial was dedicated July 21, 2008. The sculptor is Stanley Bleifeld.

Endnotes

1 Gabriel Archer, "A relation of the discovery of our river from James Fort into the main, made by Captain Christofer Newport, and sincerely written and observed by a gentleman of the colony," in Edward Wright Haile, ed., *Jamestown Narratives: Eyewitness Accounts of the Virginia Colony: The First Decade: 1607–1617* (Champlain, VA: Roundhouse, 1998), 109.

2 Mark Kurlansky, *Cod* (New York, Penguin Books, 1998), 51.

3 John Rut explored from Labrador to the Spanish West Indies in 1527; Richard Hore reached Newfoundland in 1536 in an ill-fated expedition that was marred by cannibalism among starving adventurers.

4 Haile, ed., *Jamestown Narratives*, 4-5.

5 Borgia, a Spaniard, was made a saint by Pope Clement X in 1670.

6 Clifford M. Lewis, S.J. and Albert J. Loomie, S.J., *The Spanish Jesuit Mission in Virginia 1570-1572* (Chapel Hill: Published for the Virginia Historical Society by the University of North Carolina Press, 1953), 20.

7 Ibid., 56.

8 Karen Ordahl Kupperman, *The Jamestown Project* (Cambridge: Harvard, 2007), 105. Soldiers from Jamestown attacked the major Paspahegh village, massacring its inhabitants, in 1610.

9 John Smith, "A True Relation of such occurrences and accidents of note as hath hapíned in Virginia since the first planting of that colony which is now resident in the south part thereof, till the last return from thence," 1608, in Haile, ed., *Jamestown Narratives*, 160.

10 Mary Frances Schjonberg, "General Convention renounces Doctrine of Discovery," *Episcopal Life Online* (August 27, 2009). http://www.episcopalchurch.org/79901_114001_ENG_HTM.htm.

11 "The Letters Patents graunted by her Maiestie to Sir Humfrey Gilbert, knight, for the inhabiting and planting of our people in America," in Richard Hakylut, *Principal Navigations, Voyages, Traffiques and Discoveries of the English Nation*, Volume XII, America, Part I (Adelaide: University of Adelaide Library eBooks 2010). http://ebooks.adelaide.edu.au/h/hakluyt/voyages.

12 Robert J. Miller, "Christians, Indians, and the Doctrine of Discovery," unpublished paper produced for *Consultation on the Missiology of Jamestown 1607 and its*

Implications for 2007 and Beyond (Virginia Beach, May 27-29, 2008), 2. The list of doctrines is a precise quotation from that paper. A professor at Lewis & Clark Law School in Portland, Oregon, Miller teaches Indian law courses and civil procedure. He has also been a part-time tribal judge since 1995 for many Northwest tribes and is currently the chief justice of the Court of Appeals for the Grand Ronde Tribe. Cp. Robert J. Miller, *Native America, Discovered and Conquered: Thomas Jefferson, Lewis & Clark and Manifest Destiny* (Praeger Publishers, 2006), forward by Elizabeth Furse.

13 Ibid., 1.

14 Gerald Roe Crone, "Hakluyt, Richard" in *Encyclopaedia Britannica* (8:554), 15th edition, 1974. Crone was Librarian and Map Curator of the Royal Geographical Society.

15 Hakluyt, Richard, *A Discourse on Western Planting* (1584, printed 1877. Adelaide: University of Adelaide Library eBooks 2010). http://ebooks.adelaide.edu.au/h/hakluyt/planting/, Chapter IV.

16 Ibid., Chapter XVIII.

17 Ibid., Chapter XI.

18 Edward L. Bond, untitled paper prepared for *Consultation on the Missiology of Jamestown 1607 and its Implications for 2007 and Beyond* (Virginia Beach, May 27-29, 2008), 2.

19 William L. Crashaw, "Epistle Dedicatory" to "Good News from Virginia," by Alexander Whitaker, 1613, in Haile, ed. *Jamestown Narratives*, 708.

20 Ibid., 730-732. Haile says that John Rolfe told Purchas in 1616 that he doubted Whitaker would still maintain that the Indians sacrificed children.

21 Hakluyt, *Discourse,* Chapter I.

22 G. MacLaren Brydon, *Virginia's Mother Church* (Richmond: Virginia Historical Society, 1947), 52. See also Grace Steele Woodward, *Pocahontas* (Norman: University of Oklahoma Press, 1969), 57.

23 Susan Myra Kingsbury, ed., *The Records of the Virginia Company of London* (Washington: Government Printing Office, 1905), Introduction, 14.

24 George Percy, "Observations gathered out of a discourse of the plantation of the southern colony in Virginia, 1606," in Haile, ed., *Jamestown Narratives*, 85.

25 Ibid., 94.

26 John Smith, *"General Historie,"* III:12, in Haile, ed., *Jamestown Narratives,* 332.

27 Henry Spelman, "Relation of Virginia, 1609," in Haile, ed., *Jamestown Narratives,* 482. Ivor Noël Hume, [*The Virginia Adventure* (New York: Alfred A. Knopf, 1994), 246] says "there were still close to two hundred" Englishmen at Jamestown and scattered among "friendly" native villages.

28 The stone was moved and now stands overlooking the river in Chimborazo Park, in east Richmond.

29 "A True Declaration of the State of Virginia," 1610, cited in Hume, *Virginia Adventure,* 260.

30 William Crashaw, "Epistle Dedicatory" to Alexander Whitaker's "Good News from Virginia," in Haile, ed., *Jamestown Narratives,* 700.

31 Ibid., 702.

32 Ibid., 705.

33 Peter Linebaugh and Marcus Rediker, *The Many-Headed Hydra: Sailors, Slaves, Commoners, and the Hidden History of the Revolutionary Atlantic* (Boston: Beacon Press, 2000), 12-13.

34 William Strachey, "A True Reportory of the Wreck and Redemption of Sir Thomas Gates, Knight, upon and from the Islands of the Bermudas" (London 1610) in Camilla Townsend, *Pocahontas and the Powhatan Dilemma* (New York: Hill and Wang, 2004), 97.

35 George Percy, "A True Relation of the proceedings and occurrents of moment which have hap'ned in Virginia from the time Sir Thomas Gates was shipwrack'd upon the Bermudes, anno 1609, until my departure out of the country, which was in anno Domini 1612," in Haile, ed., *Jamestown Narratives*, 509-510.

36 The Commonwealth of Virginia dedicated, on August 11, 2007, in a ceremony at the Chickahominy Tribal Center, a highway marker acknowledging the massacre. The marker is on Virginia Route 5, about a mile east of the Chickahominy River bridge.

37 Hume, *Virginia Adventure*, 299, citing William Strachey, "For the Colony of Virginea Britannia: Lawes Divine, Morall, and Martiall," (June 22, 1611), 20.

38 The Latin form of the town's name, "Henricus," is used in some sources, and "Henrico" in others. It was named for Henry, the Prince of Wales, son of King James I of England.

39 "A Brief Declaration of the plantation of Virginia during the first twelve years, when Sir Thomas Smith was governor of the Company, and down to this present time. By the Ancient Planters now remaining alive in Virginia," in Haile, ed., *Jamestown Narratives*, 900. Cited in Robert Hunt Land, "Henrico and its College," in *William and Mary College Quarterly Historical Magazine*, 2nd Ser., 18, no. 4. (Oct. 1938): 466-467.

40 Letter from Thomas Dale preserved in Ralph Hamor, "A True Discourse of the Present Estate of Virginia, and the Success of the Affairs there till the 18 of June, 1614; together with a Relation of the Several English Towns and Forts, the assured Hopes of that Country, and the Peace concluded with the Indians; the Christening of Powhatan's Daughter, and her Marriage with an Englishman," (1614), in Haile, ed., *Jamestown Narratives,* 841.

41 The southernmost point of Farrar's Island, the neck on which Henrico was located, is now occupied by Dominion's Chesterfield Power Station. During the Civil War, U.S. General Ben Butler cut through the neck's northernmost point at Dutch Gap, to bypass Southern batteries and shorten by seven miles the route to Richmond for his gunboats, destroying the remains of the town. What is left of the site is now divided between Henrico and Chesterfield County and has been rebuilt as Henricus Park. The current channel of the river is the excavated Dutch Gap channel, and Henricus Park is separated from the north bank of the river by that channel. Map of James River at Henrico and Dutch Gap is taken from the "Map of the defenses of Richmond & Petersburg" (U. S. Army, Official Records Atlas, Plate C, #2). Prepared by Nathaniel Micheler, 1865. From M. D. Gorman, www.CivilWarRichmond.com (June 20, 2010).

42 Hamor, "A True Discourse," in Haile, ed., *Jamestown Narratives,* 824-825.

43 Deanna Beacham, of the Virginia Council on Indians, points out that what may have seemed absurd to the English was in fact consistent with the matrilineal family structure of the Algonquians. (Interview with author, 28 September 2009).

44 Letter of the Virginia Company dated August 1618 in response to one from Argall dated March 1618 in Kingsbury, ed., *Records of the Virginia Company*, 2:52-53, 3:92, cited in Townsend, *Pocahontas*, 161n.

45 Hume, *Virginia Adventure*, 333.

46 Powhatan used the words "brother" and "daughter" to describe a familial relationship of trust, but not necessarily of physical origin.

47 Proceedings of the Virginia Assembly 1619 in Lyon Gardiner Tyler, *Narratives of Early Virginia 1606-1625* (New York: Charles Scribner's Sons, 1907) 274. See Kingsbury, *Records*, 3:174-5.

48 Tyler, *Narratives*, 275.

49 Sir George Yeardley to Sir Edwin Sandys, 1619-20, in Kingsbury, *Records*, 3:128, cited in Townsend, *Pocahontas*, 163-4.

50 Land, "Henrico and its College," 474-475.

51 When the Virginia Company was dissolved and all hope of the university was gone, Nicholas Ferrar, Jr. went to Yorkshire and founded, with George Herbert, a religious community called Little Gidding.

52 John Rolfe, Letter to Sir Edwin Sandys, 8 June 1617, in Haile, ed., *Jamestown Narratives*, 888. Although plans for the university as well as for cultural assimilation in the colony state this belief and recommend the strategy of raising Indian children in colonial homes or institutions, there is no indication that it proved true in practice.

53 Land, "Henrico and its College," 478.

54 George Thorpe and John Pory to Sir Edwin Sandys, May 15, 1622, in Kingsbury, *Records,* I: 588, III: 446-448.

55 Land, "Henrico and its College", 496-497.

56 Kingsbury's *Records of the Virginia Company*, cited in Land, "Henrico and its College," 493.

57 Deanna Beacham, Interview, September 28, 2009. See Frederic W. Gleach, *Powhatan's World and Colonial Virginia* (Lincoln: The University of Nebraska Press, 1997), 148-158.

58 Land, "Henrico and its College," 495.

59 Edmund S. Morgan, *American Slavery, American Freedom: The Ordeal of Colonial Virginia.* (New York: W.W. Norton & Company, 1975), 100.

60 Hume, *Virginia Adventure*, 384, citing a letter from Robert Bennett to Edward Bennett, Bennetes Wellcome, June 9, 1623. 61 Ibid., 385.

62 Morgan, *American Slavery, American Freedom*, 100.

63 Opechancanough's fortress, called "the Island," was located near Manquin, just south of Route 360, on what is now Pampatike Farm.

64 Helen Rountree and E. Randolph Turner, *Before and After Jamestown: Virginia's Powhatans and their Predecessors* (Gainesville: University Press of Florida, 2002), 154; Hume, *Virginia Adventure*, 393–394.

65 Rountree and Turner, *Before and After Jamestown,* 154.

66 Ibid., 155-156. After 1700, colonial authorities were able to identify only small groups of Indians living together as survivors of the first century of English occupation. It is certain, however, that many more existed uncounted and in unobtrusive situations.

67 Powhatan was both the name and title of the Pamunkey chief who led the group of 30 tribes who lived in and controlled Tsenacomoco when the English arrived. It was also the name of his village at the falls of the James, the location of the present-day city of Richmond. The chief's personal family name was Wahunsenaca.

68 *Captain Smith and Pocahontas,* fresco by Constantino Brumidi, 1880. Scene in the Rotunda frieze, U.S. Capitol, Washington, D.C.

69 *Preservation of Captain John Smith by Pocahontas.* Sandstone relief by Antonio Capellano, 1825. Located in the U.S. Capitol Rotunda, above west door.

70 Raymond C. Dingledine, Jr., Lena Barksdale, and Marion B. Nesbitt, *Virginia's History and Geography* (New York: Charles Scribner's Sons, 1965), 30-36.

71 John Gadsby Chapman, oil on canvas, 12' x 18'. Commissioned 1837; placed 1840, in the Capitol Rotunda. John Gadsby Chapman depicted Pocahontas, wearing white, being baptized "Rebecca" by Anglican minister Alexander Whitaker in Jamestown. She kneels, surrounded by family members and colonists. Her brother Nantequaus turns away from the ceremony while her uncle Opachisco looks on. Opechancanough and a sister are also portrayed. The baptism took place before her marriage to Englishman John Rolfe, who stands behind her. Their union is said to be the first recorded marriage between a European and a Native American. The scene symbolizes the belief of Americans at the time that Native Americans should accept Christianity and other European ways. Chapman (1808-1889), born in Alexandria, Virginia, studied in Italy. He became known for his portrait and historical paintings and his rich use of color.

72 The pamphlet was written by Chapman himself. Stephen Tompkins, Lehigh University http://www.lehigh.edu/~ejg1/natimag/pocahontas.htm, August 1998. See also http://xroads.virginia.edu/~cap/POCA/Pocanew3.html.

73 "An Act to preserve racial integrity," ch. 371, 1924 Va. Acts 534, 535. Law with hidden, specialized racial intention is an art form in Virginia legislative history.

74 Convention on the Prevention and Punishment of the Crime of Genocide. Adopted by Resolution 260 (III) A of the U.N. General Assembly on 9 December 1948. See "Letter from Treasurer and Council of Virginia to the Governor and Captain General of Virginia and Council of Estate", in Philip Barbour, *Pocahontas,* 209-211.

75 Dr. Linwood "Little Bear" Custalow and Angela L. "Silver Star" Daniel, *The True Story of Pocahontas* (Golden, CO: Fulcrum Publishing, 2007), 7.

76 Townsend, *Pocahontas,* 13-14.

77 John Smith, "A True Relation..., in Haile, ed., *Jamestown Narratives,* 160-161.

78 John Smith, *General Historie* III:46-49, cited in Grace Steele Woodward, *Pocahontas* (Norman: University of Oklahoma Press, 1969), 71.

79 John Smith, "A True Relation...," in Haile, ed., *Jamestown Narratives,* 181.

80 William Strachey, "The History of Travel into Virginia Britannia," cap. V, in Haile, ed., *Jamestown Narratives,* 630.

81 Townsend, *Pocahontas,* 73, citing Smith, *Map of Virginia,* 1:137-9.

82 John Smith, *General Historie* III:12, in Haile, ed., *Jamestown Narratives,* 336.

83 William Strachey, *The History of Travel into Virginia Britannia* III, in Haile, ed., *Jamestown Narratives,* 619-620. "They often reported unto us that Powhatan had then living 20 sons and 20 daughters [including]...young Pocohuntas, a daughter of his using sometimes to our fort in times past, now married to a private captain called Kocoum...."

84 Custalow and Daniel (*True Story of Pocahontas,* 90) say that Pocahontas has many descendants through the line of Little Kocoum, and that among those currently alive is the well-known entertainer Wayne Newton. But there is no firm evidence that she had a child by Kocoum.

85 Henry Spelman calls the town he visits Paspatanzie. It may be the same town, or another inland and several miles south. There is no certainty that the town at modern Indian Point in Stafford County was identical with the town of Patawomeck, which figured so prominently in the first decade of English conquest. The site was excavated in 1995-1996; because of its size, beauty, and prominence it is thought by many scholars to have been that town. Writing in the tribe's web site, Chief Robert "Two Eagles" Green states his conviction that this is the site.

86 "Patawomeck Indians of Virginia." http://patawomeckindians.org (3 October 2009).

87 John Smith, *General Historie* III:5, in Haile, ed. *Jamestown Narratives,* 260. Here Smith says there were thousands, but in his earlier account he says "hundreds."

88 Route 360, the "Mechanicsville Turnpike," runs just north of the line from Powhatan on the James to Orapakes on the Chickahominy to Opechancanough's home, "The Island," on the Upper Pamunkey, a distance of no more than twenty miles.

89 Henry Spelman, "Relation of Virginia, 1609" in Haile, ed., *Jamestown Narratives,* 494-495.

90 Ibid., 486.

91 "A Letter of Sir Samuell Argall touching his Voyage to Virginia, and Actions there: Written to Master Nicholas Hawes. June 1613." From *Purchas His Pilgrimes* iv. 1764-1765 in Alexander Brown, *The Genesis of the United States* (Boston & New York: Houghton Mifflin & Company, 1890) 640-644.

92 Ibid.

93 Hamor, "A True Discourse," in Haile, ed., *Jamestown Narratives,* 802.

94 Ibid., 804.

95 Alexander Whitaker, "Letter to Master Gouge, Minister of the Black Friars in London," in Haile, ed., *Jamestown Narratives,* 848.

96 Thomas Dale, "Letter to the Reverend Mr. D. M. in London," in Haile, ed., *Jamestown Narratives,* 845.

97 John Rolfe, "Letter to Sir Thomas Dale," in Haile, ed., *Jamestown Narratives,* 851.

98 Hamor, "A True Discourse," in Haile, ed., *Jamestown Narratives,* 806.

99 Ibid., 808.

100 Ibid., 809.

101 Ibid.

102 Ibid.

103 *Purchas, His Pilgrimage,* cited in Townsend, *Pocahontas,* 127.

104 Letter from Thomas Dale to Rev. D. M. in London, in Hamor, "A True Discourse," in Haile, ed., *Jamestown Narratives*, 845.

105 See, for example, Townsend, *Pocahontas*, 124-8.

106 Hume, *Virginia Adventure*, 328; Hamor, "A True Discourse," in Haile, ed., *Jamestown Narratives*, 809. Hume says Hamor's manuscript was in error and the date was more likely April 25.

107 Hamor, "A True Discourse," in Haile, ed., *Jamestown Narratives*, 831.

108 Ibid., 833.

109 Woodward, *Pocahontas*, 178-179.

110 John Smith, "To the most high and virtuous Princess, Queen Anne, of Great Brittany," *General Historie* IV, in Haile, ed., *Jamestown Narratives*, 862.

111 Ibid., 864.

112 Samuel Purchas, "*Purchas, His Pilgrimes* IV:1774" in Haile, ed., *Jamestown Narratives*, 883–884.

113 Ibid.

114 Woodward, *Pocahontas*, 174n.

115 Smith, *General Historie* IV, in Haile, ed., *Jamestown Narratives*, 885.

116 Hume, *Virginia Adventure*, 348.

117 See Custalow and Daniel, *True Story*, 83-86.

118 Ibid., 888-889.

119 It is this expression of Christianity, common at its time, which we refer to in this book as "heretical," according to the life and teachings of Jesus and the Christian scriptures.

120 Morgan, *American Slavery, American Freedom*, 387.

121 Ibid., 98, 111.

122 See Charles C. Mann, "America, Found and Lost," *National Geographic* (May, 2007). Mann believes the colonists brought malaria with them. Others speculate that the primary weakening from European diseases had come in the early sixteenth century, perhaps from Spaniards in the area that is now southwestern Virginia.

123 Cited in Hume, ed., *Jamestown Narratives*, 353.

124 For example, see the description of the Curles Neck property just downriver from Henrico in the Henrico County Historical Society web site: "The first 'Curles' patent was recorded in November of 1635 when a tract of 750 acres of land 'commonly known as Longfield' was granted to Captain Thomas Harris, 100 acres of which was due him as 'an Ancient planter & adventurer in the time of Sir Thomas Dale.' " Nathanael Bacon constructed a house there 1674-76. http://www.henricohistoricalsociety.org/varina. curlesneck.html (October 10, 2009).

125 Morgan, *American Slavery, American Freedom*, 98.

126 Ibid., 158.

127 Ibid., 163.

128 Ibid., 176.

129 See Ibid., 215ff.

130 Ibid., 110.

131 Ibid., 216.

132 Bob Deans, *The River where America Began* (Lanham, Md: Rowman & Littlefield Publishers, Inc., 2007), 139.

133 Ibid., 135. Morgan, *American Slavery, American Freedom*, 246.

134 William Waller Hening, ed., *Statutes at Large; Being a Collection of all the Laws of Virginia, from the First Session of the Legislature, in the Year 1619*, II:515. Transcribed for the internet by Freddie L. Spradlin, Torrance, CA. http://vagenweb. org/hening/.

135 Ira Berlin, *Many Thousands Gone* (Cambridge, Mass.: Harvard University Press, 1998), 45.

136 Theodore W. Allen, *The Invention of the White Race* (London: Verso, 1997), II:214.

137 *Ibid.*, 213-215.

138 John Rolfe, "Letter to the Virginia Company," in Kingsbury, *Records of the Virginia Company*, III:243.

139 Lisa Rein, "Mystery of Virginia's first Slaves is Unlocked 400 Years Later," *Washington Post*, September 3, 2006; Linda M. Heywood and John K. Thornton, *Central Africans, Atlantic Creoles, and the Foundation of the Americas, 1585-1660* (New York, 2007), 5-9.

140 I am indebted to historian Philip J. Schwarz for some of the description and analysis of bonded servitude in this paragraph.

141 Morgan, *American Slavery, American Freedom*, 299. Attempts to monopolize the trade did not succeed.

142 Hening, ed., *Statutes*, II:117.

143 Ibid., II:170.

144 Ibid., II:260.

145 Ibid., II:270.

146 Morgan, *American Slavery, American Freedom*, 312-313.

147 Ibid., 313.

148 Hening, ed., *Statutes*, II:283.

149 Ibid., II:491-492.

150 Ibid., II: 481-482.

151 Ibid., III:447-462.

152 Anthony S. Parent, Jr., *Foul Means: The Formation of a Slave Society in Virginia, 1660-1740* (Chapel Hill: The University of North Carolina Press, 2003), 121.

153 Hening, ed., *Statutes*, III:250-252; Morgan, *American Slavery, American Freedom*, 331; Helen C. Rountree and E. Randolph Turner III, *Before and After Jamestown* (Gainesville: University Press of Florida, 2002), 169-70.

154 T.H. Breen, "A Changing Labor Force and Race Relations in Virginia, 1660-1710," *Journal of Social History* 7:1 (Autumn, 1973), 3-25. The monopoly was removed in 1698 (cf. Morgan, *American Slavery, American Freedom*, 299).

155 Philip J. Schwarz, "Chronology of the Slave Trade in Richmond and Virginia," prepared for the Richmond Slave Trail Commission (Feb 2010 edition).

156 Minchinton, Walter, *et al.*, ed., *Virginia Slave-Trade Statistics 1698-1775*, Richmond: Virginia State Library, 1984, 176.

157 Lorena S. Walsh, "New Perspectives on the Transatlantic Slave Trade," *The William and Mary Quarterly*, 3rd Ser., Vol. 58, No. 1 (Jan. 2001), 168-169.

158 Allan Kulikoff, "The Colonial Chesapeake: Seedbed of Antebellum Southern Culture?" in *The Journal of Southern History*, Vol. 45, No. 4 (Nov. 1979), 527.

159 Philip J. Schwarz, *Twice Condemned: Slaves and the Criminal Laws of Virginia* (Baton Rouge: Louisiana State University Press, 1988), 62. In 1775 colonial leaders prevented importation of slaves by the British as an act of opposition. In 1778 Virginia enacted the prohibition into law.

160 Aaron S. Fogleman, "From Slaves, Convicts, and Servants to Free Passengers: The Transformation of Immigration in the Era of the American Revolution." (*The Journal of American History* 85:1 (June 1998), 44.

161 A. Roger Ekirch, *Bound for America: the transportation of British convicts to the colonies, 1718-1775* (Oxford: Clarendon Press, 1987), 113.

162 Ibid., 26. When, in 1785, the new nation refused to accept any more trade in convicts from the British Isles to America, exporters shifted their destination to Botany Bay in Australia, where the convict trade eventually totaled 150,000 emigrants.

163 David Brion Davis, *Slavery in the Colonial Chesapeake* (Williamsburg: The Colonial Williamsburg Foundation, 1986), 5.

164 Byrd to Charles Boyle, 1 July 1726, in Marion Tinling, ed., *The Correspondence of the Three William Byrds of Westover, Virginia, 1684-1776* (Charlottesville, 1977), I.355. Cited in Davis, *Slavery in the Colonial Chesapeake*, 133.

165 *Virginia Gazette*, 26 July 1770, cited in Davis, *Slavery in the Colonial Chesapeake*, 122.

166 Fogleman, "From Slaves, Convicts, and Servants to Free Passengers," 51.

167 Billy Kennedy, *The Scots-Irish in the Shenandoah Valley* (Londerry: Causeway Press, 1996), 30-31.

168 Chart from Fogleman, "Slaves, Convicts, and Servants," 44.

169 Morgan, *American Slavery, American Freedom*, 385.

170 Historian Rhys Isaac won the Pulitzer Prize in History for his study of the political and sociological impact of the Great Awakening, *The Transformation of Virginia 1740-1790* (Chapel Hill, University of North Carolina Press, 1982).

171 Charles F. Irons, *Origins of Proslavery Christianity*, (Chapel Hill: University of North Carolina Press, 2008) 35-36.

172 Ibid., 37. The location of Historic Polegreen Church, where Davies preached, is maintained as an historic site on Rural Point Road in Hanover County, twelve miles outside Richmond.

173 Michael Farris, speech given at 55th annual National Day of Prayer, Richmond, VA, 2006.

174 Derek H. Davis, *Religion and the Continental Congress, 1774-1789* (New York, Oxford University Press, 2000), 28.

175 Douglas R. Egerton, *Gabriel's Rebellion* (Chapel Hill: The University of North Carolina Press, 1993), 9.

176 Irons, *Origins of Proslavery Christianity*, 72.

177 Ibid.

178 Hickin, *Antislavery in Virginia*, 451.

179 Robert A. Rutland, ed., *The Papers of George Mason* (Chapel Hill: The University of North Carolina Press, 1970), 173. 180 Ibid., 11.

181 Deposition of John Randolph, July 22, 1793, in Flournoy, *Calendar of Virginia State Papers,* 6:452-3.

182 Egerton, *Gabriel's Rebellion,* 47.

183 Ibid., 111. The city gallows, on the hill between what became First African Church and the Negro Burial Ground, was visible from the entire valley and from all of Church Hill. Benjamin Harrison Wilkins, writing in his personal memoir *War Boy* (Tullahoma, Tennessee: Wilson Bros. Printing Company, 1938, 38-9), recounted his view across the Shockoe Valley from the cupola of what is now the Adams-Taylor House at Richmond Hill of the public hanging of seven men in 1865.

184 Jeffrey Ruggles, "The Burial Ground: an early African-American site in Richmond; notes on its history and location," unpublished monograph, 2009, 1.

185 Christopher McPherson, *A Short History of the Life of Christopher McPherson, Alias, Pherson, Son of Christ, King of Kings and Lord of Lords* (Lynchburg, Va.: 1855), 21. Available online at http://docsouth.unc.edu/neh/mcpherson/mcpherson.html.

186 University of Virginia Library, Historical Census Browser. http://mapserver. lib.virginia.edu/, 21 October 2009. Twenty-one percent of the black population of Richmond was free in 1800.

187 Patricia P. Hickin, *Antislavery in Virginia 1831-1861* (PhD. Dissertation, University of Virginia, 1968), 106.

188 Miles Mark Fisher, "Lott Cary, the Colonizing Missionary," in Carter G. Woodson, ed., *The Journal of Negro History* (Lancaster, Pa.: Assn for the Study of Negro Life and History, Inc., 1922) 25:380-418.

189 Hickin, *Antislavery in Virginia,* 253.

190 Eric Burin, *Slavery and the Peculiar Solution: A History of the American Colonization Society* (Gainesville: University Press of Florida, 2005), 14.

191 Irons, *Origins of Proslavery Christianity,* 122.

192 Cape Mesurado is adjacent to the present day city of Monrovia, capital of Liberia, at the mouth of the St. Paul River.

193 Burin, *Peculiar Solution,* 16-17.

194 *Thomas Jefferson to John Holmes,* April 22, 1820. Original in the Library of Congress.

195 Clement Eaton, *The Freedom-of-Thought Struggle in the Old South* (New York: Harper & Row, 1964, Harper Torchbooks ed.), 121.

196 Message of Gov. Wm. B. Giles to the Virginia legislature, Feb. 16, 1830, in *Journal of the House of Delegates of the Commonwealth of Virginia, 1829-30* (Richmond, 1830) in Eaton, *Freedom-of-Thought Struggle,* 172.

197 Ibid.

198 Hickin, *Antislavery in Virginia,* 133.

199 Ibid., 132.

200 Ibid., 131.

201 Delegates from urban areas, including those from Richmond, Hanover, and Henrico, were most prominent in pressing for this language in the preamble.

202 Hickin, *Antislavery in Virginia*, 151.

203 Ibid., 161.

204 *Supplement to the Revised Code of the Laws of Virginia*, (Richmond, 1833) chapter 186.

205 Ibid., 112.

206 "Resolutions relative to the interference of certain associations in the northern states with domestic slavery in the south," in *Acts of the General Assembly of the Commonwealth of Virginia, 1835-6*, 395-6.

207 Irons, *Origins of Proslavery Christianity*, 172.

208 William Meade, ed., *Sermons Addressed to Masters and Servants, and Published in the Year 1743 by the Rev. Thomas Bacon, Minister of the Protestant Episcopal Church in Maryland. Now Republished with Other Tracts and Dialogues on the Same Subject, and Recommended to All Masters and Mistresses To Be Used in Their Families by the Rev. William Meade.* Winchester, Va: John Heiskell, 1813.

209 Frederick Douglass, "Love of God, Love of Man, Love of Country." Speech delivered at Syracuse, New York, September 24, 1847. At http://teachingamericanhistory.org/library/index.asp?document=535.

210 Bailey was a Trustee of Williams College in Williamstown, Mass. Before his ordination as a Congregationalist minister, Bailey read law in Pittsfield, Mass. with Daniel Webster. The agreement between Congregationalists in the North and Presbyterians in the South enabled him to become Pastor of First Presbyterian Church in Staunton.

211 "T. J. Jackson to Prof. John Lyle Campbell," Lexington, Va., June 7, 1858 (Archives of Washington & Lee University).

212 Ellen Eslinger, "The Brief Career of Rufus W. Bailey, American Colonization Society Agent in Virginia," in *The Journal of Southern History*, 71:1 (February, 2005), 62.

213 Hickin, *Antislavery in Virginia*, 327-8.

214 Ibid., 556.

215 Judge Robert W. Hughes, "Editors of the Past," Lecture delivered before the Virginia Press Assn., Charlottesville, June 22, 1897. (Richmond: W. Ellis Jones, 1897), 15.

216 Hickin, *Antislavery in Virginia*, 563.

217 Ibid., 364.

218 Hughes, "Editors," 15.

219 "*A full Report embracing all the Evidence and Arguments in the Case of the Commonwealth of Virginia vs. Thomas Ritchie, Jr., Tried at the spring term of the Chesterfield Superior Court, 1846.*" (New York: Burgess, Stringer and Company, 1846), 15-16.

220 Rob Lopresti, "Which U. S. Presidents owned slaves?" www.nas.com/~lopresti/ps9.htm, October 20, 2009.

221 Called "the city of Richmond," Richmond was actually a town in Henrico County until incorporated as a city in 1842. Emily Salmon and Edward D. C. Campbell, ed. *Hornbook of Virginia History* (Richmond: Library of Virginia, 4th ed., 1994), 193.

222 Historical Census Browser. Retrieved 26 September 2008 from the University of Virginia, Geospatial and Statistical Data Center: 2,837 whites, 2,293 slaves, 607 free nonwhite.

223 Irons, *Origins of Proslavery Christianity*, 97ff.

224 Ibid., 131.

225 Ibid., 187.

226 *Journal of the Convention, Diocese of Virginia* (1854), cited in Edward L. Bond and Joan R. Gundersen, *The Episcopal Church in Virginia, 1607-2007* (Richmond: Episcopal Diocese of Virginia, 2007), 101.

227 Charles Dickens, *American Notes*, (London: 1842; Westvaco ed., 1970), 158-161.

228 Phillip Troutman, "African American Geopolitical Literacy and the 1841 *Creole* Revolt," in Walter Johnson, ed., *The Chattel Principle: Internal Slave Trades in the Americas* (New Haven: Yale University Press, 2005), 209-214.

229 George Hendrick and Willene Hendrick, *The Creole Mutiny: A Tale of Revolt aboard a Slave Ship* (Chicago: Ivan R. Dee, 2003), 97-111.

230 History Department of the University of San Diego, "Creole Slave Ship Revolt of 1841," http://history.sandiego.edu/GEN/civilwar/03/creole4.html (September 2, 2010). *Message of the President of the United States . . . copies of the correspondence in relation to . . . the brig Creole*," January 20, 1842, 51-52; *Niles' National Register*, December 18, 1841, 255.

231 Ernest B. Furgurson, *Ashes of Glory* (New York: Alfred A. Knopf, 1996), 20; cf. Frederic Bancroft, *Slave-Trading in the Old South* (Baltimore: J.H. Furst Company, 1931), 88.

232 Robert H. Gudmestad, *The Richmond Slave Market, 1840-1860* (Unpublished master's thesis for the University of Richmond, 1993), 13, 36.

233 Historical Census Browser. Virginia's enslaved population increased 4.4 percent.

234 Philip J. Schwarz, "Richmond and the Slave Trade," unpublished monograph for the Richmond Slave Trail Commission (2006), 8. Samuel H. Williamson, "Six Ways to Compute the Relative Value of a U.S. Dollar Amount, 1774 to present," MeasuringWorth, 2009. http://www.measuringworth.com/uscompare/.

235 "Our Slave Market," in *Richmond Enquirer* (June 29, 1859), cited in Bancroft, *Slave Trading*, 117.

236 Gudmestad, *Richmond Slave Market*, 34.

237 James O. Horton, Benjamin Banneker Prof. Emeritus of American Studies and History at George Washington University and Historian Emeritus of the Smithsonian Institution's National Museum of American Slavery, *The Future of Richmond's Past*, (Conference at the University of Richmond, September 29, 2009).

238 Bancroft, *Slave Trading*, 95.

239 Steven Deyle, *Carry Me Back: The Domestic Slave Trade in American Life* (New York: Oxford University Press, 2005), 44.

240 *Richmond Enquirer,* July 29, 1859, in Deyle, *Carry Me Back*, 56.

241 Ibid., 59.

242 Kimberly Merkel Chen and Hannah W. Collins, "The Slave Trade as a Commercial Enterprise in Richmond, Virginia," application for National Register of Historic Places (April 2007), 9; Bancroft, *Slave Trading*, 96-99.

243 Deyle, *Carry Me Back*, 4.

244 Richmond, Fredericksburg, & Potomac (1836), Virginia Central (1837), Richmond & Petersburg (1838), Richmond & Danville (1849), York River (1861).

245 Gudmestad, *Richmond Slave Market*, 49. All researchers on this topic draw heavily on the ground-breaking research of Richmonder Elizabeth Kambourian.

246 Charles Emery Stevens, *Anthony Burns: A History*, 1856. (Electronic edition, Chapel Hill: University of North Carolina, 1999. http://docsouth.unc.edu/neh/stevens/stevens.html), 171.

247 Ibid., 170.

248 Hickin, *Antislavery in Virginia*, 102.

249 Stevens, *Anthony Burns,* 1856. 187-193.

250 Eyre Crowe, *With Thackeray in America* (New York: Charles Scribner's Sons, 1893), 130-134. "Slaves Waiting for Sale" was printed on page 132 of the book and also in *The Illustrated London News* (Sept. 27, 1856), vol. 29, 315.

251 MS. recollections of Otis Bigelow, "who spent most of his manhood in the District of Columbia and Maryland, dying in 1919," in Frederic Bancroft, *Slave Trading in the Old South*. (Columbia, S.C.: University of South Carolina Press, 1996; originally published 1931), 102-3.

252 Jeffrey A. Ruggles, *The Unboxing of Henry Brown* (Richmond: The Library of Virginia, 2003), 21.

253 An exact scale replica of the box in which Henry Brown traveled from Richmond to Philadephia is located on Richmond's Slave Trail at the Canal Walk.

254 William Still, *The Underground Rail Road* (Philadelphia: Porter & Coats, 1872; digital edition, Arnold Bernhard Library, 2003).

255 Chen and Collins ("The Slave Trade as a Commercial Enterprise," 7) record increasing public recognition of the wealthy traders in the decade immediately before the War, noting that "1850s Richmond city directories listed them as slave traders, not just as 'merchants,' which had been a euphemism for slave dealer."

256 The Richmond Unity Walk had its origin when oral historian and Richmond Public Schools teacher Nancy Jo Taylor, who had carefully kept track of unmarked sites of Richmond's African-American history, shared her information with the eventual sponsors of the walk. Janine Bell and Elegba Folklore Society helped plan the walk, as did historian Nessa Baskervile Johnson. Following the walk, the City Council passed an ordinance establishing the Slave Trail Commission to develop the historic sites.

257 Identical copies of the statue stand in Richmond, Liverpool, and Benin, West Africa. The ambassador of Benin joined Virginia Governor Tim Kaine and Liverpool sculptor Stephen Broadbent at the statue's dedication, March 30, 2007.

258 Frederick Law Olmsted, *A Journey in the Back Country* (New York: Mason Brothers, 1860), 279-280.

259 Marie Tyler McGraw, *At the Falls; Richmond, Virginia, & Its People* (Chapel Hill: University of North Carolina Press, 1994), 131.

260 Virginius Dabney, *Richmond: The Story of a City* (Garden City, NY: Doubleday & Company, 1976), 165-166.

261 Currier & Ives' famous print of the evacuation fire is printed on the cover of this book.

262 See the detailed and excellent account of these events in Nelson Lankford's *Richmond Burning* (New York: The Penguin Group, 2002).

263 *Richmond Whig,* April 4, 1865, in Elizabeth R. Varon, *Southern Lady, Yankee Spy: The True Story of Elizabeth Van Lew* (Oxford: Oxford University Press, 2003), 191.

264 Historian Nessa Baskerville Johnson, in a letter to author; also Theresa M. Guzman-Stokes, "A Flag and a Family: Richard Gill Forrester, 1847-1906," *Virginia Cavalcade* (Spring, 1998), 52-63.

265 Furgurson, *Ashes of Glory,* 341-343.

266 Dabney, *Richmond,* 202.

267 Edward A. Pollard, *The Lost Cause, A New Southern History of the War of the Confederates* (New York: E. B. Treat & Co., Publishers, 1866), 751-752.

268 Michael B. Chesson, *Richmond After the War, 1865-1890* (Richmond: Virginia State Library, 1981), 75.

269 Ibid., 90.

270 *An act providing for the punishment of vagrants, January 15, 1866,* in http://home.gwu.edu/~jjhawkin/BlackCodes (20 August, 2010). "Virginia Vagrant Laws— Important Order from Gen. Terry—Modification of the Laws in Respect to Wages as far as They Relate to Freedmen," *New York Times,* January 24, 1866.

271 Account by historian Nessa Baskerville Johnson, shared with the author February 17, 2011.

272 Chesson, *Richmond After the War,* 96-97.

273 Ibid., 126.

274 Langston also founded the law school at Howard University and was the first president of what is now Virginia State University.

275 Peter Wallenstein, *Blue Laws and Black Codes: Conflicts, Courts, and Change in Twentieth Century Virginia* (Charlottesville: University of Virginia Press, 2004), 6.

276 J. Douglas Smith, *Managing White Supremacy: Race, Politics, and Citizenship in Jim Crow Virginia* (Chapel Hill: The University of North Carolina Press, 2002), 22.

277 Chesson, *Richmond After the War,* 203.

278 "The Lee Statue Unveiled; Thousands of Veterans Honor his Memory," *New York Times* (May 30, 1890), 1.

279 Fitzhugh Lee, a nephew of Robert E. Lee and a graduate of West Point, had been a major general in the Army of Northern Virginia during the Civil War.

280 Chesson, *Richmond After the War,* 188; cf. "Race and Racism at the 1886 Knights of Labor Convention," in *History Matters* http://historymatters.gmu.edu/d/44, referenced February 11, 2008.

281 Dabney, *Richmond,* 257.

282 Ibid., 270.

283 Chesson, *Richmond After the War,* 196.

284 Smith, *Managing White Supremacy*, 26.

285 Ibid.

286 Ibid., 229-233.

287 Ibid., 149.

288 Ibid., 131-132.

289 Ibid., 16.

290 McGraw, *At the Falls*, 214.

291 Ibid., 229-230.

292 In *Buchanan v. Warley* (245 U.S. 60) the court held race-based zoning to be illegal because it restricted the freedom of owners to sell their property. Xavier de Souza Briggs, ed., *The Geography of Opportunity: Race and Housing Choice in Metropolitan America* (Washington: The Brookings Institution, 2005), 221.

293 Smith, *Managing White Supremacy*, 235.

294 Robert K. Nelson, "Introduction: Race and Redlining in Richmond," in *Redlining Richmond,* Digital Scholarship Lab, University of Richmond (accessed November 7, 2010). http://americanpast.richmond.edu/holc/pages/intro.

295 The Federal Home Ownership Disclosure Act and Community Reinvestment Act provided that public comment, including comment on a bank's performance in non-discriminatory patterns of investment, was invited whenever banks sought to merge. Federal law required banks to maintain Home Mortgage data by census tract for public inspection, but Federal regulators did not examine it. In Richmond, Richmond United Neighborhoods and the Richmond Urban Institute joined to compile the data and, based on their findings, to challenge the proposed merger of the two banks. They withdrew their complaint after an agreement on reinvestment strategies was reached with bank authorities in a late-night meeting at Holy Rosary Church, in Richmond's East End.

296 HOME's initial board of directors consisted of Penny Briceland, Barbee Chauncey, The Rev. Edward Gregory, Sherman Harris, James Hecht, Randolph Kendall, Tim Langston, Melvin Law, Walter Loving, Al Matthews, Rich Miller, Martin Nordingler, Sy Dubow, George Gardner, and Nancy Day.

297 *Richmond Times-Dispatch*, March 31, 1925, 1.

298 Smith, *Managing White Supremacy*, 82.

299 Guzman-Stokes, "A Flag and a Family," 58. Richard Gustavus Forrester was the father of Richard Gill Forrester, who had raised the American flag at the Capitol the day that Richmond surrendered.

300 Smith, *Managing White Supremacy,* 133, 135.

301 Ibid., 36.

302 Dingledine, et al., *Virginia's History,* 256-257.

303 Ibid., 268, 269.

304 Smith, *Managing White Supremacy*, 136-137.

305 Clark Springs is a public playground that is directly adjacent to a portion of Hollywood Cemetery where unknown Confederate soldiers are buried and honored. On the other side of the playground is a neighborhood that African- American citizens of Richmond have called the "West End" for generations. Unaware of this tradition,

white Richmond citizens nearly universally refer to the most fashionable, virtually all-white neighborhood in the city as the "West End," and call the African-American neighborhood "Randolph."

306 Smith, *Managing White Supremacy*, 264-267.

307 Ibid., 250.

308 "Too Radical for Us," *Richmond Times-Dispatch*, July 17, 1939, 10, cited in Smith, *Managing White Supremacy*, 259.

309 The highly populated center of the Richmond metropolitan city consists of four jurisdictions—the city of Richmond and the suburban counties of Chesterfield, Hanover, and Henrico. Surrounding these are the exurban counties of Powhatan, Goochland, Charles City, and New Kent, the "eight-jurisdiction city." To the south, and included in the Richmond Standard Metropolitan Statistical Area (SMSA) by the U. S. Census Bureau, is the Petersburg metropolitan area consisting of the cities of Petersburg, Colonial Heights, and Hopewell and the counties of Prince George and Dinwiddie. In July 2008 the U.S. Census Bureau estimated the population of the thirteen-jurisdiction Richmond SMSA at 1,225,626. The four-jurisdiction central metropolitan city has 1,197 square miles. The eight-jurisdiction metropolitan city contains 2,136 square miles, leaving Richmond city with 2.8 percent of the area.

310 No governmental or nonprofit agency keeps reliable statistics on actual unemployment in Richmond. The figure given by the census and the Virginia Employment Commission (VEC) is obviously inaccurate and, as we have noted, the VEC no longer functions in the jurisdiction of Richmond city, the area of highest unemployment, but places its major offices in surrounding suburban counties, accessible only by private automobile. "Unemployment," as measured by the VEC and the Census, and regularly reported on newscasts, has become a technical term which does not apply to the situation of a significant percentage of the unemployed population. The census term "not employed" gives a clearer sense of the chronic state of unemployment and underemployment affecting major sectors of the populace. From official census data in the American Community Survey of 2009, it is clear that this situation of structural unemployment prevails in nearly the entire eastern half of the city of Richmond. In this section, representing 48% of the city's population, between 25% and 71% of adults between 20 and 64 are not employed in full-time paying jobs.

311 Christopher Silver, *Twentieth-Century Richmond: Planning, Politics, and Race* (Knoxville: University of Tennessee Press, 1984), 153. On February 3, 2009, sixty-eight years later, the *Richmond Times-Dispatch* reported: "City officials tonight showed off their plans to transform one of Richmond's toughest neighborhoods into a vibrant mixed-use community." The city announced a plan to demolish Gilpin Court and erect a new neighborhood intended as mixed income.

312 From 1912-1985 Harland Bartholomew and his firm produced comprehensive plans for 400 localities in the United States, including seventeen in Virginia. Twenty percent of these localities went to the firm for a comprehensive plan more than once. Richmond purchased comprehensive plans from the firm three times: in 1941, 1956, and 1961. Petersburg (1965) and Hopewell (1968), also in metro Richmond, sought

Bartholomew's help, as did Hanover County (1969). Eldredge Lovelace, *Harland Bartholomew: His Contribution to American Urban Planning* (University of Illinois at Champaign-Urbanna Department of Urban Planning, 1992), appendix C.

313 "Fay Heads City's Slum Clearance Program; New Surveys Set." *Richmond News Leader,* Oct. 25, 1950, 1. Cited in Selden Richardson, *Built by Blacks* (Richmond: The Alliance to Conserve Old Neighborhoods, 2007), 83.

314 Christopher Silver and John V. Moeser, *The Separate City: Black Communities in the Urban South, 1940-1968* (Lexington: The University Press of Kentucky, 1995), 150.

315 Silver, *Twentieth-Century Richmond,* 227, 235.

316 Timothy Van Schaick, "'The Sun Do Move,' But Who Moves the Highway?" unpublished master's thesis for James Madison University (May, 2008), 71.

317 Royer, *Report on the Express Highways,* cited Ibid., 66-7.

318 Silver, *Twentieth-Century Richmond,* 13, citing *Richmond Times-Dispatch,* August 2, 1955.

319 Interview by the author with Benjamin Ross, historian of Sixth Mount Zion Church, February 21, 2011.

320 Historic, multigenerational neighborhoods, with developed social relationships, some private ownership, and some variation in income, were replaced by new collections of more transient people required to be in poverty and randomly assigned to congested housing. See a chronicle of the Fulton neighborhood in Scott C. Davis, *The World of Patience Gromes: Making and Unmaking a Black Community* (Lexington: University Press of Kentucky, 1988).

321 "Separate educational facilities are inherently unequal." *Brown v. Board of Education,* 347 U.S. 483 (1954).

322 Robert A. Pratt, *The Color of Their Skin: Education and Race in Richmond, Virginia, 1954-89* (Charlottesville: University Press of Virginia, 1992), 18.

323 *Richmond Times-Dispatch,* Feb. 25, 1956; *New York Times,* Feb. 26, 1956.

324 Benjamin Muse, *Virginia's Massive Resistance* (Gloucester, MA: Peter Smith, 1969), 31-32. Muse wrote a column called "Virginia Affairs" for the *Washington Post.*

325 Ibid, 33.

326 J. Harvie Wilkinson III, *Harry Byrd and the Changing Face of Virginia Politics, 1945-1966* (Charlottesville: The University Press of Virginia, 1968), 132.

327 In Virginia, the governor is elected for a single four-year term and ineligible for the succeeding term.

328 "Massive Resistance," *Encyclopedia Virginia* (Virginia Foundation for the Humanities), http://www.encyclopediavirginia.org/Massive_Resistance (February 19, 2011). "By the time the General Assembly met in January 1956, key Byrd Organization figures were advocating a coordinated effort to block any desegregation anywhere in Virginia. Leaders such as Congressman William Munford Tuck argued against local option; only a unified resistance, they held, could prevent the 'mixing of the races.' When the Arlington County School Board members, headed by Elizabeth Pfohl Campbell, announced a plan of phased desegregation, the General Assembly reacted punitively, depriving them of their special elective status. In a series of lengthy editorials, James

Jackson Kilpatrick, editor of the *Richmond News Leader*, expounded on the idea, drawn from antebellum southern ideology, that the state could 'interpose' its power to stop implementation of federal court rulings. Acting on this belief, the General Assembly adopted a resolution of interposition. Late in February, with segregationist momentum building, Byrd made a public call for a campaign of 'massive resistance' against *Brown*."

329 Pratt, *The Color of Their Skin*, 9.

330 Attorney General Harrison argued that "racially integrated schools" were "inefficient" and "fundamentally objectionable" under the Virginia Constitution. (Harrison v. Day, 106 SE 2d 636 – Va. Supreme Court 1959). Appearing in Federal Court for the Norfolk plaintiffs, attorney Edmund Campbell argued "that the designation of which schools should close was based on race and color alone and therefore 'patently unconstitutional.'" (Muse, *Virginia's Massive Resistance*, 102. *James v. Almond, 170 F. Supp. 331 - Dist. Court, ED Virginia 1959)* The Norfolk plaintiffs had difficulty in finding a white attorney to take the lead in the case and sought out Campbell, a Lexington, Virginia native who practiced law in Arlington.

331 Pratt, *The Color of Their Skin,* 11.

332 Ibid., 132-133.

333 James Baker, "Integration is Quiet in Richmond," *Richmond News Leader*, September 6, 1960.

334 Pratt, *The Color of Their Skin*, 25. In 2009, the city closed Chandler Middle School. The most troubled middle school in the city, Chandler had been unable to meet state standards for a number of years. Forty-nine years after it became Richmond's first racially integrated school, Chandler had been resegregated *de facto* both by race and by income. The school reopened in September, 2009 as the home of the city's Richmond Community High School, an innovative and racially integrated institution.

335 "Dr. Calvin C. Green, unsung rights hero: he succumbs at 79," *Richmond Free Press*, Feb. 17-19, 2011. Green v. County School Board of New Kent County, 391 U.S. 430 (1968).1.

336 Pratt, *The Color of Their Skin*, 65-71.

337 Ibid., 90.

338 Ibid.

339 John Moeser and Rutledge Dennis, *The Politics of Annexation* (Cambridge, MA: Shenkman Publishing Company, 1982), 42.

340 White voters in Richmond city approved the merger. Black voters in the city opposed it by a substantial margin.

341 Moeser and Dennis, *Politics of Annexation*, 45-52.

342 After it was prohibited from annexing any further territory, Richmond rapidly reached its limit on bonded indebtedness, and for years has been unable to issue capital bonds except to replace those which retire each year. Bonded indebtedness per capita is three times that of the surrounding counties. The General Assembly has never, since this attempt to maintain racial segregation, made any effort to address or alleviate the paralyzing indebtedness of its capital city.

343 Moeser and Dennis, *Politics of Annexation*, 82.

344 Ibid., 108.

345 *Richmond Times-Dispatch,* November 3, 1970; September 21, 1972.

346 Moeser and Dennis, *Politics of Annexation, 177.*

347 *City of Richmond, Virginia v. United States,* 95 S. Ct. 2296 (1975) at 2307, in Ibid., 172.

348 Ibid., at 2309.

349 Cf. Jack D. Edwards, *Neighbors and Sometimes Friends: Municipal Annexation in Virginia* (Charlottesville: University of Virginia Center for Public Service, 1992), 61. Although styled a "moratorium," the action effectively ended the annexation rights of Richmond and, with other actions of the assembly, eliminated the assumption of the Virginia constitution that cities would regularly expand to take in the effective areas of growth around them. In accord with the sophisticated conventions of Virginia law on racial segregation developed during the twentieth century, a person not knowing the background, the political pressures, or the intentions of such legislation would be unable to determine its purposes or the racial conversations preceding it.

350 The five African-American councilpersons chosen in this historic election were Marsh, Willie Dell, Walter Kenney, Claudette Black McDaniel, and Henry "Chuck" Richardson.

351 "The Confederate Capital Finally Falls to Blacks," *Ebony,* Vol. 35, No. 8 (June, 1980): 45-52.

352 Willie Avon Drake and Robert D. Holsworth, *Affirmative Action and the Stalled Quest for Black Progress* (Champaign, Illinois: University of Illinois Press, 1996), 75.

353 Ibid., 77.

354 Richmond Renaissance eventually became "Venture Richmond."

355 Occupying the right of way of Sixth Street between Marshall and Grace Streets, the Sixth Street Marketplace was finally demolished in 2004 and the right of way restored. Thalhimer's and Miller & Rhoads bordered Sixth Street, between Broad and Grace streets.

356 Edwards, *Neighbors and Sometimes Friends: Municipal Annexation in Virginia,* 61.

357 Three or four other cities in the United States are "independent" from county jurisdictions, and the nation's capital is independent of state government as well, but no other state has had a consistent policy of independent cities. Virginia has had as many as 44 independent cities.

358 Redlining in Richmond was detailed in a study of data from the Community Reinvestment Act published in 1980 by the Richmond Urban Institute. The information, which rated front-page coverage from the weekly Richmond *Afro-American* and threatened to delay the merger that created Sovran Bank, was relegated to a small story in a back section in one of the two daily Richmond newspapers.

359 Individual reporters often attempted to offset the negative coverage with constructive stories on the Richmond Public Schools, but the volume of coverage itself created a distorted impression.

360 Petersburg, which is part of the Richmond Standard Metropolitan Statistical Area, has become even more demographically isolated from its adjoining suburban neigh-

bors than Richmond, and the schools have even fewer resources and a higher level of need. Most of the middle class and most of the white school students of metropolitan Petersburg live across the city line in Dinwiddie and Prince George counties and in the independent city of Colonial Heights.

361 The state composite index consistently penalizes most of Virginia's historic cities, most of which were closed to annexation in the early 1970s when schools were integrated, and most of which contain a high percentage of low- income, African-American students. The carefully engineered formula takes no notice of the median income, poverty level, or local taxation level of localities, the factors that would be essential elements in equalizing state funding for education.

362 "Appendix B: Aid for Public Education 2011-2012," in *Summary of the Governor's Proposed Amendments to the 2011-2012 Budget*, http://lis.virginia.gov/111/bud/BudSum/B.pdf, January 13, 2011.

363 Harold Fitrer, "Unfair funding cuts would leave city students stranded," *Richmond Times-Dispatch*, January 28, 2011.

364 *Comparative Report of Local Government Revenues and Expenditures, Year ended June 30, 2008* (Richmond: Commonwealth of Virginia, Auditor of Public Accounts, 2009).

Comparison of state and local revenue for Metropolitan Richmond, Virginia, and Fairfax County, Virginia, 2009		
	Metropolitan Richmond (4 jurisdictions)	Fairfax County
Population	888,549	1,017,317
Area	1,197 sq. mi.	395 sq. mi.
Population density	742/sq. mi.	2,575/sq. mi.
Total local government revenue	$3,218,182,212	$4,320,117,890
Revenue from Commonwealth	$1,102,819,761	$770,051,646
State revenue per capita	$1,241,14	$756.94
% of local revenue from state	34.3%	17.8%

Source: *Comparative Report of Local Government Revenues and Expenditures, Year ended June 30, 2008* (Richmond: Commonwealth of Virginia, Auditor of Public Accounts, 2009).

365 Matthew 23:37, New Revised Standard Version of the New Testament.

About the Author

A native of Arlington, Virginia, the Rev. Benjamin P. Campbell studied political science and political economy at Williams College in Massachusetts, and studied theology as a Rhodes Scholar at the Queen's College in Oxford. He received a Master's in Divinity and an honorary Doctorate in Divinity from the Virginia Theological Seminary in Alexandria.

He was ordained to the priesthood of the Episcopal Church in 1966. He came to Richmond in 1970 and has lived in Church Hill since that time. He has ministered to three Episcopal churches, and served as Communications Director and subsequently Program Director of the Episcopal Diocese of Virginia. He directed two non-profit corporations—the Richmond Urban Institute, and Home Base, Incorporated, a neighborhood-based low-income housing corporation. In 1987, he became Pastoral Director of Richmond Hill, an ecumenical Christian community and retreat center on Church Hill in Richmond.

He is a co-founder of the Micah Association, which links more than 100 faith communities to twenty-five inner city elementary schools in Richmond, and of the Armstrong Leadership Program, involving thirty-six students in Richmond's inner city Armstrong High School. He chairs the program committee of Communities in Schools, a program that supports volunteer efforts and social service work in the Richmond Public Schools. He is also a member of the Richmond Slave Trail Commission and the Richmond Public Schools Foundation.

Dr. Campbell is a member of the Residential Community at Richmond Hill. He is married to the former Ann Elizabeth Hopkins, a teacher at William Fox Elementary School in the City of Richmond. Their children attended and graduated from Richmond Public Schools.

Dr. Campbell is a seventh generation Virginian. His Scots-Irish ancestors first came to Berkeley Springs in the 1760s, and settled at Timber Ridge, in Rockbridge County outside of Lexington, in the 1780s.